L.M. MONTGOMERY AND CANADIAN CULTURE

L.M. Montgomery and Canadian Culture

Edited and with an introduction by
Irene Gammel and Elizabeth Epperly

UNIVERSITY OF TORONTO PRESS
Toronto Buffalo London

© University of Toronto Press Incorporated 1999
Toronto Buffalo London

Printed in Canada

ISBN 0-8020-4406-9 (cloth)

Printed on acid-free paper

Canadian Cataloguing in Publication Data

Main entry under title:

L.M. Montgomery and Canadian culture

Includes bibliographical references and index.
ISBN 0-8020-4406-9

1. Montgomery, L.M. (Lucy Maud), 1874–1942 – Criticism and
interpretation.   2. Literature and society.   I. Gammel, Irene,
1959– .   II. Epperly, Elizabeth R.

PS8526.O55Z755 1999   C813'.52   C98-932962-3
PR9199.3.M6Z784 1999

University of Toronto Press acknowledges the financial assistance to its
publishing program of the Canada Council for the Arts and the Ontario Arts
Council.

This book has been published with the help of a grant from the Humanities
and Social Sciences Federation of Canada, using funds provided by the
Social Sciences and Humanities Research Council of Canada.

Contents

Introduction

PART 1. MONTGOMERY AND CANADA: ROMANCING THE REGION, CONSTRUCTING THE NATION

Montgomery and Canadian Nationalism

Romance and the Shaping of Canadian Culture

PART 2. MONTGOMERY AND CANADIAN SOCIETY: NEGOTIATING CULTURAL CHANGE

Religion, Education, and Technology

Motherhood, Family, and Feminism

PART 3. MONTGOMERY AND CANADIAN ICONOGRAPHY: CONSUMING THE POPULAR

Anne as Cultural Icon

Foreword

ADRIENNE CLARKSON

A number of years ago, when I came to Prince Edward Island to speak at a tourism conference, I spoke about the need to take L.M. Montgomery seriously as a writer, and suggested the establishment of an institute for the study of Montgomery. Thanks to the perspicacity of the University of Prince Edward Island (from which I hold a very treasured honorary doctorate) this institute is now a reality, and this book is part of its important work.

I have loved Prince Edward Island and *Anne of Green Gables* since I first read the book when I was nine. It was given to me by the next-door neighbours in our apartment building in Ottawa, who had a beautiful baby boy whom I would go over and play with while his mother took a nap or was preparing dinner. Once I had read the first Anne book I never looked back. The entire canon of L.M. Montgomery was devoured, read and reread, in the next five years. Anne, Emily, Pat, and Jane – and Valancy – they all became my spiritual sisters. I loved them. I knew them. In this, I was no different from millions of little girls in the twentieth century, in Canada and all over the world, who identified with and entered the fictional lives of these heroines.

But more importantly, L.M. Montgomery in all her books gave me a profound understanding of what Canada is. Through the particularity and peculiarities of Prince Edward Island and these girls' fictional lives, I became a Canadian. L.M. Montgomery educated me at a very profound level about how Canada operated in a rural setting, with smart people, in the birthplace of Confederation.

I had come to Canada only six years before reading my first Anne book. My family and I were refugees from Hong Kong – just the four of us, thrust by war out of our home and into Ottawa, then a small white town, filled with snow, in the cold winter of 1942. L.M. Montgomery's world gave me an extended family that taught me about the rivalries of Tory and Grit, Protestant and Catholic, in a highly sophisticated micro-cosmic way; it was a background, a heritage that I gained literarily and that made my becoming Canadian very easy and attractive. Anne and Emily, the Story Girl, and all the others were my cousins of the imagination and the spirit, and so what they were, I became also.

Being orphaned or losing a parent, which is such a Montgomery theme, was correlated in my mind to my experience as a refugee, arriving in Canada with my parents and one suitcase each. So when Anne is found by Matthew on the railway siding, sitting on her suitcase, to me that wasn't a fictional situation. That was my situation. And Matthew and Marilla were like the safe haven that Canada was for me. In many ways they represent Canadians at their most characteristic – repressed, silent, and strictured, but decent, open-hearted, and capable of adapting to circumstances. They were a traditional bachelor and spinster, and suddenly they became parents, they became loved by someone outside of their 'family.' If that isn't a metaphor for Canada as a country that receives immigrants, I don't know what is!

But for me, the immigrant child, the world of the Cuthberts, the Lyndes, and the Barrys was the world of Canada – rural, rooted, and white – a world to which I would never have had access any other way. By this I don't mean that my public school, our friends among the parishioners of St John's Anglican Church, and my father's Ottawa Masonic Lodge weren't friendly and welcoming. The decency and kindness of Canadians – both French and English speaking – was wonderful. But the depth of understanding, the texture of generations of feuds and forgettings, the nature of the Scots-Irish Presbyterianism, constituted a reality that only fiction could convey. Only fiction can bring the truth because only fiction is not unbelievable. L.M. Montgomery understood emotions and she understood motivation; her people *are* Canada. I was taught by them as I read through her novels. Fiction, like all art, tells the truth from the inside. Any sociological study of the Islanders of the late nineteenth century would be dry, arid, seen from the outside; the Islanders would be objectified, quantified, and would emerge lacking humanity. But Matthew and Miss Tomgallon are not specimens; they're real people. It was all so real for me that I didn't even want to go to Prince Edward Island very much. I felt I knew Prince Edward Island as well as I knew Ottawa, where I grew up, and the lake in the Gatineau, where I spent my summers. I had an imaginative map of it, a vision greener than any visit could make it.

And when I was growing up, the vestal virgins of education, my public-school teachers, were not so different from Anne's school-world. Some of them *were* Anne without the decision to marry Gilbert Blythe. Anne's world was safe in love and determined economically by circumstances. Yet she comes through, even going to university, earning her own way after Matthew dies and she has to help Marilla. Her success too is a lesson to an immigrant: there are no real obstacles that hard work and planning won't overcome.

There is the sense in all of L.M. Montgomery's heroines that purpose and vision and balancing all aspects of a human life and its obligations to others, especially family, will bring the richest human rewards. The lesson is profoundly anti-materialistic, and, in that, it is the best of Canadian life too. It is not about bending the world to your will and making a fortune out of it. It is about listening to the heart and adapting to one's immediate society because one is part of it, the larger organism.

The highly structured, traditional network of the Islanders is the ideal image for an immigrant, as it echoes the general family and tribal patterns of most immigrants to Canada. Part of this idea is summed up by Malcolm Ross's phrase, 'The impossible sum of our traditions,' which is meant to include what immigrants bring here as part of their emotional, historical, and spiritual baggage and the melding that happens when they begin to graft onto the main trunks of this complex bilingual constitutional democracy.

L.M. Montgomery taught me about Canada in the First World War in *Rilla of Ingleside*. I knew nothing of Vimy or Ypres or Passchendaele until Rilla's brothers, Jem and Walter, went to war and Walter didn't return. My life had been so directly affected by war, but at least I had survived with all the members of my family intact. The impact of war on a tranquil idyllic little place where no one had ever moved more than a few miles and everyone looked and spoke like everyone else was, I realized even when I was fourteen, enormous. The reactions of the Blythe family and their housekeeper, Susan, were the intense, sometimes confused, always stoical reactions of the whole Canadian nation to cataclysm. It was an event that showed that, although they lived on an island, they couldn't be insulated from the forces that shook the world, even across an ocean.

L.M. Montgomery must have thought a great deal about the First

World War before writing *Rilla*; it's a carefully evolved response to war that treads the fine line between helpless fatalism and congenital spunkiness. L.M. Montgomery gives a breadth to the responses to cruel destiny – acceptance with acquiescence, acknowledgment without humiliation.

For the immigrant this profound lesson of attitude is invaluable. It allows all of us, whether we've been here for generations or have just arrived, a deep sense of integrity that, if it is then linked to an understanding of our wilderness (so different from the European countryside), gives the unique sense of belonging that makes a Canadian.

I owe the integrity of values, the understanding of belonging, even in trivial detail, to L.M. Montgomery. She will continue to be a beacon-light for all immigrants because of her portrayal of the Islanders, who are family. And she will continue to make everyone feel that, even though they were once alone and rejected, they now *belong*. She could take any immigrants and make them a part of her world, without their having to leave their own German or Oriental one. That is the magic of fiction; that is its transforming power.

Acknowledgments

L.M. Montgomery and Canadian Culture has a unique genealogy. Based in part on two international symposia hosted by the L.M. Montgomery Institute at the University of Prince Edward Island, and in part on solicited essays, the project quickly developed a vibrant network of connections and discussions among Canadian and international scholars that Montgomery herself would have rejoiced in. Reflecting on the Canadianness of Montgomery's writing, several of the contributors were inspired to create their own subgroups, as they read, discussed, and commented on each others' essays and arguments. We would like to thank all contributors for their willingness and patience in collaborating with each other and with the editors to produce what we hope is the unified and tightly organized book that L.M. Montgomery deserves.

Several individuals deserve special thanks: Shannon Murray, who supported the idea enthusiastically, when it was first proposed under her chairship of the L.M. Montgomery Institute at the University of Prince Edward Island; Donald Mason, who prepared the index with great care; and J. Paul Boudreau, whose taxonomical advice was invaluable in generating a flexible and unique structure for this multidisciplinary project. We have also been fortunate to work with a team of exceptionally dedicated, professional, and enthusiastic research assistants: Kim Tanner, Heather Ludlow, Tracey Noftle, and Melissa Doucette. There are others to whom we are grateful for help and support: Gabriella Åhmansson at the University of Uppsala in Sweden; Marilyn Bell, Public Archives and Records Office of Prince Edward Island; Anne-Louise Brookes, associate professor at the University of Prince Edward Island; Adrienne Clarkson, host of *Adrienne Clarkson Presents*; Bernard Katz, head of Special Collections at University of Guelph Library; Deirdre xiv Acknowledgments

Kessler, co-chair of the L.M. Montgomery Institute; Wolfgang Kloos, president of the *Gesellschaft für Kanadastudien*; Geoffrey Lindsay, assistant professor at the University of Prince Edward Island; Anna MacDonald, coordinator of the L.M. Montgomery Institute; Ian Nicholson, assistant professor at the University of Prince Edward Island; Elizabeth Percival, associate professor at the University of Prince Edward Island; Kevin Rice, registrar at the Confederation Centre of the arts in Charlottetown, Prince Edward Island; Mary Henley Rubio, professor at the University of Guelph; Philip Smith, dean of arts at the University of Prince Edward Island; and Henry Srebrnik, associate professor at the University of Prince Edward Island. We thank the three anonymous readers for their careful assessment of this project, their enthusiastic support, and their suggestions, all of which have found their way into this book. We are grateful to Emily Andrew, Gerald Hallowell, Jill McConkey, and Frances Mundy at the University of Toronto Press and to freelance editor Barbara Tessman for their hard work and expert help with the manuscript. And last but not least, we wish to thank the students of the 1997–8 L.M. Montgomery course at the University of Prince Edward Island for enthusiastically engaging with and testing some of the arguments generated by the collection.

This book has greatly benefited from the support of a Social Sciences and Humanities Research Grant, as well as University of Prince Edward Island Research Grants. We are grateful to the Macdonald Stewart Foundation for generous support for the L.M. Montgomery Institute.

Excerpts from *The Selected Journals of L.M. Montgomery*, Volumes I, II, III, and IV © 1985, 1987, 1992, 1998, University of Guelph, edited by Mary Rubio and Elizabeth Waterston, and published by Oxford University Press, are reproduced with the permission of Mary Rubio, Elizabeth Waterston, and the University of Guelph, courtesy of the L.M. Montgomery Collection, Archival and Special Collections, University of Guelph Library.

Other material written by L.M. Montgomery is excerpted with the permission of Ruth Macdonald and David Macdonald, trustee, who are the heirs of L.M. Montgomery. L.M. Montgomery's novels and short stories are published by McClelland and Stewart Ltd., Bantam Books, and Seal Books. *The Alpine Path* and *The Poetry of L.M. Montgomery* are published by Fitzhenry and Whiteside Ltd. *My Dear Mr. M: Letters to G.B. MacMillan from L.M. Montgomery* is published by Oxford University Press Canada. *The Green Gables Letters: From L.M. Montgomery to Ephraim Weber, 1905–1909* is published by Borealis Press. 'L.M.

Montgomery,' 'The Blue Castle,' 'Emily,' and 'Emily of New Moon' are trademarks of the Heirs of L.M. Montgomery Inc. 'Anne of Green Gables' and other images of 'Anne' are trademarks and Canadian official marks of the Anne of Green Gables Licensing Authority Inc., which is owned by the heirs of L.M. Montgomery and the province of Prince Edward Island.

Abbreviations

AA	*Anne of Avonlea*
AGG	*Anne of Green Gables*
AHD	*Anne's House of Dreams*
AIn	*Anne of Ingleside*
AIs	*Anne of the Island*
ASh	*Along the Shore*
BC	*The Blue Castle*
CAA	Canadian Authors' Association
EC	*Emily Climbs*
ENM	*Emily of New Moon*
EQ	*Emily's Quest*
NAC	National Archives of Canada
NCWC	National Council of Women of Canada
RV	*Rainbow Valley*
SJ	*Selected Journals*
TW	*A Tangled Web*
UJ	Unpublished journals

INTRODUCTION

L.M. Montgomery and the Shaping of Canadian Culture

IRENE GAMMEL AND ELIZABETH EPPERLY

'I went to the School of Commerce to read to the High School girls of Toronto. I had a very enthusiastic audience of about 1,500,' L.M. Montgomery records in her diary on 23 November 1921. She continues proudly: 'Afterwards I was nearly mobbed by a sea of girls wanting autographs. They nearly smothered me. I wrote about 400 autographs in half an hour' (*SJ* 3: 27). Speaking in 1923 to the Business Women's Club in Hamilton, she has an equally nice time: 'The reporters descended on me in swarms and all wanted to know what I thought of the present day girl' (*SJ* 3: 208). Montgomery's opinion made an impact in the daily media, and in 1923, the *Toronto Star* listed her as one of the twelve greatest women in Canada (*SJ* 3: 120). A Canadian celebrity, she exported Canada into an international scene with translations of her novels into seventeen languages, while at home and abroad carefully cultivating her public image for her country and era.

These examples of popular flair are easily recognized by readers of Montgomery's fiction. What has not been adequately recognized, however, is Montgomery's impact on the shaping of a distinctly Canadian culture. This lack of acknowledgment may be all the more surprising given the volubility of Montgomery's most popular characters and their uncanny ability to change their worlds through the power of the word. Her most popular girl and woman characters are readers of literature and are intimately linked to the formation of new cultural values in the young Canadian Confederation. Recitations of poetry, school concerts, and critical analyses of church sermons are an integral part of growing up in Montgomery's fictional world; the writing of letters, poetry, stories, and creative fiction is discussed and theorized, producing an important discourse on the emerging Canadian cultural tradition. Her characters grow into writers and teachers to promote their unique cultural visions in turn. For young and adult readers, these formative elements do more than heighten individual cultural awareness: they construct Canadian culture.

While Montgomery is fast becoming one of Canada's most discussed authors,[1] it seems both ironic and surprising that her shaping of Canadian culture has remained largely unacknowledged by Canadian cultural historians. As Robert Lecker has recently shown, L.M. Montgomery is virtually absent from Canada's established literary histories and anthologies. 'Did anthologists of the 1980s consider children's literature unworthy of inclusion?' Lecker asks. 'Despite their enormous popularity in their time, recent literary histories tend to treat these writers as though they didn't exist, or to express confusion about how to reconcile their earlier popularity with contemporary taste' (126). In the construction of the Canadian cultural imaginary, this gap is cavernous, drawing the critical reader's attention to the mapping of a high culture that deliberately excludes Canada's popular fiction.[2]

Such common assumptions about popular literature are echoed by Sarah Corse in her comparison of American and Canadian national literatures. In contrast to 'high-culture literature, popular literature lacks a *national*, symbolic value,' she writes (130). 'Canonical literature is "produced," in the sense of chosen into the canon, for "public" readers, e.g. school children or national populations, engaged in "public" pursuits such as schooling regarding the dominant cultural hierarchy or enculturation as "citizens"' (130). In this context, popular literature is seen to have a low-level value of entertainment and escape, ultimately serving personal rather than public needs. In this view, popular literature lacks the signifiers of national difference that are generally attached to the works of high culture; it tends toward homogenization, which makes it easy to market this literature to readers in a variety of countries.

L.M. Montgomery and Canadian Culture calls into question such polarization between high culture and low culture and their respective social functions. In effect, this collection of essays unravels the striking and ironic contradictions surrounding the reception of Montgomery's work in Canada. While literary historians in Canada have ignored Montgomery, some of the leading female icons of high culture in Canada, including Margaret Atwood, Alice Munro, and Jane Urquhart, have acknowledged their indebtedness to, and rootedness in, Montgomery's fiction. While L.M. Montgomery's fiction is not part of official school curricula, teachers from across Canada frequently turn to her novels in their teaching of Canadian literature, as the many teachers' inquiries to the L.M. Montgomery Institute testify. Montgomery's work powerfully infiltrates the institutions from below; it creates its cultural genealogies on a grass-roots level, transmitted as it is through parents reading to their children or through television or stage viewing and follow-up reading.

L.M. Montgomery and Canadian Culture is the first systematic effort to investigate the question of the Canadianness of Montgomery's writing. The essays in this collection argue that L.M. Montgomery strategically inscribes the signifiers of Canadian distinctness, even while appealing to a broad, international readership. This collection maps the important cultural, social, and popular domains of Montgomery's impact. Before sketching these domains, we offer a caveat: the collection is not designed to present an exhaustive coverage of all possible domains. For example, it excludes detailed studies of the popular television versions or series of *Anne of Green Gables, Road to Avonlea, Emily of New Moon*, or the popular stage play of *Anne of Green Gables: The Musical*, all of which will be the focus of a separate, upcoming study. To cast a wide net around the central topics and concerns of L.M. Montgomery's writing and their specific relationship to Canadian culture, this collection is organized around three core themes, reflected in the division of the book into three major parts.

The first thematic focus, and the title of part 1, is 'Montgomery and Canada: Romancing the Region, Constructing the Nation,' which investigates Montgomery's very active engagement with classical components of Canadian nationalism and identity construction in the first half of the twentieth century: immigration, the war, regionalism, canon formation, and Canadian–American cultural relations. The focal point of part 2, 'Montgomery and Canadian Society: Negotiating Cultural Change,' investigates Montgomery's work in relation to the many dramatic social and institutional changes that form the basis for distinctly different public and private lives in Canada: the women's movement, the family, the churches, the educational system, the advent of new technologies such as the automobile; they all undergo major developments and changes during L.M. Montgomery's era and are reflected and negotiated in her writing. Part 3, 'Montgomery and Canadian Iconography: Consuming the Popular,' explores Anne as popular icon of Canada, before investigating the cultural meanings and effects of the national and international ingestion, or consumption, of Anne. This area, then, turns from high culture to aspects of low culture, including material culture and cultural tourism.

Ultimately we argue that the romance of Montgomery's writing had a decidedly political dimension. With her unique combination of romance and satire, Montgomery powerfully intervened in the shaping of Canadian culture, carving out spaces of pleasure even while expressing social pains. The essays in this collection pay tribute to Montgomery's important contributions as they investigate the silencing of these contributions in Canada's literary histories. From many different angles and perspectives, this book brings together a unique blend of internationally recognized scholars in Montgomery studies and Canadian studies, in addition to new voices and new perspectives. In the editorial process, we have chosen readily available Canadian editions to regularize the source of quotations from Montgomery's works. We have subdivided the book's three focal points into six subsections. Most subsections end with a short, creative 'reflection piece' designed to highlight Montgomery's influence on recent writers as well as to accommodate topics of predominantly popular interest. Reaching across regional, linguistic, racial, and sexual boundaries, this book positions Montgomery's 'popular' fiction into the space of the national and political, ultimately reconfiguring our official signifiers of Canada.

Part 1. Montgomery and Canada: Romancing the Region, Constructing the Nation

Montgomery's loyalty was to Canada: like the writer heroines she created, she resisted the lure of quick success that moving to the United States offered Canadian women writers. Many Canadian women authors who emigrated to the United States, usually unmarried, 'blended into the American melting pot' or 'adopted an American voice' (Gerson, 'Canadian' 109). In contrast, 'those who stayed in Canada were almost all women with children who chose literary work because it allowed them to remain at home – that is, in their own houses and in their own country' (110). Indeed, as Jane Urquhart concludes in her afterword to *Emily Climbs*, this deep attachment to her geography makes Emily a writer: 'To leave New Moon and Prince Edward Island would be roughly equivalent, for this Canadian girl, to committing literary suicide' (334). The same could be said about Montgomery and her relationship to Canada.

Montgomery constructs the nation not only through the window of regional difference, but through the window of a common set of values. The region is associated with strong emotions; with the pleasure of romantic identification with the landscape and the artistic; with seductive, even erotic powers. The nation, in contrast, is associated with labour, industry, duty, courage, and noble service, illustrated in all of Montgomery's fiction, but most explicitly expressed in *Courageous Women*, a collection of biographies of mainly Canadian women, written in collaboration with Marian Keith and Mabel Burns McKinley and published in 1934. Here Montgomery and her collaborators detail women's service that was designed to build Canada: writer Catharine Parr Traill's willingness to do menial work with her hands becomes a trope that we also find in Montgomery's own self-stylization as a Canadian writer who does not shirk housework. Being Canadian implies a distinct set of values: loyalty, industry, pioneering courage, a dedication to service and humanitarian values. This element of self-sacrifice finds its ultimate expression in the war novels, *Rainbow Valley* and especially *Rilla of Ingleside*. Here Montgomery creates an idealized Canadian war bard in Walter Blythe. Montgomery believed that the common sacrifice would create a strong unity in Canada, although the war itself had shown significant ethnic and regional divisions in the country.

While the power of connection and the sentiment of loyalty to home are supreme, Montgomery also constructs the nation through difference. 'I'm a queer mixture racially – the Scotch Macneills, the English Woolners and Penmans, the Irish of Mary McShannon (Hugh Montgomery's wife) and that far-off French descent,' writes Montgomery in June 1929 (*SJ* 3: 398), evoking a uniquely Canadian genealogy in her diaristic self-construction. The 'queerness' of her mixture, which does not quite assimilate as a full unit, but is negotiated in its difference and separateness, leaves the various cultural identities in characteristic tension. This self-construction corresponds to her evocation of the different cultural groups that constitute the community of Avonlea – the Scots, the Irish, the English, the French.[3]

Through Montgomery's lens, region and nation are also presented with the notion of gendered identities. Just as the desired orphan boy ironically turns out to be a girl, so Montgomery's fiction presents a systematic reversal of gender roles and a feminization of the male figures: Matthew, better than Marilla, understands Anne's longing for puffed sleeves and shows indulgence; Cousin Jimmy, in opposition to Aunt Elizabeth, supports Emily's desire to write fiction. It is the men (Matthew Cuthbert, Douglas Starr, Mr Carpenter, Walter Blythe) who die in moments of high pathos, while the women (Marilla, Anne) recover and live, creating traditions, names, and maternal genealogies. The men die, having served as male 'muses' for the female protagonist. This feminization, we argue, is deliberate. While some English critics used cartographic metaphors to map a trans-Canadian entity, Montgomery sews the nation together through the power of sentiment. 'Can't they see that civilization is founded on and held together through senti-ment,' writes Montgomery on 27 January 1922, over three years after the end of the First World War. 'Passion is transient and quite as often destructive as not. Sentiment remains and binds' (*SJ* 3: 37). The binding power of sentiment among kindred spirits ultimately constructs trans-national connection.

Part 2. Montgomery and Canadian Society: Negotiating Cultural Change

'It is my misfortune to be a born conservative, hater of change, and to live my life in a period when everything has been, or is being turned topsy turvey, from the old religions down,' writes Montgomery in her diary on 30 October 1925. 'My aunts and grandmother lived practically their whole lives in an unchanged world. Changes came to them in the natural course of life but never were the foundations of their lives torn away from beneath their feet. For myself I have my own foundation and I stand firmly on it' (*SJ* 3: 259). The year 1925 saw the publication of *The Great Gatsby* in the United States and of *Settlers of the Marsh* in Canada. From her firm foundation, L.M. Montgomery captured these changing world spirits by negotiating them, holding on to the values that seemed to have been undone by the experience of the First World War. In effect, for Montgomery, the post-Victorian world was not one of modernist experimentation, but it was one in which she forged, ever more val-iantly, a sense of value, responsibility, and social meaning, resorting to the conventions of romance in order to heal the psychic wounds in the young nation's imaginary.

Montgomery's cultural moulding is evidenced nicely in her reflec-tions on the church, the education system, feminism, and modern technologies. After the vote for amalgamation of the Congregationalist, Methodist, and Presbyterian Churches, she mourned the loss of the 'stately Presbyterian church, with its noble history and inspiring tradi-tions' (*SJ* 3: 132); on 10 June 1925, this amalgamation would result in the creation of the United Church of Canada. As Mary Rubio documents in chapter 6, Montgomery sets a testimony to Presbyterian traditions and values in her writing, including the focus on egalitarianism, the work ethic, and agency so important in her writing and the development of her characters. Montgomery's ambivalent oscillation between social change and protection of old values is illustrated in her focus on the teaching profession. Although the school is a classical space of authority, Montgomery uses the tools of satire in her classroom settings to expose the sins of authoritarian teaching. Yet, in strange ironic reversal, her most charismatic teacher figures also hold on to the disciplinarian strategies that are linked with the old Victorian and Presbyterian tradition.

A woman with her own profession, income, and public name, Montgomery continued to adhere to the values of traditional domestic femininity, holding on to the power of women in the Victorian household. Montgomery's era witnessed the achievement of important rights for Canadian women, including the right to vote in federal elections, granted in 1918, during the last year of the First World War.[4] In 1911, Montgomery had married at age thirty-six, not necessarily for love, but to have a family. Although both before and after her marriage Montgomery adhered to the values of the traditional family, her fiction also presented new alternatives of mothering for women. The adoption of an orphan child makes possible the enjoyment of motherhood at a later stage in life, as it makes possible single motherhood without the constraints of (unhappy) marital ties. The breakdown of marriage and the transformation of the family are the topics of L.M. Montgomery's later fiction, and the restoration of the traditional family is achieved only within the context of an overt fairy tale structure. Issues of family tensions, marital separation, and child custody move into the foreground of Montgomery's later fiction, corresponding to Montgomery's own life of increased marital strain and of worries about her son Chester's impending divorce.

The most pleasurable change negotiated through Montgomery's satiric writing concerns the arrival of new technologies in Canada, most notably, as Sasha Mullally describes in chapter 8, the automobile. While automobile travel was a subject of heated debate across North America during the 1920s, Montgomery's affection for 'Daisy,' 'Dodgie,' and 'Lady Jane Grey Dort' showed an author who had thoroughly embraced the new technology. Montgomery's satiric pen helped in exploring and negotiating the changes that affected Canada's institutional lives as well as the daily lives of individuals. Far from being truly conservative,

Montgomery would often publicly condemn what she privately endorsed, and vice versa. Her ambivalence regarding feminism, technology, institutionalized religion, and discipline in raising children strategically participates in the shaping of cultural and social change, while also inscribing deeply ironic contradictions. Ultimately, this satiric negotiation does more than raise awareness of the issues addressed – it actively participates in the process of cultural transformation.

Part 3. Montgomery and Canadian Iconography: Consuming the Popular

As early as 1908, Montgomery enjoyed the glamorous status of a best-selling author, whose *Anne of Green Gables* had sold over 19,000 copies in the first five months of publication. As a popular icon, she transcended the region and country that had given birth to her and was compared with America's foremost humorist, Samuel Clemens, alias Mark Twain, who supported her writing enthusiastically. The scene most deeply ingrained in the American cultural consciousness is that of Tom tricking his friends into whitewashing a fence 'by pretending it is a great privilege and making them pay to take over the job,' as Louis J. Budd explains in 'Mark Twain as an American Icon' (6).[5] In Montgomery's fiction, the correlative episode is that of Anne breaking her slate over Gilbert's head, after he calls her 'carrots.' The scene, by far the most well known, most frequently cited, and most often reproduced in commercial products for tourists, is remarkable in that it thematizes the eruption of female temper in a space of male authority, Mr Phillips's classroom. The scene is pleasurable despite the punishment that follows Anne's transgression, as the reader sides with Anne and her rebellious spirit. And so do others: Marilla, who recognizes something of her own youthful spirit in Anne; Diana, who is in awe of Anne's daring; and Gilbert, who is truly taken with her courage. The moment of female transgression, overtly punished, is covertly praised, admired, and even eroticized, as this scene, of course, sparks Gilbert's romantic interest, initiating the romantic plot of male desire and female delay.

It is revealing that Anne's subversiveness and putative feminism were repressed in the 1934 Hollywood version of *Anne of Green Gables*: as Theodore Sheckels shows in chapter 13, the powerful female friendships are sacrificed to make room for Anne and Gilbert's romance. The subversive elements repressed in the film are significantly ones with specific Canadian implications. Frank Davey argues in chapter 12 that Anne's self-naming and creation of a new identity have become part of the Canadian memory, and are found in many later Canadian writers, including Margaret Laurence, Alice Munro, and Margaret Atwood, but also in Canada's only female prime minister, Kim Campbell, another orphan who renamed herself at age twelve. The story of Anne Shirley, a mythic Canadian story, depicts a heroine who is pulled in one direction by her drive for independence and in another by her desire to belong and to be recognized by authority. The power of self-transformation emerges strongly in Anne Shirley's story, and this power does not lead only to romantic escapism and the maintenance of the status quo. As Dianne Hicks Morrow's interview with writer Sharon Hamilton illustrates in chapter 14, the novel taught the thirteen-year-old Winnipeg reader how to transform her own negative energy into creative self-construction and self-invention, both of which involved a rejection of names created for her. *My Name's Not Susie* is the title of Hamilton's autobiographical book, which pays homage to Montgomery's Anne many decades after the first publication of *Anne of Green Gables* for providing a role model for Hamilton's own childhood spent wrestling with socially imposed negative definitions.

As described in the chapters by Calvin Trillin and Margaret Atwood, Canadian and international cultural tourists flock to see *Anne of Green Gables: The Musical,* to visit Montgomery's birth site and the Anne of Green Gables and the Macneill homestead sites in Cavendish. Japanese tourists make the long journey to Prince Edward Island to get married in the same Campbell family farmhouse parlour in Park Corner in which Montgomery spoke her vows in 1911. According to one Japanese travel magazine survey, Prince Edward Island ranks fourth in the list of favourite travelling spots for Japanese, after New York, Paris, and London. In chapter 15 Yoshiko Akamatsu explains the enormous stimulus *Anne of Green Gables* has had on the imagination of Japanese readers, many of whom have come to use it as a guidebook for life and for positive thinking. The consumption of Anne within the late-twentieth-century tourist and mass-market context has produced an equally vibrant counter-culture: *Annekenstein,* performed for the benefit of both tourists and Islanders increasingly weary of commercialized Anne, is a popular parody of the novel, the musical, and the Anne industry. In one skit, Anne, played by a male with red braids, is placed in competition with other literary orphans Huck Finn and Oliver Twist. This counter-culture itself, ironically, also presents a tribute to Anne and requires further investigation.

While scholarship over the past two decades has made important inroads in taking L.M. Montgomery seriously, this collection of essays reclaims Montgomery within the realm of Canadian literary and cultural studies. As an author who truly spans the nation, Montgomery is unique in that she reached and still reaches a broad Canadian readership: from Atlantic Canada to the Western provinces, the lower to the upper classes, rural to urban areas, young to old, female to male, English Canadian to French Canadian and Québécois. The Kindred Spirits electronic discussion group, created in 1994 and delivered through the L.M. Montgomery Institute at the University of Prince Edward Island, is the latest technology that allows Montgomery fans to connect and create a community in virtual space in order to chat about Montgomery-related matters and to revive the spirit of connection and community. Ultimately, it is this spirit of connection that makes Montgomery an important spokesperson, while her mythological and real Prince Edward Island remains deeply ingrained in Canada's cultural imaginary.

NOTES

1 In addition to the plethora of journalistic discussions in the written and electronic news media in Canada, the United States, Europe, and Japan, there have been a number of landmark scholarly studies, which will be introduced and discussed in the following chapters. Suffice it to mention three representative studies here: Gabriella Åhmansson's *A Life and Its Mirrors: A Feminist Reading of L.M. Montgomery's Fiction* and Elizabeth Epperly's *The Fragrance of Sweet-Grass: L.M. Montgomery's Heroines and the Pursuit of Romance*, both of which examine Montgomery's contributions to feminism and women's literature; and *Harvesting Thistles: The Textual Garden of L.M. Montgomery*, a collection of essays edited by Mary Henley Rubio, which deploys new interpretative strategies in re-reading Montgomery's texts in light of feminist, autobiographical, and cultural theories.
2 Several comprehensive research projects examining the politics of Canadian canonization through literary histories are currently underway in Canada, including a comprehensive study of Canada's official literary histories by E.D. Blodgett and a cross-country study of university curricula in Canadian literature by Paul Martin.
3 In *Courageous Women*, four of the seventeen Canadian women portrayed are French and two are Native: they all are strategically constructed as Canadian. The story of singer Madame Albani (alias Emma Lajeunesse) from the little town of Chambly is typical. Albani is introduced in the title as

'Canada's Queen of Song,' a strategic construction echoing today's Canadianization of Québécois sports stars (Jacques Villeneuve) or singers (Céline Dion) in the public media. Many of the Canadian portraits are those of new immigrants, English, German, Scottish; other portraits are Canadians living in other parts of the world, such as India or London.

4 *Courageous Women* pays tribute to Margaret Polson Murray, a leader in the founding of the Imperial Order Daughters of the Empire, and to Lady Tilley (Alice Starr Chipman), a leader of the National Council of Women, while Montgomery herself was one of the first members of the Women's Press Club, established in 1904.

5 The episode, of course, encapsulates the ingenuity of capitalist money making and the boy's clever manipulation of the nation's values.

Part 1.
Montgomery and Canada:
Romancing the Region, Constructing the Nation

MONTGOMERY AND CANADIAN NATIONALISM

1

'A Born Canadian': The Bonds of Communal Identity in *Anne of Green Gables* and *A Tangled Web*

LAURA M. ROBINSON

At the launching of the L.M. Montgomery Institute at the University of Prince Edward Island, Adrienne Clarkson explained that Montgomery's works helped her to understand Canada when she was a young immigrant. What is significant in Clarkson's recollection of her childhood encounters with Montgomery's novels is the power these texts had to shape Clarkson's understanding of a shared Canadian identity. Montgomery certainly brings women together in 'what amounts to a universal sisterhood, regardless of age or nationality,' as Gabriella Åhmansson has argued ('Mayflowers' 17). Yet Montgomery's best-selling novels, by their setting, their references to domestic politics, and their focus on national identity, are distinctly Canadian, an issue that has been largely overlooked. Montgomery's texts reflect distinctive trends in Canadian history, while simultaneously constructing beliefs and attitudes that, in turn, become trends and shape Canadian cultural identity for her readers at home and abroad. That she has so many readers spanning the globe makes it that much more important to examine the ideological web of Canadian identity she espouses.

Acceptance of difference is a significant part of the identity politics Adrienne Clarkson encountered in her reading of Montgomery's fiction. As Clarkson indicates in the Foreword of this book, the community of Avonlea ultimately opens its arms to welcome the newcomer, who moves through a delightful process of acculturation. Yet Montgomery's fiction, with its focus on the rural world of Prince Edward Island, also reflects the opposite – the anxiety Islanders and Canadians felt about 'outsiders,' about those 'from away' during important periods of Canadian history. In two representative novels, *Anne of Green Gables* and *A Tangled Web*, published in 1908 and 1931 respectively, the language of nationalism assumed by some of the characters is entwined with the exclusion of the foreign, even while Montgomery's overall message of tolerance looms large. The writing and publication dates of *Anne of Green Gables* belong to the first decade of the twentieth century, a period characterized by an almost unprecedented immigration wave in Canada, which resulted in concern among the native-born over the integrity of Canada's cultural traditions (Avery 31).[1] Anne, a symbol of difference who achieves acceptance in a new cultural space, also symbolizes the need for tolerance. Although immigration had significantly declined by the early 1930s because of the Great Depression, the period in which Montgomery wrote the later novel was characterized by more and disturbing manifestations of xenophobia in Canada (Granatstein et al. 266; Avery 12). Increasing suspicion of foreigners may explain why *A Tangled Web* encodes an obsession with cultural origins and ethnic purity that seems to belie a message of tolerance.

Yet despite characters' preoccupation with national, ethnic, racial, or clan identity, Montgomery's fiction continues to insist on the positive power of individual and ethnic differences. Ultimately, Montgomery uses nationalism, paired with tribalism, as the grand metaphor in these novels in order to explore the pressures to eradicate difference from within the ranks of community. Montgomery's texts expose the pernicious side to forming a rigidly fixed communal, and correspondingly national, identity. While not without her own ideological contradictions, Montgomery criticizes a xenophobic nationalism, suggesting through her support of the individual's struggle for acceptance that communal, and by extension national, identity should be one of tolerance. This embracing of difference may explain why a young Canadian immigrant such as Clarkson was attracted to Montgomery's writings in her own process of acculturation.

The Bonds of Canadian Nationalism

One ideological function of literature, according to Homi K. Bhabha, is nationalist: 'The scraps, patches and rags of daily life must be repeatedly turned into the signs of a national culture,' explains Bhabha, 'while the very act of the narrative performance interpellates a growing circle of national subjects' ('DissemiNation' 297). Likewise, Etienne Balibar describes the nationalist enterprise of creating 'a people': 'A social formation only reproduces itself as a nation to the extent that, through a network of apparatuses and daily practices, the individual is instituted as *homo nationalis* from cradle to grave' (93). Balibar suggests that nations develop unity by 'interpellating' individuals as subjects in an emotional and not a political sense: 'Ideological form must become an *a priori* condition of communication between individuals (the "citizens") and between social groups – not by suppressing all differences, but by relativizing them and subordinating them to itself in such a way that it is the symbolic difference between "ourselves" and "foreigners" which wins out and is lived as irreducible' (94). Significant individual differences within a group seem erased, in other words, by the perceived differences of ethnicity, race, and language that separate the group from the outsiders.

This pressure to eradicate differences in the creation of a communal identity is most explicitly expressed through the tangled web of Montgomery's late novel. *A Tangled Web* vibrates with fear about being an outsider; ethnic epithets and stereotypes pepper the novel in an apparently gratuitous fashion. Being drunk is referred to as 'Dutch courage' (188), while an indignant Uncle Pippin questions himself about Stanton Grundy's claim to clan identity: 'what right had this outsider, who was strongly suspected of being a Swedenborgian, whatever that was, to amuse himself over Dark whimsies and Penhallow peculiarities?' (7). Referring to a religious sect, Swedenborgian sounds non-Anglo-Saxon and resonates with the sense of something dangerously alien, essentially different from clan identity. Clan identity is shown to be a sacred entity, in which the ties of loyalty are fiercely felt and in which the desire for ethnic purity is voiced in openly xenophobic fashion.

This tangled web of communal bond and national identity finds its seeds in Montgomery's first novel. In *Anne of Green Gables*, the good folk of Avonlea set themselves apart from others as a distinct people by a discourse of inclusion and exclusion: community and outsider; Canadian and foreigner. In a prominent example early in the novel, national identity shows itself to be a strong rallying point as Marilla justifies her choice of orphan to 'all-seeing' Rachel Lynde, the town's vigilant and sometimes aggressive watchdog. Through Mrs Lynde's perspective, the narrator heightens the expected orphan's putative difference through parody, simultaneously downplaying and accentuating the foreign nature of the expected child: 'If Marilla had said that Matthew had gone to Bright River to meet a kangaroo from Australia Mrs. Rachel could not have been more astonished' (11). On one hand, emphasizing the strangeness shows the community's anxiety over outsiders; on the other, the exaggerated cultural difference – the orphan is not a kangaroo, nor is he from Australia – suggests that the child will not be as different as Mrs

Lynde expects. The narrative strategically makes Rachel Lynde's narrow-mindedness the object of irreverent parody, and revels in her shocked surprise. The over-exposure of her parochial prejudices undermines her credibility, a significant narrative gesture, as she will soon give voice to Avonlea's anxiety about strangers: 'You're bringing a strange child into your house and home and you don't know a single thing about him nor what his disposition is like nor what sort of parents he had nor how he's likely to turn out' (13).

In anticipation of this fear (and probably sharing it), Marilla goes to great lengths to vindicate her decision to Mrs Lynde. Explaining that the Cuthberts need help around the farm, she resorts to the discourse of Canadianness to diminish the potential difference of the soon-to-arrive orphan-helper.

There's never anybody to be had but those stupid, half-grown little French boys; and as soon as you do get one broke into your ways and taught something he's up and off to the lobster canneries or the States. At first Matthew suggested getting a Barnado [sic] boy. But I said 'no' flat to that. 'They may be all right – I'm not saying they're not – but no London street Arabs for me,' I said. 'Give me a native born at least. There'll be a risk, no matter who we get. But I'll feel easier in my mind and sleep sounder at nights if we get a born Canadian. (12)

Marilla's insistence on a 'born Canadian,' an orphan from an asylum in Nova Scotia, warrants a closer look. The Canadian orphan 'can't be much different from ourselves' (14), argues Marilla. In other words, the same national identity, for Marilla, means an irrefutable common bond, which keeps the risks of foreignness at a minimum; the newly adopted orphan will be given schooling, a family, and a home, all of which will help him overcome the remaining signifiers of difference.

Yet what exactly is the Canadian identity Marilla espouses? As Owen Dudley Edwards and Jennifer H. Litster argue in chapter 2 of this book, 'such avowed statements of cohesive Canadian identity' are rare in Montgomery's fiction; indeed, the explicitness of Marilla's patriotism makes her a spokeswoman for the country, an analogy to Dudley Edwards's argument that Susan Baker in *Rilla of Ingleside*, also a mature woman, represents the young Canadian nation ('Montgomery's *Rilla*'). Just as Susan Baker's Canada during wartime is formulated in opposition to the enemy, Germany, so Marilla's Canadian identity is formulated in opposition to two other countries: Britain, as signified by her rejection of the Barnardo boys, the street orphans sent from Great Britain to the Canadian Dominion for a new home; and the United States, as signified by her rejection of the hired boys who leave Canada behind in search for greener pastures to the south.

It is, of course, the opposition Marilla creates between the 'born Canadian' and the 'stupid, half-grown little French boys' that most clearly reveals the ideological prejudices of race and class in her espousal of Canadian identity. Hired boys, generally French, do not garner much respect in Avonlea, as illustrated in the treatment of Jerry Buote, the French boy hired by Matthew after the Cuthberts decide to keep Anne. While Jerry sits down to meals with the Cuthberts, the boundaries between him and the family are clear. Also, earlier in the novel, when Marilla sits in a chair at Rachel's home, Rachel suggests she move to a more comfortable chair: 'I just keep that for the hired boy to sit on' (84).[2] This distinction between Marilla's position and the hired boy's is made after Anne has made her alarming apology to Rachel. Similarly, after Anne makes her liniment cake, Marilla tells her to feed it to the pigs: 'It isn't fit for any human to eat, not even Jerry Buote' (192). Again the difference between Jerry and other people is brought up at a time when Anne has transgressed the boundaries of Avonlea acceptability by flavouring a cake with liniment rather than vanilla. At least, Marilla seems to suggest, Anne is not as different as Jerry. These references to the French in conjunction with Marilla's evocation of the 'born Canadian' create an intriguing contradiction within the text's fabric, for the Acadian community referred to belongs to the earliest settlement group in Canada. The irony of this contradiction, of course, is entirely lost on Marilla and Rachel, whose ethnic shortsightedness blends in with the endemic cultural suspicions of Avonlea. Such cultural blind spots make them perfect representatives of their communities: they are comical types, locked in their prejudices.

In Avonlea, the foreign is always suspect and the suspect is always foreign, and much of the novel's satiric energy takes as its focus Anne's perceived foreignness. It is the intrusion of Anne that will stir up and challenge some of the dynamics of communal bonding. When Anne dyes her hair green, she does so with dye purchased from a peddler, and Marilla betrays her assumptions about the peddler's nationality: 'I told you never to let one of those Italians in the house' (234). Anne, in all earnestness, corrects her: 'he wasn't an Italian – he was a German Jew' (234). Anne's response is humorous because the particular nationality is not the issue for Marilla: letting a foreigner into the house is. The joke gains further significance in the context in which it is placed. Anne's desire to dye her hair was motivated by vanity, as Marilla sees it, but as the reader realizes, it was also motivated by a desperate desire to belong to the community of Avonlea. By trying to erase the bodily signifier of her foreignness, her red hair, Anne has, ironically, dyed her hair green and she will truly stand out in Avonlea. The connection between the peddler and Anne is reinforced: he has brought dye into the self-contained community of Avonlea; Anne is wearing the signifier of excessive difference on her body. Anne's acculturation into her community follows a process described earlier by Etienne Balibar: the foreign is not so much suppressed but is first made to stand out and is then relativized, with the qualifier, however, that Anne manages to rescue important aspects of her difference, even while becoming socialized into Avonlea's community. What needs to be explored more fully now is the complex relationship between national identity and clan identity that constitutes the fabric of Avonlea.

Tribalism and Nationalism Entwined

Etienne Balibar suggests that the focus on families and lineal kinship has become displaced into 'a nationalization of the family,' that identifies nationality as a symbolic family origin (102). Therefore, nationalism can be seen as a type of 'tribalism' that reveals 'the substitution of one imaginary kinship for another, a substitution which the nation effects and which underpins the transformation of the family itself' (102). Kinship is as exclusive and disapprobative as nationalism. Michèle Barrett and Mary McIntosh argue that 'the family,' always spoken of as if it were some universal, readily recognizable, fixed entity, is not only a cultural institution but also an ideology. This ideology of the family, *familism* in their terms, can have anti-social implications if it privileges family members to the detriment of the community at large: 'The family embodies the principles of selfishness, exclusion and pursuit of private interest and contravenes those of altruism, community and pursuit of the public good. Society is *divided into* families and the divisions are deep, not merely ones of slight antipathy and mild distrust' (Barrett and McIntosh 47). Familism, like nationalist ideology, is a way of distinguishing one family as superior to another and establishing cohesion within the group by overlooking differences.

Readers of *Anne of Green Gables* will recall the Pyes as the most scorned family in Avonlea. Josie Pye is Anne's sharp-tongued, envious rival, and when Anne voices her feelings about Josie to Marilla, the consoling reply is that 'Josie is a Pye.' The Pye name itself is attached to a cluster of negative meanings, as Marilla explains: 'she can't help being disagreeable. I suppose people of that kind serve some useful purpose in society, but I must say I don't know what it is any more than I know the use of thistles' (320). Similarly, Diana comments that 'those Pye girls are cheats all round' (122). The Pyes' negative image is a clear example of familism in that it serves an important purpose: their clan serves as a distinction by which others can identify themselves positively. As such, Anne and Marilla partly affirm their ties as a newly constituted family by distinguishing themselves from another, less agreeable, one. Familial identity in Montgomery's early fiction is based on a certain degree of openness, as suggested by the unconventional family configuration of an elderly brother–sister couple adopting an eleven-year-old girl.

In the later novels, issues of blood identity, of genealogy and lineage, become more important for the creation of a cohesive community bond. Familism is the ideological focus in *A Tangled Web*, as Montgomery grapples with issues of clan identity and ethnic purity. Anxiety over kinship identity permeates *A Tangled Web* as characters struggle to validate their connection with the Dark and Penhallow lineage. Despite internal problems, the clan remains cohesive: 'They were still a proud, vigorous, and virile clan who hacked and hewed among themselves but presented an unbroken front to any alien or hostile force' (2). The key question of the novel – Who will inherit Aunt Becky's jug? – shows the distress about which individuals are considered more acceptable than others. The jug's unknown inheritor is assumed to be an upright member of the clan who has claims to closest kinship. The Darks and Penhallows marry only within the clan, and the tangled web is 'the resultant genealogical tangle' (1). They do not marry outside their clan because they feel a sense of superiority over other families. The Gibsons, for example, are not good enough for Gay Penhallow to marry into. Gay thinks to herself, 'those inbred Darks and Penhallows! Don't dare marry outside of the Royal Family!' (111). Whoever boasts the most undiluted mixture of Dark and Penhallow might be the recipient of the heirloom jug, the uncontested symbol of clan acceptance. Uncle Pippin, for example, 'knew he had no chance of getting the jug. He was only fourth cousin at best, even granting the dubious paternity about which Aunt Becky had twitted him' (5). The jug can go only to those who belong: the narrator parodies the clan's concern by asking, 'Suppose Aunt Becky left the jug to some rank outsider?' (49).

The tremendous anxiety over the jug and the clan's eagerness to prove their individual purity of kinship results in the clan's rejection of difference based on seemingly insignificant details. About Oswald Dark, for example, 'a few shook their heads over the fact that Oswald's grandmother had been an outsider – a Moorland from down east. Who knew what sinister strain she might have brought into the pure Dark and Penhallow blood?' (39). A different family from a community that could not even be that far away, given the small size of Prince Edward Island, is grounds for distress. Furthermore, the grandmother's name contains the word 'Moor,' reverberating with connotations of religious, national, and racial difference. Montgomery reveals a kinship identity that is intolerant of difference.

As Barrett and McIntosh point out, '[t]he exclusion of outsiders and turning in to the little family group may seem attractive when it works well and when the family does satisfy its members' needs. But the little enclosed group can also be a trap, a prison whose walls and bars are constructed of the ideas of domestic privacy and autonomy' (56). Since Montgomery's focus is always on individuals inside of family and community bonds, it comes as no surprise that she zooms in on the constraints and entrapments involved in such bonds. Aunt Becky writes in her own obituary: '*she longed for freedom, as all women do, but had sense enough to understand that real freedom is impossible in this kind of a world, the lucky people being those who can choose their masters, so she never made the mistake of kicking uselessly over the traces*' (*TW* 48; italics in original).[3]

While interdependence seems to be the dominant theme of these two novels, Montgomery does not lull her readers into a complacent acceptance of the status quo. Mary Rubio suggests that 'Montgomery both works within the traditional literary genre of domestic romance and yet circumvents its restrictive conventions when she critiques her society' ('Subverting' 8). Rubio illustrates that Montgomery both complies with dominant ideologies and provides an oppositional voice to them. This argument extends to the realm of kinship and national identity construction. Individuals in Montgomery's novels want approval and admission to the group identity, but acceptance often proves conditional. Ultimately, Montgomery forces readers to question the familism espoused by characters who are maligned by the narrator's wit.

The same principles that operate to establish a Canadian identity in Marilla's Avonlea based on a particular ethnicity and birthplace also operate to create families, lineages, and clans based on a sense of superiority and exclusion. Yet Montgomery's pen sharply attacks the prejudice inherent in such kinship identities in order to reveal their inherent limitations. Both novels indicate that the exclusionary politics that form the 'cohesive' group ultimately enforce conformity to it: the characters struggling to establish their own sense of identity within the family are battling the very same constructs that 'other' those outside their clan. It is the degree to which they are able to forge acceptance for their differences that will now be further investigated.

Forging Acceptance

From the outset of *Anne of Green Gables*, Anne desperately wants to belong to the Cuthberts, live at Green Gables, and be accepted by Avonlea. In one of the poignant moments of the novel, Anne swears to Marilla, 'I'll try to do and be anything you want me, if you'll only keep me' (55), suggesting that belonging is more important than individuality. Much effort is expended to shape Anne into a model girl and teenager, and Anne tries hard to learn, realizing that ridicule, ostracism, and loneliness are the cost of not conforming. After all, Anne has already experienced 'a world that had not wanted her' (48). At the same time, however, Anne's conformity is frequently a theatricalized parody of conformity, best encapsulated in her exaggerated apology to Rachel Lynde: 'I deserve to be punished and cast out by respectable people for ever' (82), she tells Rachel, while flaunting her 'otherness' under the guise of humbleness, a double discourse performed for the pleasure of both Marilla and the reader. Anne has learned the lesson of mimicking conformity, while also subverting it through parodic excess.

Of course, Montgomery's characters do not overtly defy their community. Rather, the protagonist of *Green Gables* successfully negotiates her differences in order to ensure a positive social position. Drain writes of *Anne of Green Gables*, '[t]o be adopted into the Avonlea community by the Cuthberts does not mean a comfortable sinking into conformity' ('Community' 17). Toward the end of the novel, Anne's difference from the rest of Avonlea is still pronounced, as Waterston writes in *Kindling Spirit*: 'Anne is not transformed into anything basically different from what she was at the start'; Anne is simply, Waterston contends, 'now properly recognized' (69). Miss Barry appreciates Anne because she is not like other girls: 'there is such a provoking and eternal sameness about them' (*AGG* 306). Likewise, Marilla suggests that Anne still retains a degree of outsider status when she remarks on Anne's dress: Anne looks so 'different altogether in that dress – as if [she] didn't belong in Avonlea at all' (*AGG* 296).

Likewise in *A Tangled Web*, several characters successfully insist on their differences. Quiet Margaret Penhallow is perhaps the most victorious character. She has a dream of living in a particular house and raising a child by herself. Even though the narrative takes her through an aborted engagement with the preposterous Penny, she evades socially acceptable marriage. After receiving $10,000 for a first edition of *Pilgrim's Progress*, Margaret realizes her dream by purchasing the house and adopting Brian, an abused child. Her goals are inadvertently achieved through the grand dame of the clan, Aunt Becky, who gave her the book. While Margaret pursues the unconventional path of single motherhood, her 'inheritance,' her clan identity, has enabled her to do so.

However, the power of conformity is ultimately much more triumphant in *A Tangled Web*, with the sense of entrapment already signalled in the title. From the beginning, Aunt Becky's attacks on clan members and the ever-present fear of being ostracized by the group are clear examples of the clan's attempts to control and eradicate individual differences. Aunt Becky ridicules Margaret Penhallow for writing bad poetry for the papers until Margaret gives up her writing, 'much to the clan's thankfulness' (11). Widow Donna Dark feels trapped in a role of remaining faithful to her dead husband: 'she suddenly felt sick and tired of the whole thing – of the whole clan – of her whole tame existence. What was she living for, anyhow? She felt as out of place as the blank, unfaded space left on the wall where a picture had hung' (58). The clan is distressed when she changes her behaviour, particularly because she has fallen in love with a man on the wrong side of the family feud. Donna feels increasingly ostracized: 'she had no friends – she was alone in a hostile, unfeeling clan world' (135).

Clan members who behave in transgressive ways inevitably become outsiders. Because Joscelyn had left Hugh, to the clan's disbelief, 'she had always felt a little outside of things and the feeling had deepened with the years' (*TW* 26). Like Donna, Joscelyn finds the clan oppressive: 'Joscelyn could neither tell nor live a lie – which was what had made a clan existence hard for her' (75). Gay Penhallow transgresses the wishes of the clan when she becomes engaged to Noel Gibson rather than to Roger Penhallow. She feels hostility toward her unsympathetic kin; yet, as her cousin Nan and Noel become closer friends, 'there were moments when Gay felt like an outsider, as they talked to each other a patter she couldn't talk' (142). In another case of irreconcilable differences, Big Sam refuses to continue living with Little Sam after the latter brings home an alabaster statue of a nude woman. By his admiration of the statue, Little Sam has offended Big Sam's notions of decency. Transgressions cannot be tolerated. The novel's point is that the struggle to have individual difference accepted is difficult in the face of overwhelming disapprobation. Montgomery has to resort to a *deus ex machina* or some kind of epiphany in order to facilitate community acceptance.[4] Ultimately, she does not present a clan identity that is tolerant; she merely implies it should be.

Conclusion

Literature, as one facet of cultural ideology, can have a didactic effect of interpellating the reader by presenting a subject position that the reader recognizes and uses to understand his or her own material conditions, just as Adrienne Clarkson felt that she gained an understanding of Canadian identity through the works of Montgomery. Thus, the often conflicting ideological messages imparted in narrative become particularly significant: they do not just reflect the ideology of a given historical moment, but operate to shape ideology. L.M. Montgomery exposes the rigidity of a fixed identity – whether national or familial – and lobbies for an identity that recognizes the positive power of difference. Anne, known in Canada and abroad through books, movies, and a booming tourist industry, symbolizes that difference.

In a crucial scene, Anne pleads her case with Marilla by resorting to the language of patriotism, appropriately doubling Marilla's earlier patriotic discourse. She requests permission to participate in a school concert, 'for the laudable purpose of helping to pay for a schoolhouse flag' (208). Marilla, of course, is not convinced that Anne is truly motivated by patriotism, and suspects a subversive element of fun and enjoyment behind the request. While Marilla's version of patriotism and Canada is associated with values such as duty and hard work, Anne persists in making her point: 'when you can combine patriotism and fun, isn't it all right?' (208).

As always, readers side with Anne. Anne's marrying of personal fun and public duty opens up Marilla's petrified conception of Canadian identity. And this is the crucial ideological point of L.M. Montgomery's fiction: rigid identities formed in generations of family and clan life, in danger of merging into rigid nationalism, are opened up through laughter. Laughter allows elements of difference to initiate the process of transforming the community's perception, even while the carriers of difference become transformed themselves by the community. This mixture is what continues to appeal to readers in Canada, including the newcomers such as Adrienne Clarkson. And it is this mixture that will continue to captivate Montgomery's audience, including this late-twentieth-century Canadian reader unravelling the ideological entanglements of Montgomery's creative web.

NOTES

1 For statistics on immigration in both this decade and 1931, see Kalback. Prince Edward Island was the only province not to experience a growth in 1901–11 (Granatstein et al. 42); however, the overwhelming immigration to Canada would still have affected attitudes on the Island. Recognizing the influence of contemporary politics on the writing of Montgomery's first novel, Elizabeth Waterston suggests that Anne represents Canadian moderation in the face of two superior powers, Britain and the United States (*Kindling Spirit* 75).
2 For an in-depth discussion of the representation of the French in Montgomery's fiction, see White.
3 Writing about *Anne of Green Gables*, Susan Drain echoes Aunt Becky's understanding of limited freedom: 'individuality ... is established not in contrast to a community, but by a commitment to it, and the individual's freedom is not in the isolation of independence, but in the complexity of connection' ('Community' 19).
4 Indeed, as Elizabeth Epperly has shown, several crucial voices critical of conformity throughout the text are significantly undercut 'by the positive resolution to all the stories' (*Fragrance of Sweet-Grass* 246). Struggles are resolved through events drawing attention to themselves as conventions of fiction: an inadvertent rescue from fire in the case of Donna, a book that cannot be judged by its cover for Margaret, and a sudden change of heart for Gay, Joscelyn, and the Sams.

2

The End of Canadian Innocence: L.M. Montgomery and the First World War

OWEN DUDLEY EDWARDS and JENNIFER H. LITSTER

When Marilla Cuthbert surprises Rachel Lynde by telling her that she is adopting a 'born Canadian' orphan, the Canadian setting of *Anne of Green Gables* should be identified for those readers unilluminated by the references to the Gulf of St Lawrence and Nova Scotia. By her prejudice against Barnardo boys, who are not 'native born,' Marilla also makes a surprisingly definitive statement of Canadian nationality for a character whose parents were born in Scotland and who lived on an island only recently and reluctantly confederated into the Dominion.[1] Anne's being twenty-seven at the time of the Liberal victory in the federal election of 1896 puts her birth date at 1869. Her appearance as an eleven-year-old at the beginning of *Anne of Green Gables* thus comes in 1880, only seven years after Prince Edward Islanders belatedly gathered under the Canadian banner.[2] But L.M. Montgomery's early novels seldom show avowed statements of cohesive Canadian identity: loyalty is more often given to home, to community, and to the Island itself, frequently coupled with an air of personal or collective superiority that works against other villagers, villages, cities, and provinces. Ties remain strong with the country and culture of origin, principally Scotland, but also England and Ireland; hostility and suspicion toward the United States is prevalent from a cast list who have 'no truck or trade with the Yankees.'

Such mixed loyalties reflect Canadian problems in these early years of nationhood: debates over the extent of Canadian involvement in the Boer War had illustrated both the troublesome relationship with the expansionist British Empire and the differing allegiances of anglophone and francophone Canadians; anti-American feeling was a powerful factor in Laurier's defeat in the reciprocity election of 1911. The advent of the First World War, which brought massive Canadian aid to the British

Empire and Allied countries, contrasted with initial U.S. neutrality but was by no means indicative of a new Canadian cohesion, as the largely ethnic divisions over conscription in 1917 would show.[3]

Montgomery herself had no doubts as to where Canadian loyalty should lie in 1914. Responding angrily to a claim by her pen-friend Ephraim Weber that the conflict was 'a commercial war and utterly unworthy of one drop of Canadian blood being spilt for it,' Montgomery wrote that 'it is a death-grapple between freedom and tyranny, between modern and medieaval [sic] ideals ... between the principles of democracy and militarism.'[4] Although this reasoning could have appropriately been used by those who had left the tyrannies of the mother country in search of a new freedom in North America, Montgomery countered these objections to British imperialism by recourse to what she saw as a shared ideological heritage.

Conversely, and belying this equation of British with Canadian values, she felt the sacrifices and bloodshed of war would forge real Canadian unity for the first time and produce in their wake great Canadian literature.[5] For Montgomery, war began with the death (actually stillbirth) of her second child, Hugh, and claimed her closest friend, Frederica Campbell MacFarlane, who died in the flu epidemic that followed in its wake. Montgomery's four novels written during the war and its immediate aftermath examine the ideology behind Canadian involvement in the war, express Canadian hostility at American neutrality, reflect the alterations in Canadian society resulting from the war, and witness radical changes in Montgomery's own literary style.

Montgomery's War Novels

Taking up work on her sixth Anne book, which followed the fortunes of the Blythe family and Glen St Mary community through the years of the First World War, L.M. Montgomery somewhat paradoxically wrote in her journal that *Rilla of Ingleside* would be the last of that series as Anne 'belongs to the green, untroubled pastures and still waters of the world before the war' (*SJ* 2: 309). Anne's shadowy presence and near neurasthenic condition in this novel are indeed indicative of her comparative uselessness and inappropriateness (certainly in contrast to her youngest daughter and her maid) in this crisis. Montgomery, describing herself as writing with a purpose for the first time, would seem to be quite deliberate in her intention of conveying the full horror of war by visiting its ravages on a heroine associated in the public mind both with the isolated regional idyll and peaceful pastoralism.[6]

Certainly Montgomery makes a huge chronological leap between *Rainbow Valley* and *Rilla of Ingleside* (as evidenced in their mutual discrepancies over Anne's children's ages), breaking with the close sequential nature of the earlier Anne books in order to write of the war while the experiences were still fresh. However, only the first two Anne books were written in the pre-war still waters; although set years before the shadow of conflict fell, *Anne of the Island*, *Anne's House of Dreams*, and *Rainbow Valley* are all to some extent influenced by the war. From an examination of these three earlier novels the implication is that Montgomery was moving as determinedly toward war as the arming European nations.

When Britain declared war on 4 August 1914, Montgomery was partway through writing 'Anne III,' perhaps making Ruby Gillis her first war casualty. Certainly, Montgomery's initial shock and distress are reflected in Anne's bitterness of soul at the end of her college days and in Gilbert's near-tragic illness. *Anne of the Island* closes the Avonlea part of Anne's life; its sequel removes her from an environment where 'people grew up and married and settled down where they were born, or pretty near it' (*AHD* 13), to a more global outlook: 'Stella is in Vancouver, and Pris is in Japan, and Miss Stacey [*sic*] is married in California, and Aunt Jamesina has gone to India to explore her daughter's mission field, in spite of her horror of snakes' (*AHD* 13). In *Anne's House of Dreams*, which takes lines by Rupert Brooke for its motto, the global war's influence is more explicit than in *Anne of the Island*. Through the character of Leslie Moore, the blood-red poppies at her waist and her decision to allow Gilbert to seek a cure for her 'husband,' Montgomery explores the ideology of the conflict. The poppies would be associated by readers with John McCrae's 'In Flanders Fields' (first published on 6 December 1915), the antecedent of Walter Blythe's 'The Piper.' (This early allusion to 'In Flanders Fields' may indicate that Montgomery was already planning to take the Blythe family through the war itself, using McCrae's poem as a recurring symbol in future volumes.) Leslie's reasons for supporting Gilbert's interference, dreadful to herself though its potential consequences are, seem an instructive statement of the North American view of intervention in European war, written as it was with Canada in the war on Britain's side, and the United States still out. This said, the First World War impinged on *Anne of the Island* for the writing of thirty chapters or less; neither that book nor *Anne's House of Dreams* straddled a long period of wartime in the making, however cataclysmic those first months.

Rainbow Valley, on the other hand, was written from 19 January 1917 to 24 December 1918, by far the longest wartime span – approximately

660 days (the armistice coming on 11 November 1918) – and as such must surely reflect the impact of the war on the ordinary processes of life. To say this is not to ignore the fact that *Rainbow Valley* is given the specific task of showing wartime's youthful heroes preparing for the life of sacrifice that awaits them; they do not know of this preparation, but the reader does. Any adult reader of *Rainbow Valley* when it was published just after the war's end must surely have deduced that Jem and Jerry Meredith would volunteer and fight, and probably that Walter would be killed.[7] Walter's visions of the Piper directly prefigure his reluctance to volunteer and his eventual decision to enlist. The growing authoritarianism of Jerry in particular and Jem to a lesser extent is both witness and prophesy of the rise of a Canadian officer class; Jerry's dragooning of his own siblings into a general fast, and a vigil in the rain for Carl, results in illness for Una and near-death for Carl, an all too accurate symbol of the ludicrous and worthless sacrifices officers demanded of their men, frequently to no military purpose beyond some ideal of discipline, or image, or esprit de corps. Officers in the armed forces of all belligerent countries sacrificed many lives in ill-judged strategy and tactics. But whether Montgomery's Jerry was intentionally or unwittingly used to symbolize this or not, she knew the value of her work as witness to the militarization of Canadian society and did that work well. God help the recruit who served under the real-life versions of Jerry Meredith, who drives his brother to double pneumonia three chapters after he has starved his sister into unconsciousness. When his brother is dying, Jerry, 'wild with remorse, refused to budge from the floor of the hall outside Carl's door' (*RV* 205), thus exacerbating the problems of nursing the patient; self-indulgent interference with medical attention for the troops was yet another way in which officers could keep themselves in the limelight and their troops at risk. Jem Blythe plays the role of the general behind the lines who formulates the imbecile strategies to start with – it is he who devises the regime of self-accusation and punishment ('The Good Conduct Club') that proves so dangerous to the mental and physical health of the Meredith children. But if Jerry flings himself into subsequent starring roles of self-reproach, Jem shows not the faintest trace of responsibility for inaugurating such a dangerous policy. At the end of the book he is lusting to be 'a great, triumphant general. I'd give *everything* to see a big battle' (*RV* 224). And *everyone* too, no doubt. It might be a vision of the youth of Field-Marshal Douglas Haig, whose big battle – the Somme – ended with 60,000 casualties in one day (1 July 1916).

Conclusions of this kind require vigilance regarding possible confusion of pre-war and wartime phenomena, of observation versus derivation. Canadian literature is perpetually open to influence from the United States and the United Kingdom, conscious and unconscious, positive and negative. Montgomery probably owed more to the United States than to Great Britain in originally studying form in female children's literature. The historian must be careful that what seems observation of things Canadian is not derivation from things North American. The forceful cultural, political, and international divergence of Canada and the United States, strongly exacerbated and in some respects inaugurated by the First World War (especially during U.S. neutrality), would have thrown Montgomery more directly back on British models, especially when these house Canadian perceptions of their own.

Rainbow Valley, in particular, seems to reflect British literature for children. But much of this as available in Canada would be immediately pre-war; and what might be seen as militarism born of the First World War could be the more leisured recycling of imperial patterns of children's fiction with special reference to the Boer War. For Jem and Jerry this does not matter; the characters are sketched too lightly, and their activities are too obviously local, particularistic, and manse-related to owe much to British conventions. The self-punitive feature may certainly be Scottish, but what is important is that this sort of thing surfaces in Montgomery's wartime writing, irrespective of its alleged time of happening being pre-war. For that matter, *Rainbow Valley* suggests a much more obsessively censorious adult community than is present in most of Montgomery's locations. There is always a thin line between criticism – frequently carping – and censure, but censure clearly takes over in *Rainbow Valley*. No doubt this stems from Montgomery's sensitivity as a Presbyterian minister's wife, aware of her manse being under public scrutiny and its incumbents theoretically under danger of dismissal by the community (whether formally, or informally, by congregational decline, financial decrease, and so forth). But the war evidently increased mutual social criticism and censure in Canada and moved it from a way of life into an agenda for conformity.

Walter's Altar

The most dramatic impact of war on Montgomery's characters is obviously the case of Walter Blythe, emblematic of Canadian youthful sacrifice in *Rilla of Ingleside* and overshadowed throughout *Rainbow Valley* with that inevitable destruction. Walter's fate in *Rilla* is impressive in its honest acknowledgment of Canadian cruelty to persons of conscience in wartime – as well as in its idealism and sacrifice. *Rilla of Ingleside* – and only *Rilla of Ingleside* – makes posterity understand why the most popular poem of the First World War should have been the work of a Scots Canadian. As literature, 'In Flanders Fields' cannot compete with the works of Rosenberg, Owen, Sassoon, and others; but they cannot compete with it as the perennial popular lament, perhaps the most popular latter-day bardic lament to haunt our century. John McCrae died (of pneumonia in military hospital in France) on 27 January 1918. Even if McCrae were in Montgomery's mind for his death as well as his poem, Walter had no such passive fate: representing Canada's war dead, he had to die by the violence he had hated yet adopted.

The *Rilla of Ingleside* Walter remarkably combines both the idealized Canadian war bard dying among his countrymen (as his ancestral bards died among their clansmen) *and* the sensitive artist in a crass, conformist, crusading climate, thus combining both realism and romanticism. The *Rainbow Valley* Walter is much more disturbing and, initially, much more contrived. Although he plays a much fuller part in *Rainbow Valley* than any of his siblings, he has but a few scenes centre-stage and still fewer where we see things through his mind. Montgomery had written some stories from boys' standpoints, and in portraying imaginative boys, particularly Paul Irving in *Anne of Avonlea*, she succeeds best with them as male Annes. Walter has some of Anne, but he is a much more introverted figure.

Montgomery uses the very popular convention of pre-war British stories whereby the 'muff' or 'duffer' proves to be of even more sterling stuff than the associates who taunt him. P.G. Wodehouse satirized the 'Not Really a Duffer' type in his last school story, *Mike* (1909; ch. 40), but unlike him, Montgomery had no interest in defying and deriding the 'coward' genre conventions at this juncture. She had the same purpose as so many of his immediately pre-war colleagues; the boy reader, usually less athletic and foolhardy than his Philistine fellows, would be encouraged to discover stories of supposed cowards proving heroes whence he might prove himself instead of shrinking from armed service; the girl reader might learn similar career lessons but above all must encourage boys to prove themselves heroes even when others called them cowards. Even the most unpromising prospects for future cannon-fodder required the instilment of confidence. Future wars were expected by pre-1914 scribes for children, but it was assumed they would be fought by volunteer armies, especially among the potential officer class for whom these authors wrote. In one respect the stories were usually cowardly themselves; they failed to show an actual human coward overcoming fear, merely an apparent coward gaining self-confidence.

Walter is a sophisticated case, in that he is an aesthete revolted by pain, suffering, and squalor, even by vituperation. This last is certainly exacerbated by resentment at feminization, when Walter's school colleagues taunt him with the name 'Miss Walter.' But he finally challenges Dan Reese to fight, as vengeance for the charge that Anne 'writes lies' (ignoring its possible compliment to her powers as a creative artist) and that Faith is a pig-girl and a rooster-girl. It seems important that Walter could avoid combat, given the truth of the insults, but that once he decides to fight he will not temporize, however justly.[8] Dan compounds the insults by promising to 'smash [his] sissy-face' (*RV* 121). Montgomery grants Walter verbal retaliation in one particular; he calls Dan 'a coincidence' (*RV* 120). This is charming self-indulgence; accusation of resort to coincidence was a particularly rude term of critical derision against popular authors of fiction, especially in this period.[9]

But Montgomery's primary motive was to inspire the courage of her Canadian readers for an actual war (who knew how long it would last?), where her exemplars had merely encouraged theirs for a potential one. By showing Walter's terror on the night before the fight – 'Would it hurt much? He was terribly afraid that it would hurt. And would he be defeated and shamed?' (*RV* 122) – Montgomery greatly improves on her sources by seriously addressing the psychology of fear (within limits – Montgomery could not, after all, discuss what her beloved Macaulay describes as the 'knees' being 'loosened with dismay'). In its nature Walter's terror is closer to the realism of writing during and after the First World War than to the pump-priming of heroics before it. But what actually happens at the fight reads like a cross between Roman war-fever and homicidal mania; it is a kind of literary assurance to the fearful that when the challenge comes, they will be appropriately insane. Dan strikes Walter: 'Walter reeled a little. The pain of the blow tingled through all his sensitive frame for a moment. Then he felt pain no longer. Something, such as he had never experienced before, seemed to roll over him like a flood. His face flushed crimson, his eyes burned like flame. The scholars of Glen St Mary school had never dreamed that "Miss Walter" could look like that. He hurled himself forward and closed on Dan like a young wildcat' (124). The scene is inspired partly by Macaulay's 'Horatius,' after Astur wounds Horatius:

> He reeled, and on Herminius
> He leaned one breathing-space;
> Then like a wild cat mad with wounds,
> Sprang right at Astur's face.

The fight's continuation may derive from another quarter: 'There were no particular rules in the fights of the Glen school boys. It was catch-as-catch can, and get your blows in anyhow. Walter fought with a savage fury and a joy in the struggle against which Dan could not hold his ground. It was all over very speedily. Walter had no clear consciousness of what he was doing until suddenly the red mist cleared from his sight and he found himself kneeling on the body of the prostrate Dan whose nose – oh, horror! – was spouting blood' (*RV* 124). George Bernard Shaw's new play, *Androcles and the Lion*, was published in the September 1914 issue of *Everybody's* magazine.[10] In this play, Ferrovius, the converted Roman strong man 'whose sensibilities are keen and violent to the verge of madness' (Act 1) is non-combatant because of his Christian faith but remains fearful that 'the warrior's faith, the faith in fighting' (Act 2) will overwhelm his vow of turning the other cheek. When he and his fellow Christians are driven into the arena, the frenzied Ferrovius kills, afterwards crying, 'there was blood behind my eyes, and there's blood on my sword. What does that mean?' (Act 2). Shaw sees the fate of Ferrovius as Mars triumphing over Jesus. Montgomery had no intention of allowing Christian scruples to come in the way of the god of battles, and Walter, leaving the field of slaughter, meets the Reverend John Meredith, who assures him that he was justified in avenging insulted 'womenkind.' If Montgomery was inspired by *Androcles and the Lion*, it was a fascinating case of the perversion of a source's message.

Rainbow Valley also confronts cowardice and its replacement by courage on the part of girls, specifically Faith and Una Meredith. Faith is the straightforward one, trying to recruit Norman Douglas to offset financial losses to her father's church. It is superficially a rerun of Anne's two initial interviews with Mr Harrison but has a harder and deeper psychology: 'Lacking her crimson cheeks she seemed meek and even insignificant. She looked apologetic and afraid, and the bully in Norman Douglas's heart stirred' (*RV* 112). This is a sharp reversal of another quotation of military interest but anti-war authorship, John Greenleaf Whittier's

'Barbara Frietchie.' When ninety-year-old Barbara shakes the Stars and Stripes over the heads of the Confederate forces marching in the street below her house and tells them to shoot her but spare the flag, Stonewall Jackson is moved.

> The nobler nature within him stirred
> To life at the woman's deed and word.

Montgomery produces the converse. It is not until Faith attacks Douglas with a violence quite unparalleled elsewhere in the saga that he is brought round to her: 'I am not afraid of you. You are a rude, unjust, tyrannical, disagreeable old man. Susan says you are sure to go to hell, and I was sorry for you, but I am not now. Your wife never had a new hat for ten years – no wonder she died. I am going to make faces at you whenever I see you after this. Every time I am behind you you will know what is happening. Father has a picture of the devil in a book in his study, and I mean to go home and write your name under it. You are an old vampire and I hope you'll have the Scotch fiddle!' (*RV* 114–15). This conquers Norman Douglas. It is symbolic that the only two characters in the book who appreciate the menace of the Kaiser are bullies themselves: Norman Douglas and Ellen West. It is also significant that they want to be defeated. Montgomery was too simple in the ways of international diplomacy to realize the Kaiser was actually in the German peace faction, but she seems unconsciously to have picked up on the point. Consciously, she was as hang-the-Kaiser as anyone. Una has to make her self-conquests over fear to confront people whom, with reservations, she likes but who have the potential to cause her injury: Mrs Marshall Elliott, to get her to adopt Mary Vance although she might whip up further public hostility to the Merediths, and Rosemary West, who might prove to be a cruel stepmother.

The wartime lessons are simple enough. War demands that, if necessary, women face hostile criticisms for their outspoken demands on behalf of the needs of war. The war effort may leave women vulnerable to the accusation that their behaviour is unfeminine, but they must not be distracted from their primary targets by opposition of that kind. The war requires alliances with what seem censorious or contemptuous seniors or superiors. It may mean the sacrifice of valued freedoms for the duration of the conflict; Canada has to curb its increasing independence from Mother England and accept more stringent control, even if it makes for a kind of Stepmother England.[11]

Mary Vance: The Impact of War on Montgomery's Fiction

The most drastic assertion in *Rainbow Valley* of the changes wrought by war is the violence done not only to the Anne genre but to the whole tradition of orphans in Montgomery's work. The story of Mary Vance seems a deliberate violation of almost all the Anne conventions, as though war demanded a break with the pretty literary past. Mary Vance is an anti-Anne, a Mary v Anne (easily handwritten as 'Mary Vance').[12] *Anne of the Island* gives us our fullest glimpse of Anne's parents, and the reader is assured as to their devotion to each other, their child, and their profession. Mary Vance is acknowledged to be from the same orphan asylum as Anne, but:

> 'I was two years in the asylum. I was put there when I was six. My ma had hung herself and my pa had cut his throat.'
> 'Holy cats! Why?' said Jerry.
> 'Booze,' said Mary laconically.
> 'And you've no relations?'
> 'Not a darn one that I know of. Must have had some once, though. I was called after half a dozen of them. My full name is Mary Martha Lucilla Moore Ball Vance. Can you beat that? My grandfather was a rich man. I'll bet he was richer than *your* grandfather. But pa drunk it all up and ma, she did her part. *They* used to beat me, too. Laws, I've been licked so much I kind of like it.' (*RV* 33)

This was very strong meat for Montgomery's infant readers, however desirable warnings against drink might seem.[13] Prohibition legislation in both Nova Scotia and Prince Edward Island had preceded the war, but its enforcement was heavily tightened up in wartime; by the time of writing and, indeed, of setting *Rainbow Valley*, Montgomery had an argument for making her youthful readers propagandists against liquor, and she was evidently prepared to use war feeling on the question to justify propaganda without gloves.

Yet the violence goes well beyond its occasion. One has a sense of Montgomery enjoying the mandate war had given her to shatter her own delicate conventions. Walter is not alone in being forced to confront the ugly. Little bourgeois children can no longer have their imaginary playmates limited in their misfortunes. Anne tells Marilla in the fifth chapter of *Anne of Green Gables* that Mrs Thomas 'had a drunken husband,' but we learn no more of him until he fell under a train, presumably with the assistance of alcohol; Marilla notes that Anne's had been 'a starved, unloved life ... a life of drudgery and poverty and neglect; for Marilla was shrewd enough to read between the lines of Anne's history and divine the truth' (49). There is no reading between the lines for the reader who meets Mary Vance, as far as the suicides, the booze, and the child-beatings are concerned (the latter issue is explored in more detail by Irene Gammel and Ann Dutton in chapter 7 of this book).

The revolutionary impact of war on the Anne genre becomes almost cruel in its reversal of the convention when Mary Vance is adopted by Miss Cornelia, and is promptly reformed into an atrocious little gossip, snob, and general harbinger of doom. Miss Cornelia was a highly entertaining character in *Anne's House of Dreams*; in *Rainbow Valley* she is revealed as a nasty, abrasive, censorious trouble-monger occasionally silenced by Anne (whose own kind thoughts for the young manse children are never converted into practical assistance). Mary Vance enters her new world of security and prosperity, and promptly produces a junior version of its endless carping. The book is an almost openly contemptuous protest at the community's incessant backbiting of the manse children, when no one in the community would think of going down to the manse and doing a hand's turn to clean the place, supervise the family diet, watch over the health of its members, and make new clothes for the children. If Anne or Miss Cornelia had anything constructive to add to their observations, they could intervene in the cause of the motherless Merediths' well-being. But they will not – Anne possibly because of the dangers to the doctor's practice, and Miss Cornelia because she has built her feminism on negative principles. Miss Cornelia's bluff is called by Una to the extent of making her adopt Mary Vance; but the effect is to make Mary Vance the repository and deployer of all the vicious lynch-mob responses to the family who saved her from starvation and return to the slave-auctioning orphanage. It is as though Mary Vance's conformity to Miss Cornelia's world is mockingly telling us what would have happened to Anne had she swallowed the value-system of Marilla and Mrs Rachel Lynde without question or alternative. Montgomery frequently makes gossip highly entertaining; the war seems to have encouraged her to show its aridity and destructiveness. Even nature grows more hostile in *Rainbow Valley*: 'the little path was shadowy and narrow. Trees crowded over it, and trees are never quite as friendly to human beings after nightfall as they are in daylight. They wrap themselves away from us. They whisper and plot furtively. If they reach out a hand to us it has a hostile, tentative touch. People walking amid trees after night always draw close together instinctively and involuntarily, making an alliance, physical and mental, against certain alien powers around them' (*RV* 89). The trees become a metaphor for the supposedly benevolent community.

Trees – 'forests ancient as the hills' – are an integral part of the heaven Walter Blythe imagines after reading Coleridge's description of the garden surrounding Kubla Khan's 'stately pleasure dome.' In keeping with that poem's ominous predictions, Walter has visions of a piper – drawn partly from Montgomery's Scottish ancestral voice – which would be recognized by adult readers of *Rainbow Valley* as 'prophesying war.' Walter has four visions of the Piper, two in *Rainbow Valley* and two in *Rilla of Ingleside*, the final one just hours before his death, when he is piped 'west.' His siblings fail to understand the import of these visions; Di associates the Piper with the wonderful things that may await the children who follow; Jem, hypnotized by the 'brave days of old' (*RV* 224), sees but the glorious heroism of legend.[14]

The only child of *Rainbow Valley* who recognizes the terror in Walter's visions is Mary Vance. Each time the Piper comes, it is Mary whose response captures the full import: first she admonishes him by saying 'You give me the creeps. Do you want to set me bawling?' (*RV* 55); then she protests 'I hate that old piper of yours' (*RV* 225). When news of war hits Glen St Mary in *Rilla of Ingleside*, Walter again sees the Piper, a vision prompted by Mary's question, 'What does it matter if there's going to be a war over there in Europe? I'm sure it doesn't concern us' (*RI* 33). And again Mary 'felt uncomfortable,' although her socialization into the adopting community is by now so complete that she can utter only 'Fancy now!' to those fears. That Mary Vance is the sole character who understands what Walter's visions signify (often more than Walter does himself) is surely a result of her personal experience of terror and violence. (Adults do not witness Walter's visions or, it would seem, listen to any talk of them.) The manse children, although they know grief, have no comparable experience. The children of Ingleside at this stage belong with their mother in the pre-war still waters (Di specifically links her interpretation of the Pied Piper to her mother's [*RV* 55]). But Mary Vance is scarred and therefore scared. Ultimately, Mary seems the necessary, if not altogether welcome or wanted, link between the romantic (and untruthful) past and the violent upheaval of the future.

Conclusion

Elizabeth Epperly has written that *Rainbow Valley* is imprinted with 'love of Canada and pride in the maple leaf' (*Fragrance* 96). The *maple* grove is the place, next to Rainbow Valley (itself the heaven of Mary Vance's imagination) that the children love most. But Canada had changed since Marilla Cuthbert declared her preference for a Canadian-born orphan, and L.M. Montgomery's wartime novels reflect this dramatic change. The First World War brought large-scale violence into Canadian history and culture for the first time. Unlike in the histories of the countries of origin for Canada's immigrant population and of the United States, war or frontier violence had not played a major role in the forging of national identity in Canada – in as much as one had been created – during settler history; this fact was especially true for Prince Edward Island, where even nature (consistently portrayed as the 'enemy' in Canadian fiction) was devoid of much of its hostility.

From Anne's 'Book of Revelation' in *Anne of the Island* where the 'air throbbed with the thunderous crash of billows on the distant shore' (*AIs* 235),[15] through the tragic and death-filled history of Leslie Moore in *Anne's House of Dreams,* to the mania of Walter's fight with Dan Reese and the horror of Mary Vance's childhood in *Rainbow Valley*, Montgomery was widening the parameters of her fiction to include the new reality and the new Canada that war had created. That *Anne's House of Dreams* turns on a plot where a woman shares board, and may – for all that we are ever told – have shared bed, for fourteen years with a man she believes to be her husband but who is not, shows the extent to which war was breaking fictional constraints and how far Montgomery's work had moved from *Green Gables.*

To import the language of Henry F. May, the First World War brought the end of Canadian innocence: Montgomery's revisionist history of the Hopetown orphan is one example of this dramatic change; the possibility of increased suffering for Leslie Moore if Dick is restored to his former and hideous self is another. With war came the death of innocence and the death of innocents; conversely, and with an optimism the innocent Anne of Green Gables would have admired, Montgomery also encodes in the pain of this 'death grapple' the birth pangs delivering a new country and a new art.

NOTES

We are grateful to Mary H. Rubio and Elizabeth R. Epperly for their help with this work.

1 Despite this first chapter reference to Canada, Montgomery joked in her

journal, 'Geography is not a strong point with some critics.' She went on to list various locations identified as the setting for her books: 'The scene is laid in Nova Scotia'; 'A girl adopted into a New England family'; 'rural life in New England'; 'The country of the novel is New Brunswick'; 'This detached portion of land near Newfoundland'; 'A story of life in a Breton fishing village'; 'The scene is laid in *Scotland*'; 'A play of American farm life'; '*Western* Canada is a charming setting for this story'; 'a story of American girlhood' (1 March 1930, *SJ* 4: 40–1).

2 These dates are calculated from an event in *Anne's House of Dreams*, although this 1869 birth-date for Anne contradicts that arrived at by using the dates of actual events given in *Rilla of Ingleside*. *Anne of Green Gables* is not specifically dated: some events place the setting in the 1880s, others in the 1890s. After initially refusing the 1864 Quebec Resolutions for Confederation, a decision which had widespread public support, Prince Edward Island joined the Dominion in 1873, a reversal of policy due in large part to the costly program of railway building in the colony. Marilla's patriotism may partially result from the distance between the novel's time of setting and composition, but it also shows her to be mildly more broad-minded than Mrs Rachel, who distrusts anything from off-Island including, of course, Anne herself.

3 Changing her loyalties from Liberal to Conservative in the election of 1917 and abandoning her long-held admiration for Sir Wilfrid Laurier, Montgomery wrote to Weber, 'I am now forced to believe that he has failed his country and lined himself up with Catholic Quebec and Bourassa' (25 Nov. 1917). This anti-Catholicism is repeated in a letter written to Weber between 25 September and 22 October 1922: 'you say that you do not fear a Quebec regime. I wish I could share your optimism. I know what the Catholics on P. E. Island are and they get their inspiration from Quebec' (unpublished letters to Ephraim Weber, NAC, Ottawa). Montgomery draws a strange allegiance between the Catholics of PEI, many of whom shared her Scottish heritage, and the French Canadians of Quebec. In *Rilla of Ingleside*, Susan Baker makes a disparaging comment about the Pope's proposals for peace (214).

4 Unpublished letter to Ephraim Weber, 12 Jan. 1916. Weber was at this time living in Chicago, Illinois; Montgomery continued to argue with him about the war into the 1920s.

5 In a journal entry of 27 August 1919 (*SJ* 2: 339–40), Montgomery quoted an article on Canadian literature she had written in 1910: 'I do not think our literature is an expression of our national life as a whole. I think this is because we have only very recently – as time goes in the making of nations

– had any real national life. Canada is only just finding herself. She has not yet fused her varying elements into a harmonious whole. Perhaps she will not do so until they are welded together by some great crisis of storm and stress. That is when a real national literature will be born. I do not believe that the great Canadian novel or poem will ever be written until we have had some kind of baptism by fire to purge away all our petty superficialities and lay bare the primal passions of humanity.' Montgomery raised the question of the literary effects of war in her letters to both Weber (25 Nov. 1917) and George Boyd MacMillan (16 Oct. 1914) (unpublished letters, NAC).

6 '*Rilla of Ingleside* came today – my eleventh book! It looks very well. I don't suppose it will be much of a success, for the public are said to be sick of anything connected with the war. But at least I did my best to reflect the life we lived in Canada during those four years. It is dedicated to Frede's memory. I wish she could have read it. It is the first one I have written with a purpose' (*SJ* 3: 17).

7 Despite the references to the First World War in *Rainbow Valley*, few contemporary reviews mention this background. These reviews (preserved in Montgomery's clipping scrapbooks) are largely positive; one reviewer speculates that his/her favourable opinion is 'perhaps ... because [Montgomery] has succeeded in keeping the excellent Anne almost entirely out of it, and has dealt with wickeder people' (*Evening Transcript* [Boston] 1919).

8 They are truthful insults in that Faith has ridden a pig and forced Walter to do so, and her pet is a rooster.

9 'Coincidence' was surely a term of critical derision that could have been levelled at the Dick/George Moore plot in *Anne's House of Dreams*. Given that Anne's fictional writing is otherwise of little account in the books about her after *Anne of the Island*, it seems possible Montgomery was mentally allowing Walter to fight one of her own ruder reviewers.

10 Montgomery was certainly familiar with this magazine: her short story 'The Quarantine at Alexander Abraham's' was published in the April 1907 issue of *Everybody's*, and she made it clear in a letter to George Boyd MacMillan that she considered this acceptance a literary triumph (unpublished letter dated 29 Nov. 1906). Montgomery owned several volumes of G.B. Shaw's plays (now held in the University of Guelph's collection), including *Androcles and the Lion*.

11 Arguably, the war had the reverse effect, Prime Minister Borden gaining admission to the Imperial Cabinet and winning higher consultative status than ever before, but the magnitude of this gain was evident to only a few.

12 The name may have its source in the poem 'Mary Vance' by Norman Gale: see his *Collected Poems* (1914). See also Bailey's examination of Mary Vance as Anne's 'hoydenish double.'

13 Anne accidentally intoxicates Diana in *Anne of Green Gables* and is ostracized by Mrs Barry in consequence until she saves her younger daughter from a providential attack of croup (echoed in *Rilla of Ingleside* when Mary Vance, disliked by Rilla, saves Rilla's young protégé Jims [202]). But Montgomery's telling of the story goes against Mrs Barry, and the incident draws Marilla still closer to Anne.

14 As we have noted, the language of Dan Reese and Walter's fight is partly influenced by 'Horatius,' yet the mania in evidence is far removed from romanticized 'brave days' and as such is part of the complex portrait of chivalric codes in *Rainbow Valley*. (For a discussion of chivalry in this novel see Epperly, 'Chivalry and Romance.')

15 This is an echo of Montgomery's statement that the war 'seemed to break over the world like a thundercloud' (*My Dear* 71).

ROMANCE AND THE SHAPING OF CANADIAN CULTURE

3

'Dragged at Anne's Chariot Wheels:' The Triangle of Author, Publisher, and Fictional Character

CAROLE GERSON

'Elderly couple apply to orphan asylum for a boy. By mistake a girl is sent them' (*SJ* 1: 330). As later recounted in L.M. Montgomery's revised journals, an 1895 notebook jotting eventually resulted in a 1906 manuscript that was rejected by four major American fiction publishers before being accepted by the Boston firm of L.C. Page in 1907. Issued the following year as *Anne of Green Gables*, the book soon achieved worldwide recognition as a classic novel of girlhood and adolescence. 'They took it and asked me to write a sequel to it,' Montgomery wrote in her journal: 'I don't know what kind of a publisher I've got. I know absolutely nothing of the Page Co. They have given me a royalty of ten percent on the *wholesale* price, which is not generous even for a new writer, and they have bound me to give them all my books on the same terms for five years. I don't altogether like this but I was afraid to protest, lest they might not take the book, and I am so anxious to get it before the public. It will be a start, even if it is no great success' (*SJ* 1: 331). Success indeed it was. Classed as an 'overall bestseller' by Frank Mott, who states that *Anne of Green Gables* had sold between 800,000 and 900,000 copies by 1947 (312), the book had earned Montgomery over $22,000 for more than 300,000 copies by the time a bitter lawsuit resulted in the sale of her copyright to Page in 1919 (Rubio, 'Architect' 67).

Before recounting Montgomery's long and troubled connection with her publisher, and her equally problematic relationship with her most famous character, I would like to explore the implications and expectations of Page's terms by situating Montgomery at the intersection of several specific issues. These are the contested literary and cultural value of the sequel; the publication of Canadian-authored books at the turn of the century, in particular series and sequels, and writing for

children (two formulations that sometimes coincide); and the international commodification of children's literature in children's periodicals
and series.

Positing that the sequel originates in a 'charismatic text' that has had
'an unusually powerful effect on a large reading public,' Terry Castle
opens her discussion of *Pamela Part 2* with the 'commonplace' assertion that 'sequels are always disappointing' (133–5). The same generali-
zation is applied more specifically to *Anne of Green Gables* in an article
by Gillian Thomas that begins, 'It is a cliché of popular literature that
sequels tend to be disappointing, and students of children's literature
are all too sadly familiar with the decline of writers who turn themselves
into human factories on the basis of a successful first book' (23). Disappointing for whom, one might ask. For the general reading public, the
audience and consumers of sequels, who have always been eager to buy
not only additional Anne books, but more recently have been gobbling
up associated texts such as the edited volumes of Montgomery's journals and newly issued collections of her scattered magazine stories?[1]
According to a recent analysis of Montgomery's readers, the sequels
substantially reinforce the value of the originating book because they
'tell ... what happened later' and prolong the pleasure of inhabiting the
'alternate world' of Montgomery's fiction (Ross 30). Disappointing, then,
for the publishers and marketers who realize sizable profits from such
spin-offs as cookbooks, address books, birthday books, diaries, colour-
ing books, abridged and re-written versions of the texts, as well as Anne
dolls and girl-sized souvenir wigs with red braids? For the artists who
produce and perform in television, ballet, and musical versions of Montgomery's works?[2] For the province of Prince Edward Island, and especially the residents of Charlottetown and Cavendish, whose economy
benefits enormously from the tourist industry generated by the popularity of Anne in North America and Japan?[3]

As if to emblematize the material value of Montgomery's book to
Canada as a whole, in 1994 the Royal Canadian Mint issued a twenty-
two-karat gold coin commemorating Anne, featuring (in the words of
the brochure) 'a young girl under a gazebo, daydreaming about the
adventures of Anne of Green Gables.' With a face value of $200 but
selling for $399.95, this was the most expensive item in the mint's Christ-
mas brochure – more highly priced than coins commemorating other
national cultural icons such as the last RCMP Northern Dog Team Patrol
(silver dollar priced at $17.95 or $24.50, depending upon the case), the
National War Memorial (proof loonie priced at $16.95), and the home

front during the Second World War ($100 gold coin priced at $249.95). Clearly, the charisma of *Anne of Green Gables* spills far beyond the notions of value constructed by the traditional literary critic, into a dense web of cultural activity that includes romance and popular culture, national identity, provincial and international economics, and social history. Full analysis of these concerns would constitute an intriguing cultural studies project requiring a collaborative team of interdisciplinary experts; the intention of this essay is to discuss some of the earlier historical events and contexts that underpin the later commodification of L.M. Montgomery and her works.

L.M. Montgomery and the American Market

At the turn of the century, Maud Montgomery was an unmarried woman in her late twenties, single-mindedly forging a commercially viable literary career by working her way upward from occasional newspaper poems and stories to larger commissions and serials in popular American periodicals such as *Outing* and *The Boy's World*. Trapped in the rural community of Cavendish, Prince Edward Island, as the sole caretaker of her aging grandmother, even if she had so desired she could not have followed the route taken by Janet Royal, a secondary character in her 1925 novel, *Emily Climbs*, who moves to New York to pursue a successful career as a literary journalist.[4] Nonetheless, like her Canadian-born predecessor Sara Jeannette Duncan, Montgomery well knew that 'the market for Canadian literary wares of all sorts is self-evidently New York' (Duncan 518). Although Duncan herself would later develop a substantial British readership, as would other Canadian authors with imperial connections and concerns, such as Gilbert Parker and Stephen Leacock, her 1887 comment foretold the career orientation of the majority of ambitious Canadian authors around the turn of the century.

A canny businesswoman, Montgomery recorded in her letters her preference to sell her work to American publications as they could pay substantially better than Canadian magazines. Regardless of her personal patriotism and her subsequent difficulties with Page, she declared she 'wouldn't give [an] MS. to a Canadian firm. It is much better financially to have it published in the United States' (*Green Gables Letters* 46, 59, 80). Her comments on the selection of publishers to whom she first sent the manuscript of *Anne of Green Gables* demonstrate her pragmatic assessment of the publishing industry. She began with Bobbs-Merrill as a new firm just establishing its list, then 'went to the other extreme and sent it to the MacMillan Co. of New York,' then tried Lothrop, Lee and Shepard, 'a sort of "betwixt and between" firm' specializing in juvenile series (including the series of boys' books written three decades earlier by fellow Maritimer James De Mille), then Henry Holt (*SJ* 1: 331) and finally, L.C. Page.

American publishers cater to American readers whose interest in Canada has historically been rather slight. However, these limitations appear to have been less stringent around the turn of the century, when Montgomery first broke into print. According to Pierre Berton, during the period before the Great War the American film industry was fascinated with Canada: '[t]he country, to most Americans, was almost unknown and therefore exotic' (18). In the realm of popular fiction, the situation was more complex. First of all, virtually no Canadian authors attempting to support themselves by writing could afford to publish only in Canada, with a population (and book market) one-tenth of that of the United States. Secondly, prevailing market and copyright conditions prevented Canadian publishers from easily accessing American markets. Our grasp of the situation is hindered by the fact that co-publishing arrangements are often not indicated on title pages, which therefore may imply that a book was solely a Canadian product when it was actually issued in arrangement with an American firm.[5] From my research on the papers of a number of Canadian authors, I think it likely that during Montgomery's lifetime (1874–1942) no Canadian-authored popular series appeared that was *not* published in the United States. For Montgomery, one of Page's initial attractions was the firm's recent publication of books by Charles G.D. Roberts and Bliss Carman, two major Canadian literary figures of Maritime origin like herself, who successfully established visible identities in the United States (*Green Gables Letters* 52) – although they both had to move there in order to do so, and both subsequently experienced considerable difficulty with Page.

If the primary market was the United States, how appealing was fiction set in Canada? On the one hand, a number of American publishers successfully promoted Canadian-authored popular and juvenile fiction series (sometimes comprised of sequels) with distinctively Canadian settings. These include James De Mille's Brethren of the White Cross series, set in the Grand Pré area of Nova Scotia (first published 1869–73 and still in print with the Boston firm of Lee and Shepard in the early 1900s); Norman Duncan's Billy Topsail books (1906–16), set in a New-foundland not yet part of Canada); Ralph Connor's Glengarry series, set in rural Ontario and the West (1901–33); Scribners' twenty-three-volume edition of *The Works of Gilbert Parker* (1912–23); and, somewhat later, Mazo de la Roche's Ontario-based Jalna books (1927–54) and Muriel Dennison's western Susannah of the Mounties series (1936–40). On the other hand, it is known that several Canadian authors working in the market area of juvenile and popular fiction were required to change their Canadian settings to American locations in order to secure publication, such as Marshall Saunders for *Beautiful Joe* (1894) and Elsie Bell Gardner for her Maxie series of girls' adventure stories (1932–9).[6] Still other professional writers occasionally placed their books in Canada without creating the national emphasis fostered by the geographical assertiveness of a distinct series; the list includes Zillah Macdonald, James Macdonald Oxley, and Helen Dickson Reynolds.

Enter Lewis Page, Boston Publisher

While it is always necessary to keep in mind the often precarious position of identifiably Canadian texts within the larger world of British and American publishing, more significant with regard to the development of Montgomery's career was the late-nineteenth-century explosion in commercial publishing aimed at children, particularly through the production of series. Series production, according to Norman Feltes, developed as the capitalist system's mode of controlling and profiting from commodity-texts by producing both the audience (i.e., the market) and the wares purchased and consumed by that market (Feltes, *Modes* 9–12). In the realm of juvenile literature, this occurred in conjunction with the rapid expansion of children's periodicals in the second half of the nineteenth century, in both Britain and the United States, many originating as Sunday school publications. For example, series issued under the name of the American Tract Society gave the imprimatur of respectability to the often suspect genre of fiction (Kensinger 19). Faye Kensinger, whose *Children of the Series* documents the production of juvenile serial literature in the United States, reports two specific findings important for our understanding of the atmosphere into which Montgomery launched herself as an author: series aimed specifically at girls were especially likely to follow the maturation of the main character – to be sequels rather than a chronologically static sequence of vacation adventures – and series production peaked during the second decade of the twentieth century, the decade when Montgomery produced most of the Anne books.

However, our full understanding of the production of Montgomery's books is seriously hampered by the lack of surviving archival material. Lewis Page's personal and business papers seem to have vanished, as has Montgomery's correspondence with her publishers. Although she does state in her journal that she was saving her business papers for her biographer, that package has since gone astray.[7]

Available evidence suggests that Lewis Page was an exploitive publisher who grew increasingly difficult over the years due to his volatile temperament and his costly recreations of gambling and philandering, neither of which endeared him to an author who in 1911 became the wife of a Presbyterian clergyman.[8] Intersecting with this personal level of antagonism were conflicts stemming from the changes in practices and attitudes analyzed by Norman Feltes in his two books on the evolving structure of publishing in the nineteenth and earlier twentieth centuries. Although Montgomery wanted to make money, like most authors she also aspired to literary respectability and thought of herself as an artist who should control the terms of her work. Page, however, as a commercial entrepreneur, regarded her as the producer of raw material for the process of book production over which he had absolute control (Feltes, *Literary Capital* 15). From the time he established his company in 1896, his staple was juvenile series, beginning with Annie Fellows Johnston's twelve-volume Little Colonel series, which eventually sold over a million copies (Becket and Mills 49).

In Feltes's terms, Page was a 'speculative' publisher whose acceptance of *Anne of Green Gables* was a gamble on the value of 'future texts' to be produced by Montgomery (*Literary Capital* 18, 25). Hence, while Montgomery seemed surprised and pleased that Page requested a sequel upon his acceptance of *Anne of Green Gables*, to Page, who inevitably viewed the first Anne book as the beginning of a series, there was nothing unusual about requesting a 'second story dealing with the same character'[9] long before the originating text had been produced and tested in the market. In other words, the second Anne book, *Anne of Avonlea*, was generated not by the clamour of enchanted readers, but by the current practices of market publishing; the charismatic quality of *Anne of Green Gables* was not substantive to the production of its initial sequels, but rather an incidental surprise.

In fact, in the spring of 1909 Page decided to delay the appearance of *Anne of Avonlea* until the following autumn to avoid competition with the unexpectedly brisk sales of *Anne of Green Gables* (*Green Gables Letters* 85). Moreover, Page's contracts did not distinguish between sequels and series; his reiterated demand for Montgomery's books for the next five years, whatever they happened to be, indicates that he saw his product as commodity-texts whose selling point was Montgomery's name, rather than as the on-going story of a character named Anne.[10] This interpretation is borne out by the uniform appearance of all Montgomery's books issued by Page (*SJ* 2: 134), and by his insistence on symmetrical titles.[11]

In light of the publishing structure of her era, the interesting question is whether or not Montgomery at some level expected to write a sequel to *Anne of Green Gables*: was it a text originally envisioned as closed and complete? On 10 September 1908, while she was struggling with *Anne of Avonlea*, Montgomery wrote to a friend that she agreed with reviewers of *Anne of Green Gables* that 'the ending was too conventional.' She then added: 'if I had known I was to be asked to write a second Anne book I wouldn't have "ended" it at all but just "stopped"' (*Green Gables Letters* 70–1). *Anne of Green Gables* concludes with Anne relinquishing a university scholarship in order to teach in the local school and support her beloved aging adoptive mother. In the book's social context, this decision represents a mature choice to assume responsibility and conform to community norms with regard to both class and gender;[12] yet, deliberately or not, Montgomery left open a broad range of subsequent narrative possibilities. First of all, while she initially resisted the conventional closure of marriage (it takes three books to marry off Anne, as it would later take three books to marry off Emily), one would be hard put to name a contemporary female fictional character who doesn't eventually marry – unless she dies. Moreover, in Montgomery's romance world, which permits surprise legacies and other delightful turns of fortune, there is no irrevocable reason why Anne should not get a later chance at university (as she will in *Anne of the Island*); in the meantime, her impending experiences as a teacher provide ample opportunity for Montgomery to further develop what will become her usual episodic narrative mode, composed of relatively discrete sequential stories and events unified by theme and character rather than by plot. Moreover, many earlier and contemporary authors turned the novel of adolescence into a narrative sequence on family life, beginning with Louisa May Alcott and continuing with sequential series like Coolidge's What Katy Did books and Lothrop's stories of the Five Little Peppers. In other words, while Montgomery might not have openly acknowledged (even to herself) the possibility of writing a sequel, she had nonetheless prepared the way. Once she got started, sequels and sequences proved her natural mode, only five of her eventual twenty-two volumes of fiction being unattached narratives (*Kilmeny of the Orchard, The Blue Castle, Magic for Marigold, A Tangled Web, Jane of Lantern Hill*).[13]

To support this interpretation, Montgomery's journals, novels, and letters offer ample evidence of her acquaintance with the practices of series publication outlined above. She frequently refers not only to Louisa May Alcott, whose books she knew well, but also to more ephemeral series like the Pansy books (*SJ* 1: 37) and Marietta Holley's Samantha books (*SJ* 1: 282). As well, her familiarity with periodical publishing for children necessarily brought her into contact with the interconnections between the publishing of children's periodicals and the production of series of children's books (Kensinger 16–17).

Montgomery's complex relationship with the fictional Anne Shirley is entangled with her equally complex relationship with the very real Lewis Page. The picture is further problematized by the lack of surviving primary sources other than Montgomery's journals. Her biographers suggest that she shaped her life to fit the narrative of her journals (Rubio and Waterston, *Writing* 36). However, in view of her later preparation of these personal writings for public view, with ample opportunity to adjust her wording while she recopied the text and added numerous photographs, I think it quite possible that this professional storyteller shaped her own story retrospectively. In a sense, the journals can be seen as sequels to her life and her published books.

Thus, when upon first meeting Page, in November 1910, she records in her revised journal 'I do not trust him' (*SJ* 2: 25), we cannot know if this was her actual impression at that time or a later reinterpretation, since she recopied these portions of her original diaries in late 1920 and through 1921, while in the throes of lawsuits and countersuits with Page. According to notes from her now destroyed correspondence with John McClelland, it was only in early 1916 that she began to seriously doubt her publisher: 'Three months ago, I had no real distrust of Mr. Page in any way. Since then I have heard so much against him and his methods from different quarters that I am distrustful; but the fact of his threatening me with 'the courts' is the one thing that has really turned my former loyalty into suspicion.'[14] Similarly, we cannot know whether the quotation that opens this paper represents her actual thoughts in August 1907, or if her view has been recast as the beginning of a rather gothic tale about an innocent female writer's struggle to escape the magnetism and power of a wily publisher determined to extract sequels from her for the rest of her days. Certainly her letter to Ephraim Weber of 2 May 1907, announcing the acceptance of *Anne of Green Gables*, is less apprehensive. Here she describes Page as 'a good company' that 'has published several successful books by well-known authors, including Charles G.D. Roberts and Bliss Carman.' She mentions nothing about her stingy royalty agreement, and although a little uneasy about being committed for the next five years, she takes the binding clause as 'rather complimentary' (*Green Gables Letters* 52).

When Montgomery commenced her second Anne book, her journals describe how her initial pleasure in returning to her fictional character – '*Anne* is as real to me as if I had given her birth – as real and as dear' (*SJ* 1: 332) – soon yielded to frustration: 'My publishers are hurrying me now for the sequel. I'm working at it but will not be as good as *Green Gables*. It doesn't *come* as easily. I have to force it' (*SJ* 1: 335–6). In Montgomery's case, the disappointment generated by sequels includes the plight of the author, now fearing she is 'to be dragged at Anne's chariot wheels the rest of my life' (*Green Gables Letters* 74). Trapped in Lewis Page's on-going binding contracts, she produced *Anne of Avonlea* (1909), *Chronicles of Avonlea* (1912), and *Anne of the Island* (1915) (as well as three other unrelated books: *Kilmeny of the Orchard*, 1910; *The Story Girl*, 1911; *The Golden Road*, 1912). Her journal records that in September 1913, 'I began work on a third "Anne" book. I did not want to do it – I have fought against it. But Page gave me no peace and every week brought a letter from some reader pleading for "another Anne book." So I have yielded for peace sake. It's like marrying a man to get rid of him' (*SJ* 2: 133). This troubling, ironic image (suggesting a dynamic that we now associate with battered wife syndrome) adumbrates the gendered subtext of Montgomery's narrated relationship with Page, in which her gratitude to him for having launched her career conflicts with her anger at the knowledge that his royalty arrangements have paid her less than half of what she should have received (*SJ* 2: 171). After signing two contracts promising him all her books for the next five years, she determined to break what threatened to become an eternal commitment. But in November 1910 Page cunningly invited her to Boston for a fortnight, during which visit he wined and dined her so graciously that as his guest, despite her 'disgust' with the 'binding clause' (*SJ* 2: 25) she once again signed away her books for the next five years. This would, however, be the last such contract.

Montgomery's War with Lewis Page

Montgomery does not seem to have considered seeking professional assistance until 1916, when she joined the Author's League of America. That year she gained some control over her lucrative series of Anne sequels by selecting John McClelland as her Canadian publisher and literary agent, to whom she assigned the task of negotiating a better deal with an American firm. Out of good will she insisted on giving first refusal to Page, who instead responded aggressively, with a threat to sue for the rights to *Anne's House of Dreams*. When McClelland concluded an agreement with Frederick Stokes for the American publication of Montgomery's books, there ensued a legal war with Lewis Page and his brother George, paralleling in intensity the narrative of the First World War that dominates her journal at this time.

Further complicating the picture was her view that 'The Page firm are the best bookmakers in America. Everybody admits that' (*SJ* 2: 188) – a detail that would explain why Page seemed to thrive despite the complaints of booksellers (*SJ* 2: 176), authors (*SJ* 2: 188, 193), and former employees (*SJ* 2: 182). Montgomery's suit against Page for unpaid royalties (*SJ* 2: 284) ended with his firm buying out the rights to her earlier books for $18,000 – 'nothing like the value of my books,' she fumed. 'But with a pair of scoundrels like the Pages, a bird in the hand is worth half a dozen in the bush' (*SJ* 2: 285). Page then countered with the unauthorized publication of the only known text that could be described as a 'false sequel' to *Anne. Further Chronicles of Avonlea*, cobbled together in Page's office from discards from *Chronicles of Avonlea* that were still in his possession, was manufactured uniformly with the earlier Anne books. Montgomery sued again; he threatened counter-suits, and then dealt the greatest blow of all by selling the film rights to *Anne of Green Gables* for $40,000.[15]

Montgomery's disputatious relationship with Page placed her in good company, insofar as his dealings with other Canadian authors can be determined. In 1908 Charles G.D. Roberts complained bitterly that Page had 'acted abominably' by attempting to force him into 'new & disadvantageous contracts' (287); later Roberts had great difficulty reclaiming rights to poems ever published by Page (Boone 380, 450, 589, 600, 606). Bliss Carman ran into similar copyright altercations (Miller 206, 254), as did John Garvin in compiling his anthologies of Canadian poetry.[16] The experiences of Marshall Saunders, author of the best-seller *Beautiful Joe* and other turn-of-the-century animal stories, corroborated Montgomery's view that 'the man must simply have an obsession of dishonesty' (*SJ* 2: 313).

For Montgomery, extricating herself from Page did not, however, mean extricating herself from Anne. *Anne's House of Dreams* (1917), the first Anne book issued under her new terms with McClelland and Stokes, was followed by *Rainbow Valley* (1919) and *Rilla of Ingleside* (1921). Indeed, it was the continuing appeal of the Anne books that produced terms with Stokes so good that, she wrote, they 'rather frighten me. Can I continue to write up to them? I am always haunted by the fear that I shall find myself "written out"' (*SJ* 2: 198). Upon completing *Rainbow Valley* she complained: 'I want to do something different. But my publishers keep me at this sort of stuff because it sells and because they claim the public, having become used to this from my pen, would not tolerate a change' (*SJ* 2: 278). Finally, in August 1920: 'To-day I wrote the last chapter of 'Rilla of Ingleside.' I don't like the title. It is the choice of my publishers ... The book is fairly good. It is the last of the *Anne* series. I am done with *Anne* forever – I swear it as a dark and deadly vow' (*SJ* 2: 390).

Montgomery may have been done with Anne, but Anne was scarcely done with Montgomery. Still to come were *Anne of Windy Poplars* (1936) and *Anne of Ingleside* (1939), as well as a manuscript of previously written stories linked by Anne, 'The Blythes are Quoted,' which was eventually edited by Montgomery's son and issued posthumously as *The Road to Yesterday* (1974). The production of these last books presents a poignant conclusion to the story of Montgomery's sequels.[17]

The first six Anne books form a classic *Bildungsroman* sequence, following the major character through girlhood to maturity as the captivating, iconoclastic child fades into a sedate doctor's wife. Once married, Anne slips to the margins of her books, becoming incidental to the major story – a point discussed by Gillian Thomas. Replaced as a centre of interest by her children and assorted members of the community, she presides over her household as the image of the idealized good mother (reminiscent of Alcott's Marmee) that Montgomery, orphaned at the age of two, missed in her own life and proved unable to enact with her own children. Despite Montgomery's complaints about the expectations of her publishers and public, the continued production of Anne books allowed Montgomery to have her cake and eat it too: to profit from the insatiable market for Anne books while using them as an opportunity to tell other stories, such as the experiences of women and children less fortunate than Anne,[18] as well as the depiction of daily life on the home front during the First World War presented through the maturation of Anne's youngest daughter in *Rilla of Ingleside*.[19] Because the previous texts did not present a uniform, chronological narrative, but rather discrete portions of Anne's life, Montgomery had left sufficient gaps into which she could later insert new texts. Thus the last books, set around the beginning of the twentieth century, coincide chronologically with Montgomery's own halcyon years, before the upheavals of the First World War, lawsuits, the 1919 death of her best friend, and the onset of her husband's mental illness.

Montgomery's decision to write again about Anne derives from many factors: her economic precariousness due to the Depression, the purchase of a new home, and a switch in her English publisher (from Hodder and Stoughton to Harrap); her publishers' and readers' continuing requests for more Anne books; and above all, the popular success of the 1934 film version of *Anne of Green Gables*. An avid movie-goer, Montgomery quite liked the film, despite its altered ending, although she found little connection between what she saw on the screen and her own notion of her characters.

Conclusion

In 1935, ill and depressed due to difficulties with her husband and sons, Montgomery approached her return to the world of Anne with mixed feelings. On the one hand, she wondered if she would be able to '"get back into the past" far enough to do a good book'; on the other, she found the work therapeutic: 'I had a strange feeling when I sat down to my work. Some interest seemed to return to life. The discovery that I may still be able to work heartens me. So often lately I have been afraid I never could again' (*SJ* 4: 357). A few months later, she noted that the writing of a chapter of *Anne of Windy Poplars* felt like an escape into the past. Clearly this escape was therapeutic: she noted in her journal that she was feeling healthier and was sleeping better. Similar dynamics, intensified by her ever-increasing distress at the continuing deterioration of her husband's condition, of her own health, and of the European political situation, accompanied the composition of her last Anne book three years later. At the age of sixty-three, less than four years before her death, she records than she has begun to write *Anne of Ingleside*. Her journal entry attests to her relief that, after having given up creative writing for over a year and a half, she is still able to write. Equally palpable is her joy at being back among her beloved, familiar characters: 'It was like going home' (UJ, 12 Sept. 1938).

Sequels were a determining factor in Montgomery's literary and personal life, producing the launch of her first book and her financial well-being, as well as decades of bitter dispute with her publisher and a problematic relationship with an intrusive, adoring readership. In her last years, they provided a refuge from an increasingly troubled world. By the end of Montgomery's life, sequels had ceased to be disappointing. For her publishers and other beneficiaries of the Anne industry, the sequels and spinoffs of *Anne of Green Gables* continue to produce tremendous profits. And for her public, who today still eagerly welcome every new text written by or associated with Montgomery, there can never be enough of Anne.

NOTES

I would like to thank Professor Mary Rubio for sharing some of her research materials on L.M. Montgomery, and both Dr Rubio and Nancy Sadek, Head of Archival and Special Collections at the University of Guelph Library, for facilitating my access to Montgomery's unpublished journals. I am also grateful to Anne Goddard at the National Archives of Canada and Carl Spadoni, Special Collections, Mills Memorial Library, McMaster University, for their assistance in obtaining materials relating to the publishing history of the Anne books. A version of this essay appears in Paul Budra and Elizabeth Schellenberg, eds., *Part Two: Reflections on the Sequel* (Toronto: U of Toronto P, 1998).

1 These are (to date) *The Road to Yesterday* (Toronto: McGraw-Hill Ryerson, 1974); *The Doctor's Sweetheart and Other Stories*, ed. Catherine McLay (Toronto: McGraw, 1979); and a series of books edited by Rea Wilmshurst and published by McClelland and Stewart: *Akin to Anne: Tales of Other Orphans* (1988); *Along the Shore: Tales by the Sea* (1989); *Among the Shadows: Tales from the Darker Side* (1990); *After Many Days: Tales of Time Passed* (1991); *Against the Odds: Tales of Achievement* (1993); *At the Altar: Matrimonial Tales* (1994); *Across the Miles: Tales of Correspondence* (1995); and *Christmas With Anne and Other Holiday Stories* (1995).

2 Mavis Reimer claims that a ballet version is regularly performed at Christmas in her home town (2). The musical version is a ritual component of the Charlottetown Festival held every summer in Prince Edward Island. For a discussion of the televised version, see Drain, '"Too Much Lovemaking."' Another spin-off is critiqued by Careless.

3 See Calvin Trillin, chapter 16 of this book; see also Baldwin; and Tye, 'Multiple Meanings.'

4 See Gerson, 'Canadian Women Writers.'

5 This problem is complicated by R.E. Watters's practice, in his *Checklist of Canadian Literature and Background Materials, 1628–1960* (still the closest

we have to an inclusive bibliography of Canadian literature in English),
of citing the earliest imprint (whether Canadian, American, or British)
located in a library, without seeking the variants that document co-
publishing arrangements (admittedly, a gargantuan task, as he states in his
preface, xi). Hence, for example, his listing of Ralph Connor's novels *Black
Rock* (1898), *The Man from Glengarry* (1901), *The Major* (1917), *The Sky
Pilot in No Man's Land* (1919), and *Treading the Winepress* (1925), all of
which had British and American publishers, suggests they were solely
Canadian publications (297–9).

6 Through the 1930s to the 1960s, serious writers such as Morley Callaghan
and Hugh MacLennan constantly wrestled with the problem of Canada's
viability as an internationally recognizable setting for fiction. Because he
sought an American readership, Sinclair Ross's classic novel of Depression
life on the Prairies, *As For Me and My House* (1941), contains nothing to
identify the setting as Canadian.

7 Personal communication from Mary Rubio, Montgomery's current
biographer, 13 Sept. 1995. In 1986 the National Archives of Canada
acquired eight contracts between Montgomery and L.C. Page as well as a
1919 memorandum concerning their lawsuit (MG 30 D 342). All that
survives of McClelland and Stewart's dealings with Montgomery are
several pages of notes in the McClelland and Stewart papers at McMaster
University, taken by George Parker from records that were subsequently
destroyed.

8 There is very little information available about Page, other than the entry
by Margaret Becket and Theodora Mills in volume 49 of the *Dictionary of
Literary Biography*. I would like to thank Sid Huttner at the University of
Tulsa for his assistance with references to Page. Montgomery's published
journals refer many times to Page's gambling and philandering (*SJ* 2: 117,
226).

9 L.C. Page & Company to Miss L.M. Montgomery, 8 April 1907. This is the
only letter from Page in the Montgomery papers at the University of
Guelph.

10 Another of his projects that included Canadian authors was his Little
Cousin books, a schoolroom series that included contributions by Jane
Roberts MacDonald (*Our Little Canadian Cousin 1. The Maritime Prov-
inces*, 1904), Mary Solace Saxe (*Our Little Quebec Cousin*, 1919), and Emily
Murphy (*Our Little Canadian Cousin of the Great Northwest*, 1923).

11 Montgomery wanted the second book to be *The Later Adventures of Anne*,
not *Anne of Avonlea* (*Green Gables Letters* 85), and disliked the title *Anne of
the Island* (*SJ* 2: 163). The titles of *Kilmeny of the Orchard* (*SJ* 1: 362) and

Chronicles of Avonlea were also Page's creation, the latter, in Montgomery's view, a 'somewhat delusive title' (*SJ* 2: 94). *Further Chronicles of Avonlea* (1920), the unauthorized collection issued by Page, was presented as an Anne book (*SJ* 2: 376). In addition, the maturity of the red-headed young woman appearing as the cover portrait on all the Anne books predicts the direction of the series.

12 As discussed in chapter 7 of this book, teaching school was one of the few respectable occupations for young women of Montgomery's social class who found themselves in need of financial support.

13 However, it should also be noted that none of her other sequences trailed on as did the Anne books. Rather, she limited them to pairs (*The Story Girl* and *The Golden Road*; *Pat of Silver Bush* and *Mistress Pat*) and then a trilogy (*Emily of New Moon, Emily Climbs, Emily's Quest*).

14 George Parker's notes on Montgomery's files with McClelland and Stewart, McMaster University, quotation from letter of 29 April 1916.

15 Louisa May Alcott encountered similar difficulties when she attempted to change her publisher. See Saxton.

16 Arthur Stringer to John Garvin, n.d., Queen's University, Lorne Pierce Collection, 2001b B032 F007 I13, refers to Page's 'selfish and unscrupulous conduct.' Stringer's correspondence with literary agent Paul Reynolds refers to yet another dispute with Page, eliciting from Reynolds the comment that Page 'is a smart, shrewd fellow but he will bear watching.' Reynolds to Arthur Stringer, 30 March 1905, Paul R. Reynolds papers, Box 166, Butler Library, Columbia University. I would like to thank Clarence Karr, Malaspina University College, for these two references.

17 Some pages of the manuscript of *Anne of the Island*, at the Confederation Centre in Charlottetown, are written on the backs of typescripts of what appear to be stories extracted from some of Montgomery's previously published books. While there is no bibliographical evidence that these were actually published, their format indicates that Montgomery intended to send them out to magazines. The cover page of one story, 'Anne Comes to Grief in an Affair of Honour' (chapter 23 of *Anne of Green Gables*), states that it is '1,000 words' and gives the author's address as Leaskdale, thus dating it before Montgomery's 1925 move to Norval. While not exactly sequels, if published, such stories would represent an interesting extension of the Anne books as well as an effort to get back at Page.

18 See Thomas; Mary Rubio, 'Subverting'; and Jennie Rubio.

19 See Young.

4

(Re)Producing Canadian Literature:
L.M. Montgomery's Emily Novels

E. HOLLY PIKE

During the 1920s, the definition and future of Canadian literature were under active discussion. It was 'a decade of enthusiasm for Canadian literary enterprises probably unmatched until the centennial ardour of the late 1960s,' according to Carole Gerson ('Canon' 48). This interest in Canadian literature was part of what Kenneth McNaught describes as a 'renewed' but 'loosely defined' post-war Canadian nationalism, which was apparent in the work of the Group of Seven as well (219, 238–9). Some of the attempt to define Canadian literature and identity through the establishment of a Canadian literary canon in the 1920s took place in the production of anthologies and studies of Canadian writing, and in the vivid debates surrounding those works.[1]

What constituted the Canadian tradition was an open question to the anthologists and critics of the 1910s and 1920s. In his introduction to the New Canadian Library edition of *Headwaters of Canadian Literature*, M.G. Parks notes the attempts made by Archibald MacMechan and others to come to a definition of Canadian literature, and their inclusion or exclusion of certain writers based on the criteria they establish. Both MacMechan and John D. Logan, author of *Highways of Canadian Literature*, struggle with the relative importance of Canadian birth and/ or education and Canadian subject matter or content in determining whose work qualifies as Canadian literature. MacMechan argues that even works having a Canadian subject are not Canadian if the authors 'were formed by alien influences' (100), for 'their work ... has exerted little or no influence upon the thought or life of Canada' (101). Logan distinguishes between literature written by visitors or émigrés and that which he calls the 'Native and National' literature, written after Confederation by native-born Canadians (20–1).

In the works they collect, the anthologists and critics claim to be looking for signs of a Canadian culture, which Dermot McCarthy describes as 'the myth of the consolidation of the national spirit' (38). In his book, MacMechan states that he looks for work that is 'essentially Canadian' (116) or 'distinctly Canadian' (120), that deals with images 'every Canadian will recognize' (121), identifying what constitutes Canadian culture by stating that 'spiritual purity' is the mark of all Canadian poetry (157) and that 'Nature-worship is the "note" of Canadian poetry' (170). This view of Canadian poetry is largely confirmed, at least as far as it refers to poets such as Roberts, Carman, and F.G. Scott, by Logan, who also seeks work that is 'representative of Canadian culture and of the Canadian creative spirit' (15). According to Logan, Charles G.D. Roberts was 'the first "Voice" of the Spirit of Canada,' even though his work was first published in the United States (26).

Popular Maple Leaf Romanticism

Reading many of the anthologies of Canadian literature produced in the teens and twenties, such as John Garvin's *Canadian Poets* (1916) and Albert Durrant Watson and Lorne Pierce's *Our Canadian Literature* (1922), one gets a picture of Canadian poetry that is explicitly romantic. John Garvin is not as programmatic as MacMechan and Logan are in defining what constitutes Canadian literature, but he claims that the poetry in his anthology is 'vitally, healthfully Canadian ... inasmuch as the writers have lived in this country, and have been influenced by its history and atmosphere at a formative period of their lives,' and this history and atmosphere seem to be romantic (5). In the introductions to the various poets in these anthologies, the word beauty comes up over and over, and nature poetry predominates.[2] Pierce and Garvin, of course, have been described as part of the 'conservative establishment' with a 'retrogressive cultural agenda,' attempting to 'save Canadian literature from the crudities of the modern era' (Gerson, 'Canon' 51).

Another version of Canadian literature was being formed in contradistinction to this romantic one. Writers such as A.J.M. Smith and Douglas Bush espoused the view that Canada should not be looking to the past but to the present for literary models: 'they endeavoured to induce Canadian poetry to relinquish popular Maple Leaf romanticism in favour of the literary modernism of post-war Europe and Britain' (Gerson, 'Changing' 890).[3] Rather than maintaining the purely romantic view of Canada depicted in the poetry favoured by Logan and Garvin, these writers look to the contemporary world for models, and do not concern themselves too much with Canadian identity.[4]

In a 1928 article in *Canadian Forum*, 'Wanted – Canadian Criticism,' A.J.M. Smith points to what he sees as the problem with Canadian literature: 'Of realism we are afraid – apparently because there is an impression that it wishes to discredit the picture of our great Dominion as a country where all the women are chaste and the men too pure to touch them if they weren't' (Daymond and Monkman 223). John Murray Gibbon, in an article in the July 1919 *Canadian Bookman* titled 'The Coming Canadian Novel,' made a similar point with reference to the British surprise at the efficient industrialism of Canada during the war: 'The Englishman found nothing of this in Gilbert Parker, in Ralph Connor, in L.M. Montgomery,' pointing out how far removed from 'real' contemporary Canadian life the world depicted in their novels was (Daymond and Monkman 198–9). Looking back at the period, Desmond Pacey in volume 2 of *Literary History of Canada* expresses surprise that 'reputable critics' 'came very close to ignoring the few books, such as the novels of Grove and Callaghan, that did at least come within striking distance of greatness,' while paying serious attention to novels he describes as 'romantic' (175–6).

While this debate was going on in the 1920s, Montgomery was writing the Emily novels, was actively involved in associations of Canadian authors, and was visiting other women writers on her trips to Toronto. She was one of the writers who organized Canadian Book Week in November 1921, indicating in her journal that she wrote letters and publicity materials in preparation for that event, sponsored by the Canadian Authors' Association (CAA) (*SJ* 3: 24). Her journals for the 1920s note her encounters with other writers at the events of the CAA and her private lunches with writers such as 'Marian Keith' (Mary Esther MacGregor) and 'Anison North' (May Wilson) (*SJ* 3: 4, 128, 363, 380).

Montgomery was a popular figure at Canadian Book Week events, among the writers as well as with the public. She writes in her journal for 30 April 1923 that John Logan addressed her at the CAA convention, 'Hail, Queen of Canadian Novelists' (*SJ* 3: 128) and that on another occasion John Garvin told her that he had been instrumental in arranging for the Canadian edition of *Anne of Green Gables* to be published (this at a time when there was no Canadian edition) (*SJ* 3: 364). It is significant that Garvin and Logan connect themselves with Montgomery in this way, because in their attempts at canon formation they espoused the romantic definition of Canadian literature and were among those who took seriously the writers with whom Montgomery had formed friendships and who are largely ignored in the current canon. Montgomery's journals of the 1920s show that she read fairly widely in Canadian literature, including works by W.W. Campbell, Marian Keith, Marjory MacMurchy, Susanna Moodie, Anison North, Marjorie Pickthall, Florence Livesay, Wilson Macdonald, Nellie McClung, Bliss Carman, Charles G.D. Roberts, and Arthur Stringer, writers mostly of the romantically idealist type.

Although interest in L.M. Montgomery has increased in the latter half of the twentieth century, she has generally not been considered a canonical writer in the English-Canadian tradition. Desmond Pacey's oft-quoted comment, that 'it would be silly to apply adult critical standards' to *Anne of Green Gables*, is typical of the critical response to Montgomery (*Creative Writing* 106). In volume 1 of *Literary History of Canada*, Montgomery is discussed, and her name misspelled, in a paragraph that emphasizes the shortcomings of her fiction. In volume 2 her work, with that of Ralph Connor and Nellie McClung, is described as 'working [an] even richer lode of sentimentality,' and her success is described as 'more commercial than artistic' (Egoff 138). Carole Gerson suggests that Montgomery's ex-canonical position may have been based on gender: 'Before the 1920s, L.M. Montgomery and Nellie McClung were as popular and wrote as well as their male counterpart, Charles W. Gordon ("Ralph Connor"), but lacked the canonical valorization bestowed by the latter's profession as man of the cloth' ('Canon' 54).

Nevertheless, I would argue that Montgomery was an active participant in the debate on the canon, not through participation in the production of studies and anthologies or articles in the scholarly press, but through the production of fiction about Canadian writing, and in particular through the reproduction in the work of her writer-heroine, Emily Byrd Starr, of the type of Canadian writing that she wanted canonized. In the 1920s debate over the relative merits of modernist and realist-idealist fiction and of modernist and traditional verse, Montgomery comes down firmly against modernism, and sets out her canons of poetry and fiction in the Emily books: her poetic canon is suggested through the Canadian poetry quoted or mentioned, and her prose canon is suggested through her depiction of Emily's career in fiction. Montgomery thus presents an argument that Canadian literature should comprise the types of poetry and fiction that she wrote herself, and therefore implicitly argues for her own inclusion in the canon of Canadian literature.

Emily Byrd Starr: Prototype of a Canadian Artist

In *The Fragrance of Sweet-Grass* Elizabeth Rollins Epperly establishes that romanticism plays an important role in Montgomery's reading and writing, and shows that in Emily's favourite works 'we hear the Romantic and Victorian preferences that characterize Montgomery's own volume of verse, *The Watchman and Other Poems*' (150). This preference, combined with the autobiographical elements of the Emily books – outlined by both Epperly (145–7) and Mollie Gillen (*Wheel* 134–5), and noted by T.D. MacLulich, who sees in most of Montgomery's heroines 'an element of wishful self-portraiture' (465) – makes it possible to read the Emily novels as a justification of Montgomery's own career and taste in poetry.

The references to Canadian poets in the Emily books publicly express Montgomery's position on Canadian poetry. The Canadian poetry quoted or referred to in these novels, like that preferred by Logan, Pierce, and MacMechan, tends to be in traditional stanza forms, almost invariably rhyming forms, and with careful metres.[5] For Emily, as for Montgomery, poems always rhyme. In her skirmishes with Evelyn Blake, who also considers herself a poet, Emily is more likely to comment on the faulty form of Evelyn's poems than on their content, as when she tells Evelyn in reference to the rejection of a poem she had submitted to the school paper, 'I'm not feeling badly. Why should I? I didn't make "beam" rhyme with "green" in *my* poem. If I had I'd be feeling very badly indeed' (*EC* 114). This is certainly a retrospective attitude toward poetry on Montgomery's part in the 1920s, when free verse had become the dominant form of poetry, if not on Emily's part at the turn of the century, but it does reflect Montgomery's own practice in poetry, and therefore functions to keep Emily in Montgomery's version of the Canadian tradition.

Two lines from Bliss Carman that the narrator uses in reference to Emily, referring to 'the eternal slaves of beauty' who are 'masters of the world,' sum up Montgomery's poetics: the poet is one who searches for beauty and attempts to share that beauty with others, and who has a peculiar sensitivity to beauty. Montgomery had this sensitivity herself, according to her journals, where she frequently records her response to scenes of beauty, as in the entry for 9 July 1913, where she refers to 'the rapture and ecstasy that filled my heart when from that same hill the same glimpse of the purple evening sea flashed on my eyes. That same view always brings a resurrection of that old thrill and rapture' (*SJ* 2: 123). Emily's sensitivity to beauty is experienced in the form of her flash – a sensation that comes over her when her perception of natural beauty makes her feel her immortality – what she calls her 'supernal moment' (*EQ* 165).

Also consistent with Montgomery's depiction of Emily and with her own practice as a poet is R.H. Hathaway's celebration of Carman as a poet of nature: 'As becomes such a poet, and particularly a poet whose birth-month is April, Mr. Carman sings much of the early spring. Again and again he takes up his woodland pipe, and lo! Pan himself and all his train troop joyously before us' (xiii). Carman was presented in the 1920s as a poet who appreciated beauty, who kept free from the realities of the modern world, and who celebrated the natural world. He is therefore the perfect spokesman for Montgomery's agenda, especially in the above-mentioned lines of his poetry that the narrator quotes in reference to Emily. The narrator further characterizes Emily on the same page as having 'a certain wild, lawless strain ... a strain that wished to walk where it would with no guidance but its own – the strain of the gypsy and the poet, the genius and the fool' (*EC* 155).

Like Carman, Marjorie Pickthall, another Canadian poet whose work Emily quotes, was portrayed as a romantic writer in the 1920s. Pickthall was just starting her career at the turn of the century, the time at which, according to the chronology of the novels, Emily quotes from 'O keep the world for ever at the dawn.' The poem was written by the then seventeen-year-old Pickthall to be entered in a Christmas poem contest in the Toronto *Mail and Empire* in 1900 (Pierce 36–9). Pickthall died in 1922 and was popular enough at that time to justify the publication of Lorne Pierce's *Marjorie Pickthall: A Book of Remembrance* in 1925. In his book, Pierce reinforces the view of the poet as innocent appreciator of natural beauty by emphasizing Pickthall's femininity, delicacy, and youth (she is described as a 'timid school-girl' [64]), by describing her work using such adjectives as 'charming,' and by writing that her days 'pass with an almost bewildering wealth of romance' (36).

The Pickthall poem that Emily quotes should be compared to Emily's own poetry as described in the passage in *Emily of New Moon* in which she shows her poems to Mr Carpenter. The poems she shows him are explicitly romantic, having such titles as 'Sunset,' 'A Wood Stream,' 'Wind

Song,' and 'Morning' (*ENM* 348–52), titles that are similar to those of Montgomery's poems, such as 'November Dusk,' 'The Wood Pool,' 'Rain in the Country,' and 'Sunrise Along Shore.' Similarly, Pickthall's poem is a detailed description of the natural world, and expresses a desire to keep the world unawakened. The natural world depicted is calm, smooth, and shadowy – the speaker wants nothing to do with the definite, active, or tempestuous. Each of the poem's five stanzas describes the beginning of a movement or sound and a restraining of the natural elements. The images are of birds, flowers, the sunrise, the sea, trees, and moths – all recurring images in Pickthall's poems and in Emily's and Montgomery's. The speaker in Pickthall's poem wants the world to be kept in a state of innocence, where even beauty is only half-perceived, and things are dimmed, veiled, or shadowed.

Emily quotes Pickthall's poem while sitting outside with Teddy in the early morning, using it to express her appreciation of the setting and her desire for the moment to last. In the paragraph following the quotation, the narrator recapitulates the poem, describing 'the white, filmy mist hanging over the buttercup valley across the pond,' and things half-hidden or veiled, such as the 'violet shadows' and 'plumes of purple and mauve smoke' (*EQ* 122), in a description fairly typical of Montgomery. As Epperly notes, 'Pickthall's lines are full of the images and spirit of Montgomery's own descriptions before and during this same scene' and picture 'many of Montgomery's favourite themes and moments' (*Fragrance* 197).

The imagery of Frederick George Scott's 'Dawn,' another romantic Canadian poem that Emily quotes, is much vaguer than that of Pickthall's poem, but the general topics are the same, and the idea of transcendence, of nature as a revealer of hidden truths, recurs. The experience Scott describes in the poem is something like Emily's 'flash' – a perception made by the soul beyond the physical experience and linked to nature. 'All nature' is described by Scott in the poem as the 'speech' of 'Eternal Thought,' an idea similar to that expressed by Wordsworth in 'Tintern Abbey' and elsewhere. Scott's poems have titles like 'The Storm,' 'In the Winter Woods,' 'The Unnamed Lake,' indicating that he, too, belongs to the school of Pickthall and Montgomery. 'In the Winter Woods' in particular makes an explicit connection between nature and the soul of the poet (Garvin 75–86).

Although MacMechan and Logan are concerned with the depiction of a specifically Canadian landscape and subject matter in the works they choose to include in their studies, the one thing that is missing from most of Carman's, Roberts's, Scott's, Pickthall's, Montgomery's, and Emily's poems is a specifically Canadian landscape. The trees, flowers, and sea of Carman's poems could be anywhere, like the sea of 'A Captain of the Press-Gang,' or like the non-specific dawn of Pickthall's poem, in which no detail could not apply equally to a European dawn. The lack of recognizably Canadian landscape in much Canadian nature poetry was pointed out by Huntly Gordon, in his March 1921 *Canadian Forum* article, 'Canadian Poetry': 'Lampman and the Canadians as a whole feel deeply the distinctive beauties of prairie and mountain, bushland and farm, and love their people and their ways. But one sometimes wonders whether they do not "see, not feel, how beautiful they are," so insincere sounds the sincerity of their praise, and so unreal is their description' (Daymond and Monkman 212). He sums up his comments on the poets by saying, 'There is nothing more Canadian than these subjects and nothing less Canadian than their treatment' (214). Rather than examining and representing the nature immediately around them, these poets treat nature as an idea – a symbol of their own detachment from any world but the natural world.

Rejecting the Howls of Canadian Realism

While Montgomery uses her favourite Canadian poets in the Emily books to define her canon of Canadian poetry, she defines her canon of Canadian fiction through her depictions of writing in her novels. Privately, she expressed her opinion of modernist realism in her journal comments on Morley Callaghan in 1928:

Callaghan's idea of 'Literature' seems to be to photograph a latrine or pigsty meticulously and have nothing else in the picture. Now, latrines and pigstyes are not only malodorous but very uninteresting. We have a latrine in our backyard. I see it when I look that way – and I also see before it a garden of color and perfume – over it a blue sky – behind it a velvety pine caressing crystal air – a river of silver and aquamarine – misty hills of glamor beyond. These things are as 'real' as the latrine and can all be seen at the same time. Callaghan sees nothing but the latrine and insists blatantly that you see nothing else also. If you insist on seeing sky and river and pine you are a 'sentimentalist' and the truth is not in you. (*SJ* 3: 387)

Montgomery's insistence on seeing beauty and her use of her favourite type of description to validate it, taken in conjunction with her final sentence, constitute a clear recognition that current definitions have left behind the fiction she writes and admires.

Publicly, Montgomery defines her canon of Canadian fiction and argues for her place in it through her reproduction of herself as a Canadian writer in Emily Byrd Starr. That the role of the specifically Canadian writer did not become a concern of Montgomery's until the 1920s is suggested by her earlier discussion of writing in *Anne of the Island*. There Montgomery offers some commentary on the appropriate form and style of fiction by way of Mr Harrison's comments on Anne's story 'Averil's Atonement.' Mr Harrison criticizes the flowery language and the fact that the story deals with a setting and social class with which Anne is unfamiliar, and he suggests that a degree of realism be added to the story, saying 'your folks ain't like real folks anywhere' (89). All the characters describe the story as 'romantic,' and as T.D. MacLulich points out, 'Montgomery thought of her fiction as realistic,' but 'literary realism lies very much in the eyes of the beholder,' and therefore there is no necessary contradiction between Montgomery's perception of her work as realistic and a modern reader's probable perception of it as idealistic (460).

Significantly, Anne's audience expresses a preference for Montgomery's version of realism – a familiar setting, characters who are neither all good nor all bad, and a certain amount of humour – and therefore valorizes the type of fiction Montgomery is writing. It is also significant that, unlike in the Emily books, she is not concerned with the work being recognizably Canadian, showing that that concern arose with the 1920s debate over the canon. However, in *The Blue Castle*, published in 1926 in the middle of the Emily books, the writer-character produces books full of detailed nature description, wants to publish a 'real, worthwhile, honest-to-goodness Canadian magazine' (190), and is described as having 'put Canada on the literary map of the world' (203), showing that defining a specifically Canadian literature of a type she liked had become important to Montgomery.

The development of a Canadian literature becomes an important element in *Emily Climbs*, as Emily gains some success as a writer. When Emily has the opportunity to go to New York and work for a magazine, her teacher/mentor, Mr Carpenter, does not want her to go because he thinks she will be 'Yankeefied' if she lives in the United States: 'Janet Royal *is* Yankeefied – her outlook and atmosphere and style are all U.S. And I'm not condemning them – they're all right. But – she isn't a Canadian any longer – and that's what I wanted you to be – pure Canadian through and through, doing something as far as in you lay for the literature of your own country, keeping your Canadian tang and flavour. But of course there's not many dollars in that sort of thing yet' (*EC* 310). Emily's choice to stay in Prince Edward Island can be read as Montgomery's attempt to show Canada's cultural separation from the world of commercial American literature; as Emily says, 'Some fountain of living water would dry up in my soul if I left the land I love' (*EC* 316). When Emily's novel *The Moral of the Rose* is published, Miss Royal writes to her to congratulate her and admits that the novel could not have been written in New York because 'wild roses won't grow in city streets' (*EQ* 185), a remark in which, as Ann S. Cowan writes, 'the *Canadian* novel is justified' (48). This comment places Emily's fiction in the tradition of the pastoral, beautiful, and affective and defines it as arising from her Canadian education and experience.

In her depiction of Emily as poet as well as novelist, Montgomery echoes the concerns of the critics and anthologists with the background and experience necessary for a writer to be considered truly Canadian and seems to believe that a writer needs to be insular, to be confined to his or her own time and place. In *Emily Climbs*, when Emily shows some of her poems to Mr Carpenter, he tears up a poem she had written after a walk in the woods when, she writes in her diary, 'the sounds I heard were not the cheery, companionable sounds of the daytime – nor the friendly, fairy sounds of the sunset – they were creeping and weird, as if the life of the woods had suddenly developed something almost hostile to me – something at least that was furtive and alien and unacquainted' (*EC* 251). She feels as if she had escaped from 'some fascinating but not altogether hallowed locality – a place given over to Paganism and the revels of satyrs' (EC 251). It is because the poem captures this mood successfully that Mr Carpenter tears it up. He says, 'That poem was sheer Paganism, girl, though I don't think you realise it ... that way danger lies. Better stick to your own age. You're part of it and can possess it without its possessing you' (*EC* 256). While Judith Miller sees this passage as an example of Emily being warned away from 'literature' and back to 'pretty songs,' ('Montgomery's Emily' 163) it can also be seen as an order to limit herself to her own culture rather than explore a foreign one.

Montgomery also uses Mr Carpenter to express her feelings about the new realism in fiction, which was much more a product of the 1920s, when she was writing the Emily books, than of the turn of the century, when the conversation in the novel takes place, although the naturalism of such writers as Crane, Dreiser, Norris, and Sinclair was already at issue. Mr Carpenter's deathbed pronouncement ('Don't be – led away – by those howls about realism. Remember – pine woods are just as real as – pigsties – and a darn sight pleasanter to be in' [*EQ* 30]) echoes Montgomery's journal entry on Callaghan and is just as explicit a statement of Montgomery's refusal to participate in or even acknowledge a definition of Canadian literature that includes what has come to be regarded as the mainstream of early-twentieth-century literature and the Canadian literary canon from which her work has been excluded.

Conclusion

Montgomery presents Emily as a particular type of Canadian writer, focusing on pastoral life, tied to the landscape, and dwelling on its beauty and significance. In depicting Emily's career as a version of her own, therefore, Montgomery presents a view of successful Canadian writing that validates her own views and echoes the principles expressed by Logan and MacMechan in their studies of Canadian literature – a belief that there is a recognizable Canadian literature that Canadians should identify with and value above the literature of other countries (Logan 15; MacMechan, preface). At the time, it seemed possible to some that the canon would be defined as Montgomery wished. As Lionel Stevenson put it in 1926, 'It is improbable that any sudden shift will occur in the proportion of natural and artificial elements in Canadian life. So one may venture to predict that, for some time to come, Canadian literature will provide a refreshing haven of genuine romanticism to which the reader may retreat when he seeks an antidote to the intellectual tension imposed by the future progeny of "The Waste Land" and "Spoon River"' (62). This expectation was not borne out. Dermot McCarthy states that, 'During the 1930s, a growing pressure was exerted on the canon by the influx of modernist artistic values as well as by the impact of revolutionary social and cultural events upon the traditional sense of the mimetic relation of literature to history' (44–5).

Montgomery's production and reproduction of a romantic Canadian literature in the Emily books and in the depiction of Emily's writing seem very much a participation in serious literary debate, but to accept Montgomery's version of the canon, one has to accept Emily as the type of the successful Canadian author, and the new guard of the 1920s, with their desire for 'virile' writing, apparently did not accept that portrayal (Gerson, 'Canon' 54–5). Montgomery's subsequent marginalization in terms of canonicity may be no more than the usual treatment accorded the losing side in such a debate, but the mere fact of her having dealt with the question of Canadian literature in her novels should in itself have been enough to create the serious critical attention that her work has received only in the last thirty years.

NOTES

1 Dermot McCarthy, for instance, describes the anthology as 'an instrument of literary history and canon-formation' (33), while Carole Gerson draws attention to the role of surveys of Canadian literature in canon formation and the tendency of both nationalist and modernist critics to 'conspire against the reputations of Canadian women writers' ('Canon' 46–8).

2 For example, Logan describes the work of the writers of the turn of the century – Marjorie Pickthall, Charles G.D. Roberts, and Bliss Carman – as 'notably refined in sentiment, beautiful in structure and imagery, and noble in spiritual substance and appeal' (26–7), emphasizing attitude rather than execution. In a similar vein, Garvin's anthology quotes Professor James Cappon, MA, on Charles G.D. Roberts: 'he ... strove to catch and to shape into some new line the vague, evasive, elemental beauty of nature,' again defining poetry in terms of beauty, and of natural beauty in particular (47). Furthermore, Lionel Stevenson suggests that Canadian poets share 'an instinctive pantheism, recognizing a spiritual meaning in nature and its identity with the soul of man' (12). MacMechan refers to Carman's treatment of 'the calm deep majesty of this world's beauty' to make the same point, that Canadian literature is essentially romantic (131).

3 Bush, for instance, writing in *Canadian Forum* in 1926, criticizes the poets of the early 1920s for sticking with nature poetry: 'Our writers think that tourist enthusiasms before mountain or rivulet make cultivation superfluous; indeed they seem to fear that some fundamental brain-work would take the bloom off their spontaneous emotions' (Daymond and Monkman 217). Two years later in the same journal, A.J.M. Smith makes a remark that could be read as a particular reference to the descriptions of Canadian poetry above: 'Canadian poetry, to take a typical example, is altogether too self-conscious of its environment, of its position in space, and scarcely conscious at all of its position in time' (Daymond and Monkman 223).

4 As early as 1919, John Murray Gibbon, writing in *Canadian Bookman*, points out that 'Bliss Carman is dismissed by the Chicago editors as belonging to the nineteenth century' and ridicules John Garvin's anthology by referring to it as his 'Valhalla,' and by praising poems in free verse, 'even

though they do not rhyme like Mr Garvin's galaxy of stars' (Daymond and Monkman 190).

5 Privately, in her journal in 1920, Montgomery expresses disdain for free verse, characterizing it in a mock free verse 'poem' as written by writers 'too lazy / To hunt up rhymes' (*SJ* 2: 390), thus indicating her adherence to traditional forms, just as the Canadian poets she mentions indicate her favourite content.

5

Reflection Piece –
The Poetry of L.M. Montgomery

ELIZABETH WATERSTON

When L.M. Montgomery was at school, it was assumed that reading, analysing, memorizing, and reciting poetry would help students write well. And if the talent was there, the best kind of writing would eventuate – the writing of poetry.

L.M. Montgomery always felt that her poetry was her highest achievement. Yet her poetry has fallen into disregard, not necessarily on its own merits, but largely because of a reversal of opinion about poetry itself. I propose to open this discussion of Montgomery's poetry by briefly recapping old and new conceptions of poetry – what it is, how it works, why people read it (or don't read it) today. There have been real changes since L.M. Montgomery learned and recited and eventually wrote poems. Those changes have led to the dismissal of poetry like hers.

My age will show. I too learned gobs of Walter Scott's *Lady of the Lake*, Tennyson's 'Lady of Shalott,' Longfellow's poetry, Whittier's – and even poems by Bliss Carman, a late addition to L.M. Montgomery's repertoire. Let me quote part of a poem that she learned, I learned – but that my children and my grandchildren, schooled differently, did not learn 'by heart.' (I have added some oddities of typography to Wordsworth's 1804 poem, which I will explain later.)

I wandered, lonely as a cloud
That floats on high O'ER VALES and hills;
When all at once I saw a crowd,
A *host*, of golden daffodils;
Beside the lake, beneath the trees,
Fluttering   and dancing   in the breeze ...

For OFT WHEN ON MY COUCH I LIE,
In vacant or in pensive mood,
They flash upon that inward eye
Which is the bliss of solitude.
And then my heart WITH PLEASURE FILLS
And dances   with the daffodils.

Like L.M. Montgomery, I was taught to like poetry that rhymes, and poetry that has regular rhythm. My teachers knew that to be memorizable, poetry needs the mnemonic device of recurrence: sounds that echo previous sounds, predictable repetitions of rhythm. Like L.M. Montgomery, I learned Wordsworth's 'Daffodils' by remembering the rhyme words – cloud/crowd; hills/daffodils – and the beat of the stanzas: ta-tum ta-tum ta-tum ta-tum; ta-tum ta-tum ta-tum ta-tum ... Having 'learned by heart,' I kept the poem in my heart *and* my mind for its deeper, more complex values. I can still recite it – just as L.M. Montgomery could recite line after line after line of the poems learned by her heart, in her schooldays.

She of course learned that the charm of regular rhythm consists in part of the occasional irregularities that give it spice and surprise. You can't make a 'ta-tum' rhythm out of 'fluttering and dancing': it must be 'fluttering (pause) and dancing' – with the kind of memorable variation that imitates the momentary ruffle and halt in nature's seasonal pace. The rhythmic variations must be appropriate, supportive. If the line pauses in the middle, the pause must permit a shift in thought: 'fluttering and dancing' not of their own will, but in response to something else in nature, 'in the breeze.' Those incidental irregularities give the reciter of a rhythmic poem a chance to display sensitivity and individuality. Similarly, elementary classes in 'English' taught L.M. Montgomery (and me) the value of rhyming 'daffodils' with 'hills,' and (at the same point in a later verse), 'solitude' with 'mood.' The 'long word,' a refreshing substitute for more obvious and simple rhymes ('chills'? or 'food'?), lets the reader or reciter slow the pace, relish the 'big word,' and prepare for something more complex than the 'moon/June' verses of popular songs. To work well, rhymes should be subtle, surprising, apparently inevitable.

The down side of poems with regular rhythm and rhyme is contortion and contrivance. In Wordsworth's poem, as the mark of its age, there is 'Poesy': ornate diction, not the language of ordinary life, but 'vale,' and 'o'er,' and 'oft.' There is inversion, words wrenched out of their normal syntactic order to make a rhyme: 'when on my couch I lie,' 'my heart with pleasure fills.' (I have set these bits of 'poesy,' words and phrases, in capital letters.)

And then there is sound play: the internal links between floats and flutter and culminating *flash*, wonderfully effective in this case. We know L.M. Montgomery learned in school about alliteration, consonance, onomatopoeia: open *The Poetry of Lucy Maud Montgomery* at any page for proof. We do not know whether Professor MacMechan, in that brief one-year course, Introduction to British Literature at Dalhousie University, taught her to recognize the subtler word play in poetry. Perhaps she learned to appreciate Wordsworth's poignant use of the word 'host,' a surprising, evocative word, with multiple suggestions of hospitality and of religious sacrament, as well as of crowds. Perhaps appreciation of such subtleties had to wait for the 'new criticism,' the in-depth analysis of the 'well-wrought urn' sort.

But sensitive readers, from Wordsworth's own day on, have recognized and ingested the shift in the poem, from the dancing daffodils to the dancing heart. There in the poem is the distinction between seeing and remembering, between gazing and accepting the workings of the inward eye, the movement from mere loneliness to the *bliss* of solitude. (I have used italics to underline the phrases, words, sentences that seem to me to pack the poem with verbal and intellectual power.) All the mnemonic tricks in Wordsworth's poem contribute to lines that are worth memorizing.

Then the sensitive reader, becoming an effective oral performer of this poem, can convey a clear, though perhaps subtle and complicated message, a clarification of something 'that oft was thought but ne'er so well expressed.' Given a meditative, rhythmic performance, the message slips in quietly, but surprisingly. The listener receives not only an unforgettable picture of a breezy golden lakeside, but also an insight into the paths of the mind.

Now let me look at L.M. Montgomery, who is working in somewhat the same mood and tone. Her poetry rhymes and has regular rhythm: witness 'Buttercups,' a poem first published by 'Maud Cavendish' in the *Mayflower* in 1899, three years after her Dalhousie exposure to *Standard English Poems*, and republished in *Farm Journal* in 1910, the year before she married and left Cavendish.

Like showers of *gold* dust on the marsh,
   OR AN INVERTED SKY,

The buttercups are dancing now
Where *silver brooks* run by.
Bright, bright,
As *fallen flakes* of light.
They nod
In time to every breeze
That chases shadows swiftly lost
AMID these grassy *seas*.

See, what a golden frenzy *flies*
Through the light-hearted *flowers*!
In mimic fear they *flutter* now;
Each FAIRY blossom cowers.
Then up, then up
Each shakes its yellow cup
And nods
In careless grace once more –
A VERY *flood* of sunshine seems
ACROSS THE MARSH TO POUR.

The rhythm is varied and graceful, nodding lightly like the fragile flowers. Effective in repetition, too, the poem teases the mind with the sequence of 'gold dust,' 'silver brooks,' 'golden frenzy.' There are some clever antitheses – the kind of yoked opposites that we recognize in metaphysical poetry: showers of dust pour as a flood in the final line; the inverted sky narrows to a yellow cup.

But at least one rhyme overpowers the syntax: 'across the marsh to pour.' And the archaisms pile up: 'amid,' 'a very flood,' 'fairy' (again I have used capitals to highlight the elements that seem to me to weaken the poem). Alliteration seems pushed too far: 'fallen flakes ... flies ... flowers ... flutter ... flood' – stop! stop! And a chain of water allusions, 'showers ... brooks ... seas ... cup ... flood ... pour,' does not seem to cohere in a new impression of the buttercups, or add to any intrinsic movement of thought about the flowers. No single word in the poem carries the concentrating power or suggestiveness of Wordsworth's 'host.' Instead, there is a diffusion of meaning in the image of the 'inverted sky.' It is hard for me to see how dancing buttercups resemble the sky even if the sky is turned upside down – with flakes falling from it. Perhaps the linking of archetypes, flowers and waters and sky, lifts the poem to something universally recognizable, and perhaps that is as good a function for poetry as the more esoteric insights of academic, elitist verse.

But what is the residue? An image may flash across the inward eye, yes, but the flash is followed by no mind-catching enlightenment about experience, memory, imagination, or (to use its own terms) grace and carelessness.

I'd give L.M. Montgomery B+ for this poem.

Montgomery, however, gave herself A++ for all her poetry. She considered the writing of poetry her highest calling, and her achievement in verse her greatest gift. She became puzzled and angry at its reception as the years passed. Sometime just before or during the First World War, poets had begun to slip away from regularity, rhyme, and easily marked rhythms, and from archetypal topics, prettiness, and 'fairy blossoms.' The world was too slippery, too pointless, too off-key, too irregular in beat, to be caught in tidy verse. Poets began to shudder at the neatness of poems like Montgomery's. They were moving toward a kind of poetry epitomized by this poem by William Carlos Williams, published in 1913:

Flowers through the window
lavender and yellow

changed by white curtains –
Smell of cleanliness –

Sunshine of late afternoon –
On the glass tray

a glass pitcher, the tumbler
turned down, by which

a key is lying – And the
immaculate white bed

'Nantucket' begins like a Montgomery poem, with a singing, simple rhythm; then comes change. Change to 'non-poesy,' to the reality of 'pitcher, key, bed'; to clarity and evasion of message. An easy poem to admire – though it is a hard poem to memorize or to recite. And not one for children to learn in primary grades, to keep for comfort, inspiration, and solace in adult years.

When teachers in the post-war years coped with the post-war moods and modes, the old kind of poem faded out of school readers. Canadians found sharp, taut little poems like A.J.M. Smith's 'The Lonely Land' (1936) preferable to Montgomery's prettiness:

Cedar and jagged fir
uplift sharp barbs
against the gray
and cloud-piled sky;
and in the bay
blown spume and windrift
and thin, bitter spray
snap
at the whirling sky;
and the pine trees
lean one way ...

But for children in the 1930s and 1940s there was still nothing like the Tennyson, Wordsworth, Longfellow, or Bliss Carman poems. Teachers began to encourage little children not to memorize poems, but to compose them, directly from their own hearts and experience (if any). At college, in the 1940s and 1950s, older students toiled through difficult, un-memorizable poetry; staccato in rhythm, with tortuously internalized rhymes and complex, metaphorically inverted, undercut meanings. Unmemorizable, to be read and footnoted rather than recited. Consequently, very few adults now read poetry, memorize it, recite it – although many feel they are writing poetry when they let their innards hang out in obscure short lines.

I would like to make a case for returning, at least in school classes, to Burns and Scott, Wordsworth and Tennyson, Whittier and Longfellow, Robert Louis Stevenson and Kipling and Vachel Lindsay. And to L.M. Montgomery? For the moment, I reserve judgment.

John Ferns and Kevin McCabe, editors of *The Poetry of Lucy Maud Montgomery*, selected one out of five poems to make up this first volume, and they conclude their volume with some of her earliest and strongest verses. This raises a question about her development as a poet. Did she change her poetic mode with the years, as we know Tennyson did, and Wordsworth? Did the sombre realities of her mature life (as we now know of them) lead to darker, heavier, more introspective poems? Did she still see buttercups as fairy blossoms, cowering, in the days when she was fighting her publishing battles, or struggling with marital dismays? Can we see in her poems of the 1920s and 1930s the same release of high spirits, gaiety, satiric perception, that bubbled up, in spite of troubles, in her prose fictions of the same period? I hope that the next book of her poetry to be edited by Ferns and McCabe will date each entry, so that we can study the links or breaks between her works in the two channels, prose and poetry.

Meantime, for me, L.M. Montgomery's best poetry seems to be prose poetry, the poetic prose of her novels. That is one reason I will conclude by quoting from a totally contemporary poet – not English or American or Canadian, this time, but Scottish. Robert Crawford was thirty-two when he published this poem; he is now thirty-six years old, Montgomery's age when she wrote *Anne of Green Gables.* The rhythm is elusive, and a kind of rhyme appears only in that repeated 'At first I was jealous.' There are elements here – that outside toilet! – that dear L.M. Montgomery would have kept out of her poetry (though she rushed the Earl Grey incident into her journal, with considerable relish).

Anne of Green Gables
Short moneyless summers at West Kilbride you sat out
On the back steps with a view of the outside toilet
Reading the Anne books, one after the datestamped next,

Anne of Windy Willows, Anne of Avonlea,
Anne of the Island, Anne's House of Dreams.
No books were ever as good as these

From West Kilbride Public Library
That had always to go back.
When we got married, one by one

You bought the whole set, reading them through. At first
I was jealous when you sat not speaking,
Then put the books away on your own shelf.

'"How white the moonlight is tonight," said Anne
Blythe to herself.' At first
I was jealous. Not now.

The illumination that the poem brings is the dawning understanding of what reading meant to a girl as she moved through an unbeautiful life. Her husband comes to realize the qualities the Anne books instilled in her, including the love of lilting language. He realizes, and we realize with him, that he loves his wife partly because she has learned to love beauty, and beautiful language, through her immersion in Montgomery's writing. And how modern to choose an over-rhymed phrase to epitomize that catalyst of character!

Part 2.
Montgomery and Canadian Society:
Negotiating Cultural Change

RELIGION, EDUCATION, AND TECHNOLOGY

6

L.M. Montgomery: Scottish-Presbyterian Agency in Canadian Culture

MARY HENLEY RUBIO

Culture is a force that spreads as much through stories as it does through political revolution. L.M. Montgomery was a storyteller supreme, and her worldwide impact is only now being charted. The cultural impact of Montgomery is part and parcel of the enormous influence wielded by the Scottish immigrants to Canada. This impact is deeply rooted in the religious and cultural ethos of the Scottish-Canadian society in which she was raised; that ethos, in turn, is a continuation of unique ideas about education, egalitarianism, and agency that her ancestors brought from Scotland. Montgomery is inescapably a descendant of ancestors who came out of Scotland's Presbyterian culture.[1]

The principles of Scottish Presbyterianism – specifically, those placing emphasis on empowerment of *all* classes of people through education, on participatory democracy in church and civic government, on constant self-examination through one's reasoning faculties, on 'plain speaking' and accessibility in rhetorical style and public discourse, on valuing intellectuality and achievement – were deeply held beliefs that the Scottish emigrants took with them wherever they settled. They were ideals that gave them a sense of agency. Also, the Scots have had great impact in creating imaginative literature, coming as they did from a culture that valued *both* the oral tradition and the written word. They also recognized the power of story in the transmission and critiquing of cultural values.[2]

Montgomery's genius was to embed in narrative, and particularly in narrative about women and ordinary people, many of the basic ideas and energies that fuelled the rest of the Scottish colonial enterprise.

Montgomery is vigorously against cant, hypocrisy, and authoritarianism. She has a sense of 'social class,' but she sees status as maintained through people's behaviour, not just through their class at birth. She admires moral seriousness, but she shows how it often is misguided in a strict religion that has become somewhat calcified. She grows up in a society that values reason and the intellect above all, but she uses her fiction to show that the intellect is often driven by the emotions. And, very important, she values education – for women as well as for men – which undercuts the Presbyterian exclusion of women (in her era and earlier) from official positions of power, although women were not excluded from getting a basic education in itself. In short, she continues in the tradition of her Presbyterian ancestors from Scotland who used 'common sense' and learning to constantly renew their evolving society. She certainly was not one to accept the status quo without critiquing it. Hers is essentially a subversive approach – one that challenges authoritarianism and that creates a space for elevating women within a society supposedly built on egalitarian principles. Narrative is her chosen medium, and it has been uniquely effective.

Montgomery's Presbyterian Heritage

L.M. Montgomery grew up on the north shore of Prince Edward Island in an enclave of Scots who were militantly proud of their ancestry, their literacy, their educational system, and their cultural heritage in general.[3] Her ancestors on both sides had been in the first wave of emigrants who came to PEI, and were from a higher socio-economic class than many later Scots, especially the impoverished Scots who came as the result of the Highland Clearances in the early nineteenth century. Her ancestors had done well after they left Scotland, obtaining or purchasing land in Prince Edward Island in the late eighteenth century. Their clannishness, their moral seriousness, their Presbyterian belief in the Protestant work ethic, their faith in the possibility of human improvement, and their insistence on setting up the best possible school systems for all their children without the prejudice of social class – all this contributed to their success and their subsequent pride in this success. The Scots came from a country that had long allowed exceptionally able 'lads o' pairts' to rise out of humble beginnings. By contrast, many of the English emigrants, who were also drawn from the farming and lower classes, often came with far less education, as well as with an internalized sense of inferior social class that often held them back.[4] Long accustomed in their native land to being patronized by the

English, the better-educated Scots thrived abroad, taking root with the tenacity of the famous Scotch thistles.[5]

The early Presbyterians in Scotland had been religious fanatics, but they created a democratic mechanism that had enormous social impact the world over when they were able to institutionalize their belief that education should be accessible to all classes of people. Scotland's first Education Act, in 1496, prior to the establishment of Presbyterianism, had consolidated power in the hands of the literate elite, namely the Catholic clergy and the landowners. Presbyterianism was first established as the national religion of Scotland by an Act of Parliament in 1560 (Bone 13), and strongly affected Scottish education from then on. The Presbyterians countered the idea that education was only for the elite by legislating a second Education Act in 1696 which proclaimed that a school was to be established in every parish, and that all children, rich and poor, male and female, should at least have access to education, though they were not forced to attend school.[6] (This system was far more deliberately egalitarian than England's, which did not nationalize education for the lower classes until the Education Act of 1870.)[7]

While the education system in Scotland was quite variable in quality, was only erratically available in the remoter highlands, and was one that favoured boys, it still educated a great number to a basic level, and exceptionally talented children of a poor class could theoretically rise through merit. Some did. And a large number of Scottish young people achieved a solid basic education. Thus, Scots had a deeply ingrained respect for education from a very early era, which gave them a great advantage as colonizers.[8] Thus in Scotland, where religion and state education were not separated, and where the Presbyterian religion promoted education, this religion, which was itself militant and rigid, became an instrument that eventually fostered the seeds of democratic egalitarianism.

Scottish education was not just learning facts. The Scots were particularly adept at conceptualizing because in the Scottish educational system they had studied philosophy as a base for further specializations. From their understanding of first principles, they then proceeded to the study of specialized subjects like mathematics, science, medicine, and law.[9] The Scots felt their educational system – as well as much else about their culture – was markedly superior to England's, which was more focused on specialization, and is satirized in Charles Dickens's *Hard Times* through Mr Gradgrind's educational approach.

A further skill that the Scots admired and honed was that of fluency and force in oral argument. Arguing fine points of theology, philosophy, and law had long been a national pastime in Scotland, and the effects had been both good and bad: over the centuries, the disputatious and polemical Scots had carried many of their arguments to the battlefield, and the history of their country is full of bloody encounters. But they had also carried their arguments into the halls of learning, producing an extraordinary flowering of knowledge during the Scottish Enlightenment in the eighteenth century.

Finally, the Presbyterians held that education should be offered to anyone of ability, not excluding women.[10] For Montgomery, this meant not only that she had access to good schools, but also that she learned in those schools to respect the prime Scottish educational ideals of reasoning and rhetoric. Montgomery's novels make a strong stand for the education of women. She believed that women, as well as men, should be able to use education to give self-direction to their own lives. Montgomery's novels and stories gave agency to the women of their era, showing that women could have considerable power if they exercised it. They could talk, harass their husbands, gossip (a very powerful form of social control in small communities), and, in her own case, write humorous accounts of patriarchal church structures that annoyed women. The internalized notion that people hold about what it is possible to achieve strongly affects what they are actually willing to try achieving: thus, the Scottish Presbyterians' belief in education for everyone, and for using that education to critique and improve society, eventually became a liberating social force, despite the inherently repressive nature of the early Presbyterian church.

Montgomery also retained from her Scottish heritage a belief that telling stories was a slow but effective way to change public attitudes. In addition to being a nation that particularly valued written texts and book-learning, the Scots also valued the oral tradition and were storytellers par excellence.[11] Their storytelling is often attributed to the vague 'Celtic legacy,' or to the Highland culture, which was primarily an oral culture. However, among literate Scots, having access to the stories of the Bible, which their education allowed them to read in the vernacular, was another site of cultural enrichment – again a point where religion and education intersected. The Bible was, of course, more than a source for theological points to argue about – it was full of good stories, as well as examples of teaching through stories and parables. And it was read daily in the homes of the Presbyterians of Cavendish, where Montgomery grew up. Montgomery's fiction draws on the storytelling of her cultural milieu, too, as well as on the general ethos of Presbyterianism.

In the narratives of L.M. Montgomery, we see a community that is always examining itself. This too is part of the intellectual, emotional, and social heritage of Presbyterianism. Presbyterians were taught by their religion – a particularly fervent one – to constantly examine their own lives for signs of slackness. Since humanity's responsibility was to enact God's teachings (as laid out in the Bible), constant self-examination was in order. Intense self-examination became a habit of mind with them.

More important, perhaps, Presbyterians enthusiastically extended the process to an examination of the lives of their relatives and neighbours. The Scots Presbyterians in Cavendish could be very hard on themselves, but they could be harder on others, for it is human nature to find faults in others in order to mitigate one's sense of one's own imperfections. Montgomery's stories are laced with judgments about people's morality, theology, behaviour, and general rectitude. This constant judging of others is a religious exercise in the purest sense, for it shows up the people who are mean-spirited, selfish, and otherwise unworthy of God's grace. Her cast of fictional characters always includes those yeasty souls who take it as their 'Christian duty' to gratuitously detail others' faults to them. Montgomery's texts grow full of verbal sparks when well-meaning (and less-well-meaning) people take aim at others, delivering hurtful remarks, all in the service of being good Christians. They justify their 'plain speaking' easily: since barbs keep others humble, and since humility is a prerequisite for getting into Heaven, it follows that the induction of humility can only be good. Besides presenting sharp-tongued characters, she herself revels in examining the foibles of men and women, grown-ups and children, the pious and the reprobates.

However, the ultimate sense that readers get from Montgomery's fiction is that Avonlea is a safe place to be: however much people prick and rub their neighbours' skins raw, they also care deeply about each other. Their society is run by law and order. They intend to be fair-minded even when they are not. Thus, the ever-present Scotch thistles are ultimately contained and neutralized by the coddling wool of community caring. These are good people at heart, and very predictable. They constitute a society that has high standards of personal moral earnestness, a reverence for rational individual thought based on careful discernment, and a deep commitment to civic good. One's 'social class' means far less to them than the state of one's soul with God. It is a society that believes everyone has the right to respect unless he or she forfeits that right by unacceptable behaviour. The Scots who emigrated to Canada, and elsewhere, came with these ideas.

Montgomery and Religious Satire

When she was Mrs Reverend Ewan Macdonald, L.M. Montgomery felt in her core that the Presbyterians were a special breed apart from the other Protestant sects – to say nothing of Catholics. (Her son told me that when he was training at St Michael's Hospital in Toronto, she lived in constant fear that he might fall in love with a Catholic nurse and marry her. He didn't.) However, when she is writing fiction, Montgomery can be objective and satirize her own prejudices, which were those of her beloved Cavendish, a typical tightly knit nineteenth-century Scottish community, with life organized around its church.[12]

It is remarkable that Montgomery was able to have such sport with religion in her novels – in an era that still took denominational rivalry very seriously – and yet not offend her readers. Her techniques are subtle: she puts the most partisan remarks (which are often offensive) in the voices of the people who are already flagged as comical characters, like Miss Cornelia Bryant or other mouthy or opinionated sorts who are baited if they are adults (or scolded if they are children). If, for instance, the grown-up Anne of Green Gables, as the respectable Mrs Dr Gilbert Blythe, were to comment seriously on the superiority of Presbyterians, Montgomery's novels would have become offensive religious propaganda. But Miss Cornelia can say anything and get away with it because the reader knows that everyone is laughing at her for her opinions. Still, they like her.

According to the church theologian and historian Professor Gavin White, the doctrine of predestination[13] was no longer taught in the theology school at Glasgow by the time that Montgomery's husband, Ewan Macdonald, studied there in 1906. The Glasgow theological school ceased teaching this doctrine to young ministers in the late nineteenth century, but it was an idea deeply imbedded in the cultural memory of older people, and many of them thought a minister's theology was not 'sound' if he did not preach about it. Letters about predestination were still surfacing in the PEI newspapers her grandparents read in Montgomery's childhood and early youth.[14] This theology tormented Montgomery's husband in his periods of mental illness after their marriage.

The doctrine of election offers Montgomery many chances for satire. In *The Blue Castle*, Roaring Abel praises drunkenness for setting him free, 'free for a little while – free from yourself – yes, by God, free from Predestination' (80). In *Magic for Marigold*, Uncle Jarvis hopes 'gloomily that Leander's baby was an *elect* infant' (17; my italics). In the same book, a child is rejected: 'She is plainly not of the elect and she is too wicked for you to play with' (248).

In *Anne of Green Gables*, Montgomery creates a little girl whose first presence in a Presbyterian church results in her shocking report to Marilla that she spent her time in church looking out the window and dreaming. Montgomery is undoubtedly reflecting some of her child-hood feelings of being cooped up in a church when she might have been out running through the fields and playing. She also is touching on a theme that comes up repeatedly in her novels: long prayers and tedious sermons that a captive child – and indeed captive adults – must endure.

However, there is more to her dissatisfaction than mere child's memory of churchly incarceration on beautiful Sunday mornings. One needs to read her characterizations of ministerial style in light of the ideas of Hugh Blair's widely circulated and immensely influential 1783 *Lectures on Rhetoric and Belles Lettres*, the best-known of the many books that he wrote in Scotland during the eighteenth century. These lectures were originally given at the University of Edinburgh and heard by thousands of young men going into the ministry, commerce, law, or education. The lectures were also printed and widely distributed throughout the English-speaking world. Not only did these ideas of the Scottish Enlightenment come across with the early Scottish settlers, and later with the ministers who were sent out to the colonies, but native-born Canadians who went to Scotland to study would have had renewed contact with them. In Montgomery's own immediate family, her academically gifted Uncle Leander Macneill (oldest brother of her mother) was sent to Edinburgh for his university education. Later, Montgomery's husband studied theology at Glasgow. Uncle Leander became a very successful minister. Parishioners of the Reverend Ewan Macdonald told me that, when he was well, he gave excellent sermons: they were learned, accessible, and interesting.

In *Church and University in the Scottish Enlightenment*, Richard Sher talks about the impact of Hugh Blair's ideas: sermons were not to be read, as was the custom in England (170); they were to be delivered extemporaneously. A good sermon was a persuasive sermon: 'the end of all preaching is to persuade men to become good' (169). To achieve this, ministers had to be interesting, show both 'gravity and warmth,' and be free of abstruse 'doctrinal discourse.' The Scots rated oratorical skills very highly, and 'ostentatious swells of words or a pointed ornamented foppery of style' was regarded as the nadir of pulpit oratory (169). The Scots valued fluency, but they hated pomposity for its own sake, in the pulpit or anywhere else. They regarded the purpose of language as communication and persuasion, not obfuscation.

This attitude is still prevalent in the Scottish culture in all intellectual circles, not only in religious ones. Professors and ministers who read formal written texts are regarded as weaker specimens of their profession. Montgomery makes the comment a number of times in her works that 'dullness' is the cardinal sin. Anne of Green Gables says: 'It was a very long text. If I was a minister I'd pick the short, snappy ones. The sermon was awfully long, too. I suppose the minister had to match it to the text. I didn't think he was a bit interesting. The trouble with him seems to be that he hasn't enough imagination' (*AGG* 92–3). Another character rebels against a 'portly, dignified old man with silver hair and gold-rimmed glasses, who preached scholarly, cultured sermons and was as far removed from [her] personal life as a star in the Milky Way' (*ASh*, 'The Unhappiness' 213). Miss Cornelia chimes in, 'What I had against Mr. Dawson ... was the unmerciful length of his prayers at a funeral. It actually came to such a pass that people said they envied the corpse' (*AIn* 199).

Some children (in *The Story Girl*) might both be impressed by pompous preaching and have sport with it: 'Not a motion, or glance, or intonation escaped us. To be sure, none of us could remember the text when we got home; but we knew just how you should throw back your head and clutch the edge of the pulpit with both hands when you announced it' (198); but an Emily, one of Montgomery's later characters, could roundly criticize it: 'That sermon was a most inconsistent thing. Mr. Wickham contradicted himself half a dozen times. He mixed his metaphors – he attributed something to St. Paul that belonged to Shakespeare – he committed almost every conceivable literary sin, including the unpardonable one of being dull' (*EC* 248–9).

There was another kind of sermon that Montgomery also satirized: the thunderous 'old-style' minister's sermon that stressed hellfire and brimstone. Before the Scottish Enlightenment, there had been a 'persistent stereotype,' no doubt with some justification, 'of Scottish Presbyterian ministers as [being] ignorant, bigoted, and narrow-minded fanatics' (Sher 57). This type of minister, trained in the older theology, and coming out to the colonies, was still occasionally found in the rural areas. In *Rainbow Valley*, an adult bully who won't come to church sends a message to the minister: 'You tell him that if he wants to keep me [Norman Douglas] in good-humour to preach a good rip-roaring sermon on hell once every six months – and the more brimstone the better.

I like 'em smoking. And think of all the pleasure he'd give the old maids, too. They'd all keep looking at old Norman Douglas and thinking, "That's for you, you old reprobate. That's what's in store for *you!*" I'll give an extra ten dollars every time you get your father to preach on hell' (117).

L.M. Montgomery's view is not necessarily that of her characters, of course. She stands enough outside them that she knows when their viewpoint, put in plain English, will sound quite comical, not only to the Presbyterians who will read her novels, but also to millions of other people with different religious beliefs who are equally convinced that their own religious view is superior to every other. In other cases, she takes aim at those whose practice of religion misses its spirit. However, Montgomery's point of view is very complex and often unstable, and it changes at different points in her life. The Montgomery who writes the novels is often not the Montgomery who writes the journals. As a writer, Montgomery can take the ironic perspective, but as a human being she is often heir to the prejudices that she satirizes in others. This is clear in her fiction when she satirizes the view of Presbyterians that they are superior to others, while in her journals she often speaks disparagingly of other denominations.[15]

Changes and Dissension in the Presbyteral System

There were two churches in Cavendish: the Presbyterian, which was in the centre of the community, and the Baptist, which had been founded by break-away Presbyterians, at the edge of the community. Unlike many English-Canadian villages, Cavendish had neither a Roman Catholic Church nor an Anglican one. In Montgomery's mind, and often in her novels (although she could be inconsistent), Protestants are subdivided into three classes: the Presbyterians (the superior group but nevertheless the subject of much satire), the Episcopalians/Anglicans and Methodists (the next best, although she again took shots at various practices and individuals within these groups, such as the dreadfully pompous, stuffy, and insensitive Stirling clan in *The Blue Castle*), and the Baptists (doctrinally anathema to Presbyterians because they believed in total immersion when being baptized, although in fact Montgomery often attended their church activities in Cavendish for social reasons).

Old religious dissentions lingered in the Canada of Montgomery's childhood. Religion was still the strongest organizing force within local communities. But these divisions were not just between Presbyterians

and Episcopalians, or between Presbyterians and Catholics. It is important to understand the role that the Presbyterian Church structure had
in creating a sense of agency in ordinary people, making them resistent
to any authoritarian structures imposed from above. The Presbyterian
Church structure was built on the 'presbyteral system,' a type of government that vested power in ordinary people at the grassroots level. Much
of the political and religious strife in Scotland from the sixteenth century onward had been centred around the question of whether authority should be organized around the 'presbyteral' or the 'episcopal' system.
Scotland favoured the former, England the latter. The presbyteral system held that authority should begin at the most local level: a community would designate its own lay leaders (called the 'church elders') and
select their own minister. This minister was 'ordained' in the church,
but was subject to the 'call of the people.' This system had the effect of
consolidating considerable power in the hands of ordinary lay people
because power moved upward from the local level to the next level,
through a reasonably democratic process of selection. The church elders
and the local minister constituted the 'local Kirk [church] session.' A
gathering of local sessions constituted the next level, called the
'presbytery.' A subsequent gathering of 'presbyteries' made up the 'regional synod,' and the top level was the 'General Assembly,' which had
supreme authority. But it did not have the power to impose a minister
on any local group – each community 'called' its own minister, and
could dismiss him.

The episcopal system was very different. In the Church of England
(and, similarly, in Roman Catholicism), power was vested in the hands
of a higher pastoral order headed by bishops, under whom were priests,
followed by deacons. Although both systems provided for a hierarchy of
power, the episcopal system vested greater authority at the top, whereas
the presbyteral system placed much authority at the non-clerical, local
level. Those favouring the presbyterial system in Scotland opposed any
system that they thought smacked of 'popery,' where authority was
vested either in all-powerful bishops (as in the Church of England) or a
pope (as in the Roman Catholic Church).

As a result of their church's grassroots organizational structure, the
Presbyterians had always found enough things to fight about among
themselves; in the mid-nineteenth century during the period of the
church 'disruptions' in Scotland, the Presbyterian Church essentially
split, and these bitter schisms were carried abroad wherever the Scots
emigrated. Eighty years later, in the early 1920s, another massive church

upheaval occurred in Canada when the vote over church union occurred. In 1923, a preliminary vote paved the way for the Presbyterians,
Methodists, and Congregationalists to merge into the United Church of
Canada. However, at the local level, many Presbyterians voted in 1925
to stay separate, and they retained the name Presbyterians. Montgomery's journals reveal that she and her husband remained adamantly
Presbyterian when local parishes voted in 1925: 'I feel I have no longer a
church.' At the time of the national vote, Montgomery had written in
her journals on 12 June 1923. 'My Presbyterian Church has gone – I owe
and feel neither love nor allegiance to its hybrid, nameless successor
without atmosphere, tradition or personality' (*SJ* 3: 132). Montgomery
stuck to her belief that the Presbyterians should stay Presbyterian, and
not turn into the United Church of Canada.

At the same time, however, Montgomery describes a community that
is always in a state of renewal and improvement. In *Emily Climbs* (1925),
a congregation faces a threatening kind of new vision in the church, one
that actively tolerates other religions: when Emily remarks, 'Mr. Johnson
... said in his sermon last Sunday that there was some good in Bud-
dhism,' Aunt Elizabeth indignantly replies, 'He will be saying that there
is some good in Popery next' (25).

More important still, in Avonlea and Montgomery's other fictional
villages, the old and the new ministers have different Gods. The old fire-
and-brimstone ministers had the Old Testament God of retribution,
which the early Puritans had made so vivid in their sermons, no matter
whether they were Presbyterians or from other protestant sects. The
newer God – and the one that Montgomery favoured – was the one
described by Emily of New Moon's father: '"You can't help liking God. He
is Love itself, you know ..." Emily didn't know exactly what Father meant.
But all at once she found that she wasn't afraid any longer – and the
bitterness had gone out of her sorrow, and the unbearable pain out of
her heart. She felt as if love were all about her and around her, breathed
out from some great, invisible, hovering Tenderness. One couldn't be
afraid or bitter where love was – and love was everywhere' (*ENM* 26–7).

An even more important change is registered in *Rilla of Ingleside*,
Montgomery's war novel. Here, a woman once violently opposed to the
union of Presbyterians and Methodists says, 'Well, in a world where
everything is being rent and torn what matters one more rending and
tearing? Compared with Germans even Methodists seem attractive to
me' (226). That passage, from a 1920 novel, points to the enduring
quality and depth of Montgomery's writing: she takes us where the real

action comes from, someplace in the unfathomable mysteries of the human heart. Here, evil merely shifts its manifestations in human society. Montgomery here registers the massive shift in the twentieth century away from a teleological world to a secular one: theology is losing its position as the site for human discussion of evil.

This change is also noted by two 'old-timers' on Prince Edward Island in a delightful book of social history edited by Island historian David Weale. He asks these two men what the biggest change in their lifetime has been. Both comment on the decentring of religion. The first says, 'There have been many great changes in my lifetime, but I do believe that the greatest change of all is the change that has come over God ... when I was growin' up, God was something to be feared. Oh yes! The fear of God was drilled into us every chance they got' (108). Another notes: 'I can tell you right now I didn't like Him [God] much. Who would? He seemed to disapprove of the very appetites He had put in us. Not only that, He watched all the time, every little misstep. And if you stumbled, He was right there, on the spot, to wag his big finger' (109). Montgomery's books catch this era of change, and considering the force wielded by popular literature that is widely circulated and repeatedly reread, they undoubtedly also contributed to it. They are social criticism writ large into comedy, but she laces her morality with humour, rather than thundering away like John Knox.

Conclusion

In Cavendish, and the fictional Avonlea, people believed – just as their strict Scottish forebears had – that humanity's chief goal on earth was to prepare for entrance into Heaven. Religion was at the centre of their world and their daily consciousness (as was the case, of course, in other denominations, too). It provided the measure of their every thought and deed and dictated the kinds of pleasures they could allow themselves. As the character Miss Cornelia puts it, 'Politics is for this world, but religion is for both' (*AHD* 211). Montgomery herself would have agreed. Montgomery's family (the Macneills) had provided the property on which the Presbyterian church was located, adjacent to their farm, and her grandfather and uncle were elders in this church. The Presbyterian Church was the measure of her personal world.

In her fiction, Presbyterian faith was core to her central characters' identity, and so was their Scottishness. L.M. Montgomery remains a thinking and judging Presbyterian to the core, always studying herself and the wider human society to see how it might be improved. Like her forebears, she believes that human society can be improved. In her own writing endeavours, she knows the powers in story – a lesson learned as a captive little Presbyterian lass listening to Sunday school lessons and Bible stories, as well as to ministerial sermons, which were all designed in the most practical and immediate sense to alter human behaviour for the better. That attitude underlies Montgomery's fiction and has made it empowering for many to read: she conveys a sense of personal agency.

At the beginning of a new century, Canadian culture is a dynamic, evolving organism, influenced by people from many different countries and cultures, but the influence of the Scots and Scottish Presbyterianism was deeply influential in Canada's early history.[16] A disproportionate number of early writers in Canada were Scots, as any perusal of early Canadian anthologies will show. The Scots' continuing influence has been felt in the twentieth century through the writing of many well-known authors such as Montgomery, Hugh MacLennan, Sinclair Ross, Margaret Laurence, and Alice Munro. There are many others who, if they don't write *out of* the Scottish ethos, write *about* a culture that contains it. The pervasive Scottish influence, by the late twentieth century, resides partly as 'myth,' and partly as 'reality.' Adrienne Clarkson writes in the Foreword to this collection about how reading Montgomery led her to a better understanding of her adopted land. In Montgomery's case, the extreme popularity of her writing has resulted in her having secondary influence on subsequent generations of younger writers and other professionals, especially women.

The Scottish-Presbyterian legacy still lives. It is encoded in Montgomery's texts, which themselves have travelled all over the world, wielding their own influence. Those who have thought of Montgomery as a superficial writer of romances for little girls may be startled to learn that Montgomery's books have had a wide-ranging political and social influence, both in Canada and internationally.[17]

NOTES

I am deeply indebted to those who have read and commented on a longer draft of this paper: Elizabeth Waterston, Catherine Kerrigan, Elizabeth Ewan, Linda Mahood, Jennie Rubio, Owen Dudley Edwards, Jenny Litster, and Gerald Rubio. I also thank Mike Kennedy for information about Scottish emigration.

 1 The Presbyterian Church was institutionalized as the National Church of

Scotland. One should note, however, that there were a number of Roman Catholics in Scotland, and many of them migrated to the New World also, but with different religious institutions. In the old country, and often in the new, there was a great deal of mistrust between Presbyterians and Catholics.

2   In his essay on the oral tradition in Scotland, Hamish Henderson notes that 'in 1951 the renowned American folklorist Alan Lomax ... carried out two energetic recording tours in Scotland' for Columbia Records, and when he documented his findings in *World Library of Folk and Primitive Music*, he wrote about Scottish folk culture: 'The Scots have the liveliest folk tradition on the British Isles, but, paradoxically, it is the most bookish. Everywhere in Scotland I collected songs of written or bookish origin from country singers, and, on the other hand, I constantly encountered bookish Scotsmen who had good traditional versions of the finest folk songs.' (Henderson 161).

3   Montgomery's Montgomery and Macneill ancestors were both proud of their status as being among the first immigrants after Prince Edward Island fell under English ownership in 1763. The Montgomeries are believed to have arrived in PEI between 1769 and 1772, and the Macneills in 1775. Her grandmother's Woolner ancestors did not come to PEI until Lucy Ann Woolner was twelve years old, in 1836, which made them lower in status. Also, the Woolners were English, not Scottish, which gave them a different religious and cultural heritage.

4   L.M. Montgomery's maternal grandmother, Lucy Ann Woolner Macneill, came from Dunwich, England, a borough in a very wealthy area of southern England (East Suffolk) that had been unusual in having an exceptionally good educational system for several centuries. Lucy's parents were working-farmers, but very successful and capable ones. Hence, when she married into the Scottish Macneill family, she was literate, and she valued education as much as the Scots did. In fact, she was more supportive of the young L.M. Montgomery's desire for advanced education than was her husband, Alexander Macneill.

5   North Americans frequently treat England and Scotland as a single country when they are discussing the literatures or the colonizing history of these two countries within the British Empire. Although the two countries are geographically attached, and although they did intermingle and share a government structure in England (from 1707 until the Scottish vote for devolution in 1997), it is essential to understand that they are nevertheless two distinct peoples with two different national histories: at certain points in history they were less 'kissing cousins' than 'killing cousins.' When

Scotland united with England and Wales to become Great Britain in 1707, the Scots managed to keep control of three of their institutions: the religious, educational, and legal systems. These institutions, which grew out of cultural difference between Scotland and England, maintained and furthered these cultural differences.

6 For a transcription of the original documents, see Insch. Rendall also reproduces many of the legal and cultural documents that underlie the development of Scotland's distinctive society and gives commentary on their significance.

7 England was much slower than Scotland in instituting education for the poor for several reasons. For one, the English looked at Scotland and thought that the Scottish mixing of state education and religion was dangerous. In addition, W.O. Lester Smith's history of English education notes that the effect of bitter feeling in seventeenth-century England between the Anglicans on one side and the Dissenters and Roman Catholics on the other had the effect of aligning religion along class lines (with Dissent entrenched in the middle and lower classes and Anglicanism in the gentry): this bitter rift made these classes further distrust state control of education (42). It was only in the last quarter of the eighteenth century that the English began to seriously debate the question of whether mass elementary education should be offered to the lower classes (Wardle 1). Though England had assorted church and charity schools for the working classes in the early nineteenth century, these were local initiatives, not state-sanctioned institutions. Charlotte M. Yonge's novel *The Daisy Chain* (1856), for instance, describes the setting up of one of these schools for the poor by some idealistic young people of the educated classes. But in England there was widespread resistance to mass education, partly because of the fear that, as the poet Alexander Pope put it, a 'little learning was a dangerous thing': education for the masses might, the reasoning went, upset the class system by making 'members of the working class discontented with their lot' (Wardle 7) or it might become an instrument of the state by increasing 'the power of the government by allowing it to assume responsibility for the private lives of its citizens' (Wardle 3–4). According to many historians, there was deep resistance to educating the poor in England, particularly after the French Revolution, when there was talk among politicians of introducing a bill to suppress Sunday schools (Silver 17) because they taught the poor to read. Thus, England's late start in national education for all classes put the English working class at a disadvantage when they were competing in the colonies with the aggressive and better-educated Scots.

8 Ewan Macdonald's niece, the late Mrs Mary Furness of PEI, told me how their family came from the Highlands where there had been little access to education. But they came with the idea that education was the way to escape grinding poverty and servitude, and every child with aptitude in the family was encouraged to go on in school. Ewan's brother became a very successful medical doctor with a substantial clinic in Warsaw, Indiana, and Ewan himself worked to get a good education for the ministry.

9 A massive shift in the Scottish educational philosophy began after 1872, when there was pressure to bring higher education in Scotland closer to the English model of specialization, but this was long after Montgomery's ancestors had emigrated to Canada, so it did not affect them.

10 Helen Corr points out that although women were not excluded from educational opportunity, in practice they generally acquired far less education than men. The point is, however, that literacy was not closed to women.

11 The Scottish oral tradition's influence on Montgomery is inadequately explored to date, although some scholars (see Tye, 'Women's') have begun to look at it. Montgomery was influenced by Sir Walter Scott, whose popular novels about Scottish life were read all over the British Empire in the nineteenth and early twentieth century. Elizabeth Ewan of the history department, University of Guelph (personal communication) believes that most of the actual Scottish history that Montgomery learned would have come to her through the oral tradition and through Sir Walter Scott's novels. For the influence of Scott on Canadian culture, see Carole Gerson's chapter on Sir Walter Scott in *A Purer Taste*. See also Michael Lynch's comments about Scott's influence in 'Scottish Culture in Its Historical Perspective.' It is important to understand that in Montgomery's time, and well after, the history of 'Great Britain' was essentially taught as the history of 'England.' This resulted in Scots being denied learning the history of their own country, written and taught from a Scottish perspective, well into the twentieth century. Their continuing resentment of this helped fuel the vote for 'devolution' in Scotland in 1997.

12 See another Canadian's account of growing up in a Scottish-Presbyterian community in the Harvard economist John Kenneth Galbraith's *The Scotch*. Like Montgomery, he regards his strict childhood upbringing with a comic eye.

13 Predestination was that austere doctrine that held that before each child's birth God had determined on high whether a person was of the 'elect' (chosen for salvation in the afterlife) or the 'damned' (consigned to Hell in the afterlife).

14 Many old-timers believed in the doctrine. See, for instance, the *Charlottetown Examiner* for 27 February 1890, in which the Archbishop of Halifax attacks 'Predestination.' A letter on 8 June 1893 also attacks the doctrine, calling it fit for the Dark Ages. On 15 June 1893, there is another letter complaining that some Presbyterian ministers teach old dogma they don't believe in, just to keep the older parishioners happy (especially the 'elders' who might dismiss them).

15 The Presbyterian distrust of Catholics is registered various places in Montgomery's novels. Montgomery lets some of her characters show their prejudice against Catholics – the same prejudice she herself felt – but she satirizes it nevertheless. See, for instance, *A Tangled Web*: 'Little Sam looked doubtful. He had been bred up in a good old Presbyterian hatred of Catholics and all their ways and works, but somehow he didn't think even they would go so far as to represent the Virgin Mary entirely unclothed' (125). In *Emily of New Moon* 'Lofty John' is a Roman Catholic, and he terrorizes Emily with his practical jokes and his threat to cut down her favourite bush. She seeks the intervention of his priest because 'Catholics have to do just what their priests tell them to, haven't they?' (203). After his priest talks to him, Lofty John says to Emily: 'your Aunt Elizabeth said a number av things that got under my skin ... So I thought I'd get square by cutting av the bush down. And you had to go and quare me wid me praste bekase av it and now I make no doubt I'll not be after daring to cut a stick of kindling to warm me shivering carcase without asking lave av the Pope' (217). Earlier in the novel, Emily fears 'he would burn us all at the stake if he had the power ... [H]e winked at me and said Oh, we wouldn't burn nice pretty little Protestants like you. We would only burn the old ugly ones.' Emily notes, 'That was a frivellus reply' (141). Montgomery is here giving voice to age-old Presbyterian (and in a wider sense, Protestant) views of Roman Catholicism and satirizing them, even though her son told me she still held prejudices against Catholicism late in her life.

16 The Presbyterian stress on starting up schools and then universities wherever they colonized abroad continued to sustain their power.

17 See Barbara Wachowicz's article in *CCL* (46) about the reception history of Montgomery in Poland. This article was written before Communist rule was relaxed in Poland, however, so she was unable to say anything controversial about Montgomery's real impact in Poland, part of which came through Montgomery's challenges to authoritarianism in any guise.

7

Disciplining Development:
L.M. Montgomery and Early Schooling

IRENE GAMMEL and ANN DUTTON

'I cannot help feeling furious over this matter. That this creature should dare to pose as my early "guide, philosopher and friend" when she was my bitterest enemy' (*SJ* 3: 358). The 'creature' referred to in this 29 October 1927 journal entry is 'Izzie' Robinson, Montgomery's teacher when Maud was twelve years old. The 'matter' Maud refers to is Izzie Robinson's 1927 interview with the *Toronto Star* in which the former schoolteacher proudly remembers 'Lucy Maud's' school adventures. The humiliation suffered in school, the public chastising of the sensitive child by Robinson, remained ingrained in Montgomery's memory: 'My soul burned within me over the cruel and wanton injustice of her attack – and it burns yet as I write. I should like to meet that woman to-day and tell her exactly what I think of her for uttering such a speech to a child who had not been doing or saying anything to provoke it' (*SJ* 1: 384).

Indeed, more than three decades after the events, Montgomery's sense of injury and injustice remained so vivid and acute that she would take her revenge, confronting the former authority on her own turf: 'I wish she knew that she served as the model for "Miss Brownell" in *New Moon*,' she writes in 1927, 'I don't think she would go about then posing as my early and always admirer' (*SJ* 3: 358). Miss Brownell appears as a demonic teacher figure in *Emily of New Moon*, who commits the unpardonable sin of shaming the child in front of the class, publicly ridiculing her early attempts at writing poetry.

The tyrannical Miss Brownell is only one of many teacher figures in Montgomery's fiction. Montgomery's spectrum of pedagogues ranges from the incompetent Mr Phillips in *Anne of Green Gables*, through the charismatic Miss Stacy in the same novel, to the exacting Mr Carpenter in *Emily of New Moon*. Montgomery's own experiences as an Island schoolmarm are documented in Anne's teaching career in *Anne of Avonlea* (1909). From an insider's perspective, Montgomery presents her readers with an invaluable historical investigation into the social and psychological dynamics of the one-room school in rural Canada, capturing a slice of Canadian pedagogical history.

Montgomery's impact and contribution are profound, for she gives voices to the humiliation, anger, and even hatred created in the hearts of children and young adolescents at the hands of insensitive and mediocre teachers. She is acutely sensitive to, and critical of, the sins of bad teaching and the abuses of power that accompanied it. As a writer, she powerfully argues for a space of imaginative freedom within the disciplinary confines of school life, allowing the rebellious child to push against the boundaries of rigid conventions. At the same time, Montgomery's writing displays important ambivalences on the topic of appropriate discipline, for she is equally supportive of some 'corrective' Victorian-style disciplining techniques, which are strangely at odds with her sympathies for the pain of children. For Montgomery, writing becomes a field for her own psychological and moral wrestling with the question of appropriate discipline, a question never adequately resolved, as the unresolved tension in her fiction testifies.

Montgomery as Island Schoolmarm

In July 1894, Montgomery's impressions of Bideford school, her first post, were far from romantic. The school was 'artistic as a barn, and bleakly situated on a very bare-looking hill'; it was 'big and bare and dirty' inside (*SJ* 1: 115–16). On her first day at Belmont she was greeted by the sight of trustees 'putting up the [stove]pipe and the children huddled around' (*SJ* 1: 164). Trustees usually arranged for one pupil to unlock the school and light the fire ahead of class. Montgomery, however, often found the school locked and the boy gone to Summerside with the key; she has to wait hours for a duplicate to be found. Once inside, there was no fire on, and, once lit, the fire 'sulked the whole morning' and the room was bitterly cold (*SJ* 1: 167). 'I can't live in that school thro' this winter in the condition it is in,' she writes in the fall of 1894 (Bolger, *Years* 144). Given her grievances, it is ironic, that, in retrospect, Montgomery in 1910 describes her year at Bideford as a pleasant one, and 'the last happy year of my life' (*SJ* 1: 390).[1]

Material conditions in rural schools across Canada left much to be desired, as Jean Cochrane's study *The One-Room School in Canada*

(1981) documents. Stoves provided by the trustees were frequently metal barrels on their sides; they either glowed red-hot or smoked, and their long pipes often fell, emitting smoke and soot (18). Children near the stoves roasted, but those further away shivered near huge windows that let in the light but were draughty in winter and let the bugs in during the summer (17). Parents would each provide a load of wood, split and cut to length for the stove, in lieu of taxes.[2] School trustees were held responsible for neglect and inefficiency in the school system, and the relationships between trustees and teachers were frequently adversarial. Montgomery, for instance, calls them 'those rotten old trustees' in a letter to Pensie MacNeill (Bolger, *Years* 144).

These conditions, of course, have historical roots. In early-nineteenth-century Prince Edward Island, the quality of education varied a great deal, ranging from Hannah Bullpitt's excellent school as early as 1810 through informal home teaching to instruction by itinerant teachers. John McNeill, the Island's first school visitor, did not mince words in his report to the Board of Education in 1845, describing some of the teachers to be 'persons of ship-wrecked character and blasted prospects in life' for whom teaching was the 'occupation of last resort' (quoted in Peabody 49). This point is echoed by Captain Jim in *Anne's House of Dreams,* when he describes teachers as 'clever, drunken critters who taught the children the three R's when they were sober, and lambasted them when they wasn't' (31).[3]

By mid-century, however, Prince Edward Island was at the forefront of educational reforms in Canada. The Free Education Act of 1852 was the foundation for the educational system in the province for the next fifty years. Premier George Coles's enlightened legislation aroused much interest in Britain, because Prince Edward Island was the first territory in the empire to introduce free education.[4] As Ian Ross Robertson reports, under the act, the colonial treasury would pay for the schools and a small portion of the teachers' salaries. The quality of education increased in Prince Edward Island and the rest of Canada, and by 1905 'all provinces except Quebec had laws requiring young children (initially those between the ages of seven and twelve) to attend school for certain minimum periods' (Prentice et al. 155). The improvement of classroom education went hand in hand with reforms in teachers' training, although many problems remained.

Teaching was one of the few professions through which unmarried women could support themselves in late-Victorian Canada. A low-status, badly paid profession, it attracted women and teenage men, the latter quickly moving on to more prestigious and better-paid professions, or quickly being promoted to principal and school superintendent (Prentice et al. 156). The gruff Mr Carpenter in *Emily of New Moon* works in 'a district school for a pittance of a salary' (307–8) because he has failed in 'real' life and is given to bouts of drinking. To be a male 'country school-teacher at forty-five with no prospect of ever being anything else' clearly invites the community's and students' speculation and pity. Conversely, the promising Gilbert Blythe gives up teaching at White Sands for a better profession – medicine: 'I want to do my share of honest, real work in the world,' (*AA* 53) he enthuses to Anne, who remains tied to the gender-traditional teaching profession (Epperly, *Fragrance* 44).

Given the profession's low status, it is no surprise that Montgomery's grandfather Macneill did not think highly of women as teachers, and refused to take her to interviews, which decreased her chances of securing a good post: 'Unless you applied in person you had very little chance of getting a school,' writes Montgomery (*SJ* 1: 389). In Prince Edward Island, as in other Canadian provinces, the responsibility of hiring teachers lay with a board of three trustees elected in each district. With a shortfall in funds, trustees frequently could not afford to pay teachers with the best licences.[5] Montgomery bitterly denounces the trustees' practice of hiring third-class, or even failed candidates, who gladly took any school with no salary supplement (*SJ* 1: 389). In *Anne of Green Gables*, Montgomery's portrait of Mr Phillips satirizes the shortfalls of such a system. Mr Phillips simply ignores his pupils, who do 'pretty much as they pleased': they eat apples, draw pictures, and race crickets in the aisles, while he is busy courting Prissy Andrews (123).[6]

'I have 38 on the roll now and am getting fond of them all. They are a nice little crowd and very obliging,' Montgomery writes in August 1894 (*SJ* 1: 117). By Christmas there are over forty-eight pupils, but she seems well able to cope; she has twenty-three students present for the Inspector's examination. Her pride in her chosen profession is evident: 'And now here I am, a genuine live school teacher myself,' she writes, and adds, '[I] wouldn't be a bit surprised if the kiddies were to rise in open rebellion and refuse to obey me' (*SJ* 1: 119). About her third school in Bedeque (1897–8), she writes, 'I simply *love* teaching here. The children are all so nice and intelligent' (*SJ* 1: 203). Montgomery truly enjoyed the actual teaching, and would have continued but for her grandfather's death in 1898, which put an end to her teaching career and forced her to return home. It is the happy memories of her first and last teaching posts that provide the basis for *Anne of Avonlea*.

If Montgomery highlights her positive experiences in the main themes of the novel, her negative ones are relegated into the subtexts and the journals. In *Anne of the Island* (1915), Stella writes to Anne that she is 'tired of teaching in a back country school' with nine grades and having to 'teach a little of everything' (65). Stella is likely modelled on Montgomery's close friend Frederica Campbell, about whom Montgomery writes in her journals: 'She was, I knew, tired and discouraged, seeing nothing before her but endless, monotonous years of teaching country schools for a mere pittance' (*SJ* 2: 303). Moreover, even Montgomery, who loved teaching, knew some of the problems first hand, in particular through her experience at Belmont school in 1895–6, where she taught a 'scrubby lot of urchins ... from rather poor homes' (*SJ* 1: 164). 'I will not teach in Belmont another year. The work is too hard,' Montgomery writes on 9 April 1897. 'I have been very nervous lately, I sleep badly and I seem to have constant colds – the result of doing two teachers' work all winter and being half frozen most of the time' (*SJ* 1: 183).

Yet Montgomery did return to teaching in her fiction. Focusing on the learning child and the teaching adult, she reveals her deep ambivalence about crucial issues of discipline in child rearing and early Canadian schooling.

Spare the Rod: Debating Corporal Punishment

'Different Opinions' is the appropriately entitled chapter in *Anne of Avonlea* in which Anne Shirley and Jane Andrews discuss teaching philosophy and discipline. Unlike Anne, 'Jane was not troubled by any aspirations to be an influence for good'; her ambitions are to 'earn her salary fairly, please the trustees, and get her name on the School Inspector's roll of honor' (26). To accomplish these goals, she will 'keep order' by being cross if need be, and punish her pupils by whipping them. Anne is horrified: 'No, if I can't get along without whipping I shall not try to teach school. There are better ways of managing' (27). Jane is unmoved, even when Anne reminds her that at Avonlea Miss Stacy kept order without whipping, and that Mr Phillips 'was always whipping and he had no order at all' (27). The social importance and social acceptance of corporal punishment is emphasized by other characters in the novel, including Mr Harrison, who tells Anne that she will never be able to manage the class unless she 'keep[s] a rod in pickle for them' (30). Even gentle Gilbert Blythe tells Anne, 'Corporal punishment as a last resort is to be my rule' (27).

Despite her good intentions, halfway through the novel Anne Shirley abandons her ideals and whips Anthony Pye, whom she has not been able to win over by affection: '[T]he pointer nipped keenly and finally Anthony's bravado failed him; he winced and the tears came to his eyes' (97). The episode highlights Anne's legendary temper, which belongs to her survival kit. The pain inflicted creates a paradoxical mix of intertextual reading pleasures, connected as it is with the memory of the earlier slate-breaking episode in *Anne of Green Gables*: Anthony occupies the position of Gilbert Blythe when punishment strikes at the hands of Anne. Yet Montgomery makes her point even more explicitly. Anne's transgression, namely, the violation of her own professional ideals, the outburst of anger after a bad night's sleep, ultimately turns into a *felix culpa*, resulting in the conversion of Anthony Pye, who now pays Anne respect. '"I never expected to win him by whipping him, though," said Anne, a little mournfully, feeling that her ideals had played her false somewhere' (100).

While still a teacher at Bideford, Montgomery refers to herself as a 'sedate Bideford "schoolmarm" well versed in the mysteries of rod and rule' (*SJ* 1: 125). Looking back on her teaching career, she writes: 'I was enthusiastic and had many "ideals" – which suffered a good deal from contact with the real; but I was never wholly false to them nor they to me' (*SJ* 1: 389–90). These comments, coupled with Anne's (beneficial) whipping of Anthony Pye, suggest that Montgomery favoured the 'last resort' philosophy on corporal punishment, as popularized in the United States and Canada by Lydia Maria Child in a best-selling motherhood manual and advocated in *Anne of Avonlea* by Gilbert Blythe. Her own child-rearing practices confirm that she was not shy in exercising stern measures.[7]

In his landmark work *Spare the Child: The Religious Roots of Punishment and the Psychological Impact of Physical Abuse* (1990), Philip Greven traces the widespread practice of corporal punishment to the Bible's concept of eternal damnation (6). According to Greven, spanking advocates in white Protestant circles, 'especially those from evangelical, fundamentalist, and Pentecostal backgrounds,' claim that spanking is different in kind from child abuse, the latter defined by 'slapping and hitting with fists' (81). A variety of implements may be used in spankings, including a leather belt, switches, rods, and hands – although hands are the least effective (75). Advice books counsel that punishment should be administered calmly and deliberately: 'spanking should be a ritual' and 'a controlled administration of pain' (76, 77).

Given Montgomery's Presbyterian background, as discussed by Mary

Rubio in chapter 6, where does Montgomery stand? Brought up by her strict grandparents, Alexander and Lucy Woolner Macneill, Montgomery attended revival meetings at the 'Big Brick,' the Knox Presbyterian church in Charlottetown, when she was a student at Prince of Wales College (*SJ* 1: 105). Three years later, however, she acknowledged a gradual fading of her beliefs: 'My belief in the fine old hell of literal fire and brimstone went first' (*SJ* 1: 197). Montgomery thoroughly abandoned the notion of hell, even satirizing the fire and brimstone sermons of Presbyterian ministers, as Rubio illustrates. Yet she continued to struggle with the concept of corporal punishment and gave voice to this struggle in her fiction.

Rainbow Valley, the novel completed at the close of the First World War, investigates corporal punishment, child abuse, and violence in its subtexts. This dark vision was likely created by the horror of the war, as shown by Owen Dudley Edwards and Jennifer H. Litster in chapter 2. The dramatic, violent school-yard fight between sensitive, gentle Walter Blythe and name-calling Dan Reese (quoted in detail by Edwards and Litster) is a fascinating study in psychology. Walter feels compelled to defend the honour of his mother and of Faith Meredith by challenging Dan to fight. Walter fears pain and loathes physical violence; yet once Dan strikes the first blow and Walter feels pain, he attacks the other boy in an uncontrolled fury. Overwhelmed by the unexpected onslaught, Dan quickly folds. Since Susan Baker (*RV* 2), as well as Gilbert and Anne ('Penelope' 106), spanked the Blythe children when necessary, it can be inferred from Walter's behaviour that the release of anger, suppressed after spankings in early childhood, was triggered by the pain of Dan's blow. As Greven shows, corporal punishments entail pain and fear, engendering anger and hatred (122–3), both of which have to be internalized by the child, since to express either is to invite further punishment. Montgomery hints at this cycle in *Rainbow Valley*. Walter has no other relationship with Dan, and nothing to lose in releasing his anger – only himself.

The scene gains further significance when contextualized by two episodes relating to corporal punishment. Early in the novel, Mary Vance, a runaway girl, appears in the village of Glen St Mary, her scrawny arms 'black with bruises' from beatings administered by her mistress, Mrs Wiley. 'My, how I hate her!' says Mary, the novel exposing a case of shocking child abuse (31). In contrast, the Meredith children have never experienced physical punishment. Their mother is dead, and their gentle father, a minister, is too absent-minded to guide their growing up. In a crucial scene, entitled 'Carl Is – Not –Whipped,' the minister, who has never whipped a child, is faced with punishing his son: 'What was used to whip boys? Rods? Canes? No, that would be too brutal. A [l]imber switch, then?' (215). At the last moment, he cannot bring himself to do it: he 'threw down the switch. "Go," he said, "I cannot whip you"' (216). What is significant in this scene is that neither characters, nor readers are allowed to relish a sense of comic relief. John Meredith retreats into 'undisturbed solitude' (216), a wording highly sarcastic for a father accused of neglecting his children's welfare and education earlier in the novel. The children are left to discipline themselves.

These episodes become even richer in implication when we consider that Mr Meredith is modelled on Ewan Macdonald, Montgomery's husband. On 8 June 1922, three years after the publication of *Rainbow Valley*, she complains that Ewan 'indulges [the children] and never punishes [them]'; Montgomery is left alone in disciplining Chester's pranks, since the boy's teacher, 'a somewhat weak and inexperienced young girl,' is not much help either. 'It is not fair,' she writes, accusing Ewan of shedding his duties as father, 'and at times I feel very bitter about it' (*SJ* 3: 58). The minister's wife in *Rainbow Valley* is dead, while the subtext presents the reader with an abusively disciplining mother figure, Mrs Wiley; both perhaps nightmare projections of Montgomery's own feelings of guilt about the punishment she has inflicted on her own sons. Conversely, the main text – focusing on the channelling of the son's murderous rage into chivalric fight when 'womenkind are insulted' (RV 125) – may very well be the author's projected wish fulfilment. Her focus on chivalry, discussed in detail by Epperly (*Fragrance* 95–111), exposes her psychological system of rationalization; the son's anger resulting from early punishment is released in purified and sublimated form to defend his mother's honour. Ultimately, Montgomery's message is an ambivalent and uneasy one, signalling her own wrestling with the issue.

Montgomery's ambivalence is all the more important, as corporal punishment remained an unchallenged reality for the nineteenth- and early-twentieth-century classroom in Prince Edward Island and the rest of Canada. School visitor John McNeill observed that some teachers used little corporal punishment, whereas others could not imagine managing without it (13).[8] Montgomery's Uncle Leander taught at Prince of Wales College, but '[h]e could not keep order without thrashing several of them every day,' an exercise that was 'rather too strenuous' (*SJ* 2: 135). Similarly, in Manitoba, almost two decades after Montgomery's teaching career, Canadian writer Frederick Philip Grove made ample use of the strap in his teaching, even strapping his wife's pupils, 'the older ones that Mrs Grove couldn't handle,' as his former students report (Stobie 49). After catching one student swearing, Grove 'took him into the room and gave him a strapping. He didn't swear any more after that. He stripped him, you know. When he gave him a licking' (Stobie 49).[9] Women teachers did not engage in physical fights with their pupils, but some became rigid martinets, as illustrated in Montgomery's Miss Brownell.

Montgomery keenly registers the psychological imprinting on the child, the invisible scars being often deeper than the physical ones. And yet the conflict between her awareness of psychological wounding and the corrective demands of discipline is never completely resolved, not even in Montgomery's teacher ideal.

Montgomery's Teacher Ideal

On 30 June 1892, Montgomery's diary records that Miss Gordon is leaving for Oregon: 'I have lost a true friend – the only one in Cavendish who sympathized with me in my ambitions and efforts' (*SJ* 1: 81). *Anne of Avonlea* is dedicated to Hattie Gordon, 'in grateful remembrance of her sympathy and encouragement.' Hattie Gordon was the first of Montgomery's teachers to require the writing of compositions: 'Every week we of the advanced classes had to write one at home on a given subject, sometimes selected by ourselves, sometimes by the teacher' (*SJ* 1: 385), while Friday afternoons were reserved for recitations of poetry, dialogue, and songs, a 'dramatic joy' for Montgomery. Small wonder that Hattie Gordon became the model for Montgomery's fictional teacher ideal, Miss Stacy in *Anne of Green Gables*, who is a 'bright, sympathetic young woman' capable of 'bringing out the best that was in [her pupils] mentally and morally' (206). Like Hattie Gordon's, Miss Stacy's innovations include physical culture ('fiddlesticks,' says Marilla), recitations on Friday afternoons, and field trips in nature study (208). Hattie Gordon, Miss Stacy, and Anne Shirley all exploit the pleasures of learning, giving their pedagogical innovations an added transgressive element in a pleasure-denying and duty-oriented society.

Montgomery's male teacher ideal, Mr Carpenter in *Emily of New Moon*, similarly relies on performance – on play-acting of historical characters, on declamation of speeches – in order to awaken the dormant creative talents and need for expression in Ilse Burnley, Perry

Miller, Teddy Kent, and Emily Byrd Starr. Yet he encounters opposition: in a conservative Island community, the teacher fostering the creative mind with unconventional methods does not always win the trustees' respect. 'The trustees were quite scandalized over some of the goings on' in Mr Carpenter's classroom and 'felt sure that the children were having too good a time to be really learning anything' (310), just as in *Green Gables*, Marilla and Rachel Lynde are suspicious of Miss Stacy.

During the 1920s, theories of childhood were undergoing radical changes through the insights of Jean Piaget and Maria Montessori, and Montgomery was particularly drawn to the theories of Professor Blatz at the University of Toronto, as Elizabeth Waterston reports. Blatz postulated that 'jealousy and shame are stimulating and exhilarating forces in infants'; they are not necessarily negative ones, 'since they energize responses and expedite conflict which is the beginning of knowledge' (Waterston, 'Marigold' 159). Given Montgomery's adoption of the conflictual model of psychological development, her characters are not stunted in their growth but move on to the next stage of development after having overcome frequently traumatizing events in their lives. Anne and Emily grow through painful experiences – death of loved ones, humiliating punishment, even near-death experiences. As Canadian writer Jane Urquhart has argued, Emily, the day-dreaming girl 'is met with enough resistance from the ordinary world to instill in her the knowledge that she is "apart" (yet not so much as to silence her).' The pitfalls and conflicts ultimately 'strengthen rather than destroy her' (333).[10]

Mr Carpenter's teaching is also based on a conflictual model that causes pain, a model shown to contribute to Emily's growth. Mr Carpenter's is an archetype of classical comedy, a self-deprecating *eiron* figure (Frye, *Anatomy* 172–4). His didactical comments belong to the realm of satire; often they are painful, as satire always debases and dissects. He is a mocking, analytical, and dissecting figure, and his methodologies are surprisingly close to Miss Brownell's, whose cruelly sarcastic and satiric vision ultimately stifles creativity and autonomy and makes her a terrifying figure. Yet Mr Carpenter emerges as a 'good' teacher, an ultimately positive influence in Emily's life: he is an important catalyst for the cultivation and emergence of Emily's voice as a future writer.

The important differences between the two teachers lie in their opposite responses to Emily's creativity. Mr Carpenter recognizes her talent in an unflattering satirical sketch Emily has written about him: 'Thanks to her dramatic knack for word painting, Mr Carpenter *lived* in that sketch' (*ENM* 353). The sketch is crucial for our understanding of Montgomery's pedagogical vision. In her sketch Emily holds up a comical and critical mirror, dissecting the teaching authority she observes, and it is here that Mr Carpenter recognizes the independent authority of her voice. 'By gad, it's literature – *literature* – and you're only thirteen' (354). To allow for, indeed encourage, such creative reversals of authority is the essence of the true pedagogue. Like Miss Brownell, Mr Carpenter poses as an agon, but he also invites the pupils to push back.

Moreover, Mr Carpenter's name – suggestive of the craftsman, rather than the artist – is appropriately limited. Like Miss Brownell, he does not really understand Emily's vision; but Montgomery's point is that he does not need to. He is a mere catalyst, and his *ironic* methodologies, while drawing on the same sadistic energy that propels Miss Brownell, are ultimately constructive and energizing. They open a space for Emily to generate a new text, to experiment with conventions, to defy, parody, and exploit them. Only in this irreverent play can the artist be born.

Conclusion

'Teaching is really very interesting work,' writes Anne Shirley to a Queen's Academy chum. This sentence opens a chapter in which Anne receives a love letter from one of her female pupils, Annette Bell: 'You are so beautiful, my teacher. Your voice is like music and your eyes are like pansies' (*AA* 88). While the uncritical adulation expressed is satirized (indeed, the love letter is plagiarized from a letter Annette's mother received from an admirer), the adulation expressed is not different in kind from Anne's crush on Miss Stacy: 'I love Miss Stacy with my whole heart, Marilla. She is so ladylike and she has such a sweet voice' (*AGG* 207). It also echoes Montgomery's own preoccupation with Hattie Gordon, as she remembers her affectionately, 'dressed in the brown velvet coat and smart little toque she wore that winter.' 'We were always much interested then in what our teachers wore and how they dressed their hair,' writes Montgomery (*SJ* 1: 386), highlighting to what extent the female teacher was incorporated into her female pupils' imaginary as an object of fantasy and adulation. The female role models become part of an active girls' culture, shaping their positive identification with women.

Yet Montgomery's teachers are far from perfect: they all have explosive temperaments. If Mr Carpenter 'burst[s] into flame at least once a day' (*ENM* 308), Anne Shirley has her 'Jonah day,' during which her rigid commands lead to a literal explosion of firecrackers in the school stove (*AA* 95). Even Montgomery's beloved Miss Gordon had 'a very quick temper' (*SJ* 1: 386) and 'rather terrifying ways by times' (*SJ* 1: 6). If the explosive temper humanizes Montgomery's otherwise perfect teacher, the recurring patterns of such bouts of anger and aggression still constitute an important psychological and sociological subtext, calling the romance plot of the school novel at least partly into question. Frustration and rage voiced by teachers against pupils hint at negative social realities (gender imbalance, low remuneration, low status, overwork) that teachers were often not able to change. Strict discipline and order may indeed have been a pretext for release of sadistic anger.

Finally, Montgomery pays homage to the efforts of those teachers who made a difference, and who are remembered fondly by students even decades after their schooling. The task of inspiring students – generally eight grades in a one-room school with the complexities of organizing reading and arithmetic – may seem quixotic today. Yet it was accomplished by the likes of Hattie Gordon, who 'had the power of inspiring a love of study for its own sake and of making the dry bones of the school routine alive with interest' (*SJ* 1: 385). As an innovative, enthusiastic teacher, she accomplished much; the energy that went into field trips and school concerts produced a 'tie of common friendship' (*SJ* 1: 23), a bond to be cherished even many years later. As a teaching pioneer, Hattie Gordon served Montgomery as an inspiration and allowed her to create a strong counterpoint heroine, one that would exorcize the demon of Izzie Robinson.

NOTES

1 An inspector in New Brunswick comments in 1858 that the province's schools were always 'the smallest, dirtiest, shabbiest [building] in the settlement' (Peabody 27). Many rural schools had dirt floors, windows without glass, poor ventilation, and were unfinished and unplastered (Peabody 28). In March 1890, when Maud was a student in Cavendish, her diary records that the Cavendish school 'has never been cleaned since last winter' and 'the trustees won't bestir themselves' (*SJ* 1: 17). The pupils heat water on the stove to wash blinds, windows and walls; they scrub maps, desks and the door, but the floor was so dirty, 'A shovel would have been the best thing to tackle it with' (*SJ* 1: 17).

2 Many children lacked the proper footwear or clothing suitable for school,

and parents improvised items such as 'shoe packs' filled with straw, or layered their children with hand-me-down sweaters, as coats were unobtainable. The children would sit all day in their damp clothes without a hope of drying out, and then face their long homeward journey of wet and cold snow (Cochrane 42–3).

3 For a historical account of education and schooling on Prince Edward Island, see Dianne Morrow's 'A Little Learning'; see also Mary E. Doody Jones's 'Education on P.E.I.' As Dianne Morrow reports, in Charlottetown, Hannah Bullpitt, wife of a missionary from London, established a 'dame' school in the parsonage in 1810; the Island's first premier, George Cole, was one of her pupils.

4 See Ian Ross Robertson's intriguing argument that the lack of land ownership and the necessity to sign complex contracts with landowners for leasing land forced the tenants of Prince Edward Island into accelerated access to education as early as 1855.

5 The turn-of-the-century salary for a one-room schoolteacher was between $180 and $230 a year (*SJ* 2: 304). In Charlottetown, teachers with first-class certificates, including principals, received a salary of $300, supplement of $150, and bonus of $20 up to a maximum total of $470. Peabody writes that in Nova Scotia a Class A female teacher received just under 60 per cent of her male counterpart's salary and 'in Prince Edward conditions were often much worse' (53). See also Alison Prentice's 'The Feminization of Teaching.'

6 Montgomery may also have modeled Mr Phillips after Mr Mustard, her high school teacher in Prince Albert, Alberta, in 1890 who was 'a very poor teacher'; although Maud disliked him 'professionally and personally,' he 'fell in love with [her] and suggested marriage' (*SJ* 1: 386–7).

7 In an 11 April 1915 diary entry, Montgomery describes the punishment used to discipline her two-year-old son Chester: 'The hall closet is where he is sometimes imprisoned when he is naughty until he promises to be good' (*SJ* 2: 165).

8 Peabody paints a picture of the poorly trained male teacher, little older than the bigger boys, and his struggle to maintain order. The rougher, rowdier boys would not submit to his authority willingly; they would rush about the schoolroom, drowning out his voice with their noise, overturning benches, and even breaking windows. Sometimes the teacher would fight them before he could exert any control over them (59).

9 While trustees were reluctant to renew Grove's contracts and while he rarely stayed longer than two years in one place as a teacher, corporal punishment is not an issue that Grove is criticized for; rather trustees perceived him as 'overbearing,' 'arrogant,' 'self-righteous,' and 'impatient' (Stobie 25–55).

Grove gave up teaching once he was able to make a living with his fiction writing. Strapping students did not keep Grove from theorizing education in Rousseauistic terms. In an educational article entitled 'Rousseau as Educator' (1912), Grove argued for the importance of nature study (as Montgomery's Miss Stacy might). Dismissing straight lecturing as bad pedagogy, Grove argued for an educational approach that will lead 'the children into a field of triumphant discoveries' (Stobie 37), emphasizing the hands-on didactic also practised by Miss Stacy, Anne Shirley, and Mr Carpenter.

8

'Daisy,' 'Dodgie,' and 'Lady Jane Grey Dort': L.M. Montgomery and the Automobile

SASHA MULLALLY

Automobile travel was a subject of heated and at times bitter debate in rural communities across North America before the 1920s. Nowhere on the continent was anti-automobile sentiment more strongly expressed than in L.M. Montgomery's home province of Prince Edward Island, where the local legislature first banned automobiles between 1908 to 1913, and then severely restricted their use until the end of the First World War. While L.M. Montgomery shared the concerns expressed by her fellow Islanders, she also used the automobile as a powerful symbol of freedom in her fiction, most notably in her 1926 romance for adults, *The Blue Castle.*

The deep ambivalence toward early automobiles in the records of Canada's rural history is powerfully dramatized in Montgomery's writing. For social historians, Montgomery's oeuvre presents an invaluable resource for a study of the conflicting attitudes toward technological advances in Canada. Both her public and private narratives shed important light on the uneven and uneasy integration of automotive engineering into rural societies, and the ways in which people made sense of the social changes such technologies wrought on their social and cultural landscapes during the turbulent first years of the twentieth century.

Automobiles and the Pleasure of Speeding

'Just where Lovers' Lane debouched on the street, an old car was parked. Valancy knew the car well – by sound, at least – and everybody in Deerwood knew it' (*BC* 28). The noise from Barney Snaith's car – an old Grey Slosson, ironically dubbed Lady Jane Grey – jolts and disrupts life in fictional Deerwood, Ontario. Barney's noisy car also signifies the jolt of modernity to the values and strictures of Victorian society. The novel's main character, Valancy Stirling, teetering on the edge of spinsterhood, chafes under the burden of Victorian 'respectability.' Forsaking the mores and the company of her anachronistic clan and the burdens of filial obedience, Valancy conquers her fear of the world. Her transformation is facilitated and symbolized by the mobility and freedom Barney Snaith's automobile provides her.

While the automobile stands as a symbol of social, geographical, and psychological freedom in *The Blue Castle*, Montgomery uses the automobile to outline both the social setting of Deerwood as well as the mental states of her main character. Montgomery describes the novelty of automobiles in the small town; no Stirling had yet 'condescended' to own one. Her heroine had never driven in a motor car, and was in fact rather afraid of them 'especially at night,' for 'they seemed to be too much like big purring beasts that might turn and crush you – or make some terrible savage leap somewhere' (21). Automobiles splash her as they pass by on the street, issuing 'insulting shrieks' at the downtrodden girl. Valancy's sheltered life and fear of the unknown keep her bound to her family and make her tolerate their devaluation of her as a woman and an autonomous person.

Valancy's family shares her fear of automobiles, especially when linked to strangers like Barney Snaith. Barney is a man with a shadowy background who drives his beaten-up old car – 'the tinniest of Lizzies' (28) – in and around their small town. The possibilities for illicit and unsupervised courtship and sexual encounters multiplied with the advent of the automobile, as automobility meant greater freedom and privacy away from the eyes of protective older relatives. A scandalized Uncle Wellington and cousin Olive find Valancy with Barney Snaith in his car, after dark and unchaperoned.

And yet she was enjoying herself – was full of a strange exultation – bumping over that rough road beside Barney Snaith. The big trees shot by them. The tall mulleins stood up along the road in stiff, orderly ranks like companies of soldiers. The thistles looked like drunken fairies or tipsy elves as their car-lights passed over them. This was the first time she had ever been in a car. After all, she liked it. She was not in the least afraid, with Barney at the wheel. Her spirits rose rapidly as they tore along. She ceased to feel ashamed. She ceased to feel anything except that she was part of a comet rushing gloriously through the night of space. (109–10)

Valancy's initiation to the pleasures of the car, of course, encode the tropes of courtship and sexuality. It is during this first car ride that Valancy falls in love with Barney Snaith. The powerful awakening of intense new feelings represent Valancy's rejection of repression. Montgomery uses the episode to support the idea of Valancy's sexual autonomy, and prepares this character for the eventual stripping of all conventions when she later proposes marriage to Barney for the sole reason of pleasing herself and enjoying what she believes to be the last months of her life.

The speed of motoring dissipates Valancy's shame, symbolizing new possibilities of escape and pleasure. Driving with Barney through Port Lawrence at twilight, she felt 'crazy with the delight of speeding' (118). 'I admit there is witchery in speed,' Montgomery wrote in her journal in August 1925 on a spontaneous two-hundred-mile trip to see Bertie MacIntyre in Trenton. 'We had a delightful drive and the effects of the early morning mists along the creek and river valleys were more exquisite than any I had ever seen' (*SJ* 3: 245).[1] Montgomery was at a loss to completely explain her love for speed, musing to herself, 'Is it because it gives us the subconscious feeling that we are *escaping*?' (*SJ* 3: 337). Given the constraints in her private life, Montgomery, like Valancy, had good reasons to fantasize about escape and pleasure.

This association of the automobile with freedom is given an important gender focus in Montgomery's writing. Montgomery's positive conceptualization reflects the role women played, and the place they occupied, in Canada's emerging automobile culture. As Heather Robertson points out in *Driving Force: The McLaughlin Family and the Age of the Car*, Margery Durant, daughter of one of Canada's premier automen, drove her own Buick. By this action, she 'was leading a rebellion. She was proving to women that they could drive, and they could drive alone, by themselves, wherever they wanted to go' (119).[2] Montgomery's work recognizes the full potentialities of this freedom, while it also mirrors some of the limitations for women of the automotive revolution.

In *The Blue Castle*, Barney's Slosson transforms the social boundaries of Valancy's life, but is she more economically and socially autonomous after marriage? Automobility has given her the power to choose her friends, her husband, and her entertainment, but it does not empower her to transform the gendered sphere of work and her dependent station within the household. The presence of these limitations in the text of *The Blue Castle* bolsters the novel as an accurate piece of social commentary. While automobiles 'enabled rural women to participate in town life much more frequently than they had in the days of horse and foot transportation, to more easily combine household duties with sociability' (Scharff 144), one must not overestimate the car's transformative impact on gender identity and structure. In the words of historian Ruth Cowan, in many cases the automobile merely meant 'more work for mother' (82–5).[3]

Thus both the potential and the limitations of automobile travel receive an apt portrayal from Montgomery's pen. While Montgomery's *Blue Castle* heroine never actually sat behind the wheel, Montgomery did not perceive or construct her automotive dependency as an obstacle to her personal freedom. Whether her access was direct or indirect, Valancy reaped immense social benefits from automotive freedom.

L.M. Montgomery and the Trouble with Autos

Speeding tourists seeking the same escape to nature Montgomery glorifies in *The Blue Castle* often disrupted the rural communities through which they passed. Horses, unfamiliar with the noisy, sputtering new machines, would bolt, balk, and run away, sometimes injuring themselves or their drivers. Livestock met untimely deaths on the grills of the speeding motor cars. This generated a fear of automobiles and of the perceived dangers of automobile travel, fears often exploited by those who harboured a grudge against this new mode of transportation. Prior to his own conversion to the moror car, Robert McLaughlin, whose family would eventually found General Motors of Canada, commissioned an advertisement that featured a shining new McLaughlin buggy blissfully sailing past an overturned car in the ditch (Robertson 95–6).

Historians have documented anti-automobilism during the early years of automobility, such as legislative measures and vigilante activity. In 'Dependant Motorization: Canada and the Automobile to the 1930s,' Donald Davis describes several cases of anti-auto vigilantism in Canada. Davis documents how a rural representative in the provincial legislature threatened to 'blow [the] brains out' of any 'nabobs of Toronto' who ventured by automobile in their community (124). While death threats were uncommon, Heather Robertson relates a more typical anecdote of a motor enthusiast in Bathurst, New Brunswick. Feeling the thrill of driving an automobile for the first time, he blew his horn twice at a passing streetcar. A young boy, unimpressed, leaned out of the streetcar window and shouted, 'Get a horse!' (95). If the automobile was the harbinger of modernity and city values, the rural areas of Canada were not interested in the chaos such modernity brought with it and, in the very early years of motorization, strove mightily to turn back the motor car.[4]

The community that had the most success in turning back the tide of automobility was Montgomery's home province of Prince Edward of Island. Christened a 'fad of millionaires and fools' by one Island commentator, automobile travel was banned outright on the Island between 1908 and 1913. From 1913 to 1919, motor car travel was allowed but restricted to very few roads, and, even then, one could drive only on non-market days: Monday, Wednesday and Thursday. People were automatically forbidden to drive the motor car on the Sabbath (Davis 124–5; Stewart 9–10).

The origins of this backlash are worth exploring. Some scholars believe this negative and 'irrational' response to early motor cars was a reaction against the freedom automobility gave the individual. Michael Berger, for example, has argued that traditional rural values of communalism and the ability to enforce social codes through collective community pressure eroded with the advent of the car (Berger 206–8). Certainly, in *The Blue Castle*, Barney's automobile provided Valancy with a wide choice of entertainment and companionship, and it irrevocably undermined her family's ability to enforce social codes of 'respectability.'

Yet rural areas had embraced the automobile by the First World War, and by the 1920s, automobiles were ubiquitous on the rural scene. By 1908, Henry Ford had developed the Model T Ford and succeeded in revolutionizing the market for automobiles by making them affordable to the average North American. Farmers' ability to put the automobile to a wide variety of uses was another integrative factor.[5] By the 1920s, North American farmers had accepted the automobile as a means of transportation, realizing that an auto with a detachable back seat could serve as a small truck. Farmers demanded that the automobile engine have conversion capabilities to run butter churns, water pumps, hay balers, fodder and ensilage cutters, corn shellers, or washing machines as the situation required (Kline and Pinch 775). One Canadian farmer converted his 1915 Overland into a tractor by replacing the car's rear wheels with larger, steel, reaper wheels attached to a heavier axle. His innovations became the prototype for manufacturer's 'conversion kits' sold to transform any Model T Ford (Kline and Pinch 787).

While PEI was initially the bastion of anti-automobilism, affordability and farm utility soon gave the automobile a very broad, democratic appeal. Ford advertisements in Island newspapers, for example, tried to make a strong statement in favour of the financial benefits of owning a car. With the company's 'Universal' cars, ranging in price from $535 to $750, the buyer could eliminate many costly items, including 'your driving horse and buggy ... the single harness, blankets, whips, curry combs, brushes, horse-shoes, pitchforks, feed bins, etc.' Such advertisements touted the automobile as 'the utility car for the busy farmer and his family' (*Charlottetown Guardian* 5). Special events centring around the automobile had also achieved tremendous popular appeal by the 1920s. A 1919 automobile show held in Charlottetown was attended to overflowing. The crowd was composed mainly of farmers, a group that had formed the backbone of anti-automobilism on the Island. Motor registration statistics show that between 1913 and 1925, the number of automobiles registered in PEI increased 113 times, from only 26 in 1913 to 967 in 1919 and 2,955 in 1925 (*Canada Year Book* 687).

Montgomery realized that the advent of the automobile was a mixed blessing for the Island. As the automobile makes Prince Edward Island ever more accessible to motor tourists from across North America, Montgomery complains bitterly to G.B. MacMillan in 1928 that 'Cavendish is being overrun and exploited and spoiled by mobs of tourists and my harmless old friends and neighbors have their lives simply worried out of them by car loads of "foreigners" who want to see some of Anne's haunts' (*My Dear* 130). It seems from this narrative that L.M. Montgomery was of two minds about automobiles and the uses of such new forms of transportation technology. Like anti-automobile agitators at the beginning of the century, Montgomery initially finds her true home altered and threatened by automotive travel. However, like them, she ultimately finds that auto travel benefits her social life more than it hampers it. By her 1927 visit to PEI, she is motoring around as a matter of course.

Montgomery's ambivalence is perhaps best illustrated by an anecdote reported in her journals. On one motor outing, Montgomery and her friends came upon 'a certain grim old dame' who refused to rein in her horse and let the motorists pass. Although they were 'ingloriously ditched' because of the woman's stubbornness, Montgomery wrote, 'in my heart I believe I sympathized with the old girl. Had I been a spinster lady, driving along with my own nag ... I believe *I* wouldn't have stirred a finger either when some obstreperous car honked behind me. No, I should have sat up as dourly as she did and said "Take the ditch or the devil for all of me!"' (*SJ* 2: 250–1).

In the spring of 1918, Montgomery and her husband invested in their first car. The event marked a new 'epoch' for Montgomery and her family, and she marvels in her journal how common automobiles were becoming in her husband's parish – 'as thick as hops.' Through her excitement, Montgomery owns she will miss 'a buggy with a nice lovable horse.' She concludes, 'But I realize a car's good points also, as time and distance-savers. And one must "keep up with the procession"' (*SJ* 2: 247). Initially, she finds she is 'not wholly pleased' with cars, mainly because of sentimental attachment to horses. Like most families, they christened their new car – in this case, the called it 'Daisy' – perhaps in an attempt to personify the machine and render it somehow more 'lovable,' like a horse. But automobiles are neither lovable nor romantic for Montgomery. She writes to MacMillan, 'I'm glad *my* courting days were over before the cars came!! There is no romance whatever in a car. A man can't safely drive with one arm! And loitering is impossible' (*My Dear* 85). Especially during trips home to PEI, Montgomery finds herself nostalgically yearning for the days of buggy travel.[6]

In an 1922 letter to MacMillan, she proudly announces that she and her family had motored 'all the way to P. E. Island and back – almost 3000 miles. A wonderful trip in many ways but pretty fatiguing, especially for children.' During the trip, she indulged herself in the view of the 'grey, misty breakers' along the New England coast to Portland, Maine (*My Dear* 106). In 1924, Montgomery, Ewan, their two sons, and friend Bertie MacIntyre take a motor trip to Kentucky to see the Mammoth Caves – 'a very delightful motor trip of 1817 miles (*SJ* 3: 196), with neither one drop of rain nor any car trouble.' This trip was made in their second car, a Grey Dort, affectionately called Lady Jane Grey, foreshadowing Barney Snaith's fictional Slosson. She and Ewan went on two trips up to Muskoka by automobile. The second trip, taken in 1928, was occasioned by a drive through virgin forest along the new Ferguson Highway past North Bay: 'To me every moment of it was a delight, and the greatest delight of all was the innumerable lakes starred with water lilies' (*SJ* 3: 375). She and Ewan and their two sons made good use of the automobile as a leisure vehicle, which undoubtedly affected her position toward its social contribution to middle-class family life.

Interwoven into the virtues of vacationing by automobile, however, is a thread of anxiety concerning the dangers of motor travel. Like Valancy, Montgomery never learns to drive an automobile herself, finding she hasn't enough 'nerve' to learn. She and Ewan were involved in a number of automobile accidents, one involving a lengthy lawsuit that caused her years of anxiety. 'My nerves have been somewhat racked,' Montgomery confesses to her journal when her son Chester began to drive. 'I have seen so many things go wrong with a car, no matter who is driving, that I never see him starting off without a pang of dread' (*SJ* 3: 377). Montgomery's opinion about automobiles gives insight into the means by which this writer and her generation dealt with social changes wrought by new technologies.

L.M. Montgomery and Modern Technology

The automobile is a crucial icon for Montgomery in that it stands as a symbol for much more sweeping technological changes, including innovations in communications and entertainment that affected, shaped, and transformed the daily lives of Canadians. While embracing new technologies, Montgomery was also aware of the price they frequently extracted, demonstrating her ambivalence on numerous occasions. Montgomery constantly wonders about the social ramifications of radio, air mail, and even talking movies. 'This evening Ewan and the boys and I motored down to Uxbridge to hear the radio,' she reports in her journals on 27 October 1923. 'We hear music in Chicago and a speech in Pittsburg [*sic*]. It is a very marvellous thing and will probably revolutionize the world in another generation. But it had made me feel a little unhappy and unsettled some way' (*SJ* 3: 150–1). In 1927, she remarks that, '[t]hey are carrying the mails over to P. E. Island now by aeroplane. A wonderful bit of progress – or would be if the letters so carried were any sweeter or more vital thereby' (*SJ* 3: 364). In 1929, she and her family go to see a 'talkie.' Montgomery does not care much for the mixture of sound and picture, finding it difficult to follow. She closed her entry in her journal that evening by observing that '[n]ew inventions crowd on each other's heels – each more amazing than the last. But the trouble is – no one is happier or better because of them' (*SJ* 3: 401).

Her concern with happiness and betterment plagues her throughout her middle age, and was a constant theme in her journals around the time she was writing *The Blue Castle*. The Great War had troubled her terribly. During the 1920s, heated debate over whether to support the union of the three Protestant churches darkened her entries, as Mary Rubio reported in chapter 6. Along with lawsuits over the automobile accident and her lawsuit with Lewis Page (discussed by Carole Gerson in chapter 3), Ewan's mental health was unstable and her two sons were growing up and leaving for school. As she considers the future, in the context of all this social upheaval and personal strife, Montgomery is desperate to ease the strain and uncertainly. She finds some relief by accepting a faith in science and the technologies that had previously 'unsettled' her.

Considering the possible demise of the Presbyterian Church and its traditions, which are important to her, Montgomery concedes in 1925 that perhaps the church had 'served its day as God's instrument.' She writes, 'He is using another now – Science. Through Science the next great revelation will come' (SJ 3: 238). When in 1924 Ewan's mental health takes a sharp turn for the worse, Montgomery reads in a popular health manual of new findings in endocrinology that might explain Ewan's condition. Immediately, her moods lifts and she prophesies in her journal: 'I feel that we are on the threshold of a new and amazing revelation. The world needs it. The older revelations have exhausted their mandate. I believe the next one will come through science. What form it will take I cannot guess ... Two thousand years ago Jesus burst the bonds that were stifling the human race ... – outworn dogma, dead superstitions. It will take something as tremendous as his message of spiritual freedom to destroy those bonds again. But it will come ... and presently there will be light' (SJ 3: 182). In her vision, scientific 'revelations' will be the next tool for humanity to break 'bonds' that arise from ignorance.

Montgomery's reconciliation with the technologies of her day in life and in literature reflects generally the way rural societies reconciled themselves to the transformative possibilities of the automobile. Montgomery ultimately mirrored the culture of cautious technological optimism, which established a positive image for the automobile in such societies during the early twentieth century.

Conclusion

L.M. Montgomery's view of the automobile as a symbol and vehicle for freedom in *The Blue Castle* comes at the end of a long and varied personal experience with many new and potentially transformative technologies. Throughout the course of her adult life, Montgomery reconciles feelings of deep ambivalence about automobiles with the obvious benefits she and her family derive from its use. She was 'unsettled' by radio, found 'talkies' difficult to follow, and questioned whether the fast-paced world would be any better for such achievements. Nonetheless, she concludes that science would succeed with great revelations and innovations – 'I am as certain of [that] as I am that the sun will rise tomorrow morning' (SJ 3: 238).

Montgomery seemed to comprehend the transformative social potential of the automobile in rural societies just as that potential became manifest to rural communities, and her depiction is balanced between cautious optimism and critical accuracy. The largely positive portrayal of automobiles earmarks her among many of her literary contemporaries. War-weary, 'lost generation' American writers of the 1920s were ambivalent at best about all forms of technology, including the automobile. In F. Scott Fitzgerald's *The Great Gatsby*, Gatsby's yellow car stands as a measure of social status, but also as a harbinger of moral decay and destruction. In Canada, humorist Stephen Leacock mercilessly mocks middle-class adventures in motor touring. In a 1929 piece, 'Travel Is so Broadening,' Leacock lampoons the average Canadian motor tourist in Europe, who is obsessed with mileage and the volatility of European grades of gasoline (*Iron Man* 117). In 'The Gasoline Good-bye,' Leacock caricatures the unromantic automobile itself. Upon taking leave from friends, no matter how touching and heartfelt the good-bye, one could always count on the auto to add the same punctuation – 'Phut, phut-BANG!' – and then refuse to move (*Winnowed Wisdom* 96–7).

Unlike her literary contemporaries who either satirized automobiles and motoring or found the automobile a handy symbol for moral laxity and social decay, Montgomery used it as a symbol for freedom, pleasure, and escape. Her optimism in the positive transformative powers of automobiles and other science-based innovations was not unqualified, however. Privately she believed that this progress does not come without a price: 'We will fly around the world and solve the secret of the atom – but there will be no more Homers or Shakespeares' (*SJ* 3: 361). Only in her romance for adults is her message clear and unequivocal. In *The Blue Castle*, the transformation of Valancy Stirling from a repressed and downtrodden spinster into a liberated and pleasure-seeking woman stands as a tribute to the positive power of technological progress in Canada.

NOTES

The idea for this article originated with Irene Gammel, who also provided excellent advice and editorial comments. My thanks also to Donald Davis for sharing his considerable interpretive insight on the history of automobiles and automobility.

1 Two years later, 'spinning along the highway at an ungodly rate' on a trip to Toronto, she comments on this 'witchery' a second time.

2 In her recent work on women and automobiles, *Taking the Wheel*, Virginia Scharff shows how the automobile 'more than any other consumer goods' available for the first time by the 1920s, 'offered women new possibilities for excitement, for leisure and for sociability' (135).

3 See also Ruth Cowan 173–4; Jellison 122–4; and Neth, 246–7. Kline and Pinch argue argument that, despite automobility, rural women 'stayed within their traditional supportive gender roles when they shopped for domestic goods or went to town in an emergency to buy parts to fix the tractor' (781).

4 Canada's development with respect to automobility parallels that of the United States. David Flink argues that '[a]lthough feelings against the speeding automobilist were extreme in some localities ... anti-automobile sentiment among farmers remained localized, was directed against speeding and reckless driving, and was pretty much confined to the years 1904 through 1906' (27). Michael Berger's *The Devil Wagon in God's Country* tells how rural communities across the United States passed local ordinances banning automobile travel in their districts. Sometimes elaborate proceeding were required, such as in Vermont, where each automobile passing through had to be preceded by a person 'of mature age' carrying a red flag. Rakes, saws, glass, and barbed wire kept delinquent motorists at bay from one end of the country to the other (26–8).

5 According to Ronald Kline and Trevor Pinch, the 'users' of new technologies often play a dominant role in shaping its meanings and ultimate designations, social and economically. The automobile had, for rural people, 'radical interpretive flexibility'; the 'devil wagon' quickly became the farmer's best friend (766, 772–3).

6 She does express some pleasure with pending legislation allowing unlimited auto travel, for 'I have hated to hear the Island made fun of for its prejudice against motor cars' (*My Dear* 87). Yet she allows that she harbours some resentment against the 'strident honk, honk' of the auto, which now jarred the 'ancient peace' of PEI. She was happy to note in her journal that 'faeries' still abide in Lovers' Lane: 'Even the motor cars cannot scare them away' (*SJ* 2: 252).

MOTHERHOOD, FAMILY, AND FEMINISM

9

Knitting Up the World: L.M. Montgomery and Maternal Feminism in Canada

ERIKA ROTHWELL

Since the war broke out women have done a great deal of knitting ... The woman's outlook on life is to save, to care for, to help. Men make wounds and women bind them up, and so the women, with their hearts filled with love and sorrow, sit in their quiet homes and knit ... Women [however] have not only been knitting – they have been thinking.

Nellie McClung, *In Times Like These*

Nellie McClung (1873–1951) is best remembered for her feminist activism and political essays. In her activism, she focused on Canadian women's suffrage, domestic violence, and issues of alimony and child support. In contrast, L.M. Montgomery is still best remembered as the author of 'tales of sweetness and light for girls,' as Rea Wilmshurst ruefully notes (7). Even so, Montgomery was far from unaware of the darker side of women's lives. Although not as vocal as McClung, Montgomery shaped the politics of maternal feminism in the years that preceded, encompassed, and followed the First World War. Through her fiction, she actively participated in the sweeping changes that altered the lives and circumstances of women in Canada.

McClung paints a vivid and compelling image of women knitting and contemplating their status during the war years. Similarly, Montgomery features knitting women in her fiction. In *Anne of Green Gables* (1908), *Rilla of Ingleside* (1921), and *Jane of Lantern Hill* (1937), knitting functions as a metaphor for maternal feminism, revealing a decided progression in Montgomery's portrayal of the maternal across this historical period. In the beginning, Montgomery depicts the maternal as a strong, positive force rooted in tradition. This influence is then used by rising generations, who gain power, demand change and reform, and finally attain suffrage. Eventually, however, the maternal becomes subject to challenge and inquiry and alters, losing much of its power to nurture and to effect good, while pointing toward the need for remaking feminine identity and power.

L.M. Montgomery and the Matriarchs of Avonlea

In *Anne of Green Gables*, Avonlea is insular and relatively untouched by technological innovations. It is peacefully pastoral, for it belongs to 'the green, untroubled pastures and still waters of the world before the war' (*SJ* 2: 309). It is a predominantly maternal world: strong women knit up the substance of Anne's domestic, educational, political, and religious experiences. Marilla oversees Anne's domestic education; Mrs Barry regulates her friendship with Diana; Miss Muriel Stacy reigns over Anne's intellectual development; and Miss Josephine Barry is a cultural mentor. As Carol Gay has observed, a rereading of *Anne of Green Gables* with the tools of feminism reveals 'a distinct woman's world existing within a dominant patriarchal society' (9). Women organize many of the church charities and societies, which essentially constitute the social services of Avonlea. The Sunday school teachers are both female. Anne's world is a decidedly matriarchal one in which the power of decision making belongs to the women: they are, so to speak, the social housekeepers of Avonlea.

In portraying this world of female guardians who nurture Anne and Avonlea, Montgomery identifies herself with maternal feminism, a powerful branch of the women's movement in turn-of-the-century Canada. Its ideological position is summarized by Veronica Strong-Boag: 'Women themselves, like virtually everyone else in Canadian society, identified their sex with a maternal role. A re-invigorated motherhood, the natural occupation for virtually all women, could serve as a buttress against all the destabilizing elements in Canada' (181). Similarly, in 1893, Lady Ishbel Aberdeen, the head of the National Council of Women of Canada (NCWC), spoke of mothering as the 'grand woman's mission.' Delegates promised to 'conserve the highest good of the family and state' through philanthropic service among the sick, poor, and elderly, although the council held 'aloof from issues pertaining to women's rights' (Roberts 21–2).

Like Aberdeen, Montgomery endorses and even enshrines maternal capabilities and power. *Anne of Green Gables* does not actively campaign for change, or even directly confront issues such as the drive for female suffrage, which had begun as early as 1877 in Canada.[1] Montgomery's maternal guardians on the whole have a healing and nurturing effect; they were engaged in activities officially endorsed by women's organizations of the time. In contrast to Montgomery, the more radical Nellie McClung campaigned vigorously for suffrage from 1912 onwards, when she joined the Winnipeg branch of the Political Equity League, identified by Catherine Lyle Cleverdon as 'one of the most enterprising and successful suffrage organizations in the Dominion' (55). Montgomery, like the NCWC, held aloof from this stance at the time. 'Montgomery was not a radical, and herself chose to fit into respectable society and take on the responsibilities her culture designated for her,' as Elizabeth Epperly observes. '[S]he created heroines who also embrace traditions' (*Fragrance* 17).

Montgomery's vision of maternal feminism is steeped in realism. Not all the mother figures in *Green Gables* are ideals. Mrs Hammond and Mrs Thomas use Anne as a maid-of-all-work, and Mrs Peter Blewett, who has quarrelsome children, consistently wears out successive serving maids. Even positive maternal figures are not paragons: Mrs Lynde is gossipy and overbearing; Marilla is initially dour and repressed; Mrs Barry lacks insight and is stubborn. Thus, even at this early stage Montgomery gently undermines the political vision of maternal women as centres of what Sylvia B. Bashevkin calls 'pure reformist motives,' which many maternal feminists believed 'promised a restoration of traditional moral values in both the home and the state' (255). Montgomery's women are too humanly flawed to provide for a perfect world merely through their own empowerment. Readers leave *Anne of Green Gables* with the hope that 'Anne will do better than Mrs Lynde in reconciling the contradictions and the tensions' that surround being female in her society (Drain, 'Feminine' 47).

Avonlea perpetuates its traditional, maternal nature in accordance with the practice of mother-monopolized child rearing. Anne, for instance, easily slips into the groove of continuing maternal influence and activity in Avonlea and Green Gables, remaining in 'the dear old place,' or on the home front secure in her feminine identity (*AGG* 324). The last chapter of *Green Gables* anchors Anne's maternal commitment. Anne finds Marilla 'in the kitchen, sitting by the table with her head leaning on her hand. Something in her dejected attitude struck a chill to Anne's heart. She had never seen Marilla sit limply inert like that' (321). Anne's turn for knitting up the world of Avonlea has come with the threat of

Marilla's blindness. Instead of going to college, Anne becomes a mothering and nurturing figure to Marilla, a role further enhanced by her new responsibility of teaching the Avonlea school and bringing up a new generation of children. As Anne assumes her matriarchal heritage, *Green Gables* closes with Anne quoting Robert Browning's *Pippa Passes*, 'God's in his heaven, all's right with the world' (330). Yet the comfortable and romanticized insularity that characterizes the Anne series is undeniably ruptured and destroyed by the First World War.

L.M. Montgomery, Suffrage, and the War

In 1917, Nellie McClung achieves an echo of Montgomery's last words in *Anne*, writing:

In the quiet old days of peace perhaps there was some excuse in women saying all was well, the world was going along quite nicely without their help, but in these days of terrible destruction, of desolation and loss, of pillaged homes, orphaned children, broken hearted women, I cannot see how any woman who has any red blood in her heart can sit idly at home comfortable, warm, fed and clothed and say that all is well. (quoted in Savage 119)

In their evaluation of the war, Montgomery's and McClung's positions converge. *Rilla of Ingleside* (1921) is Montgomery's portrayal of the day-to-day lives of the women who waited on the home front while the men went to war.[2] The novel opens with the 'big, black headline' (1) announcing the assassination of Archduke Ferdinand erupting into the domestic world of Avonlea.

In *Green Gables* Mrs Lynde's knitting suggested the confident control and influence she exercised over the social fabric of the community of Avonlea; in *Rilla*, knitting for the soldiers now grows out of the Ingleside women's sense of helplessness and anguish in the face of the war. It is a coping mechanism that helps women bear stress and anxiety. Their men are gone, and they can do nothing but knit and wait. The women of Glen St Mary (a name that aligns them with Christian maternal tradition) resort to traditional maternal activities, symbolized by their knitting.

Yet there are important changes, for knitting now mingles with politics. '"No, Woodrow, there will be no peace without victory," said Susan, sticking her knitting-needle viciously through President Wilson's name in the newspaper column' (203). As the women of Ingleside await the results of the December 1917 conscription election, they take up their needles. Such is the tension over the election that Rilla later finds her mother, Anne, 'ravelling out four inches of her sock. She had knitted that far past where the heel should have begun!' (228–9). Traditionally opposed discourses – the domestic and the political – have become deeply and inextricably intertwined. The formerly apolitical Susan becomes intimately acquainted with the politicians of the day and bestows her judgment upon their actions.

Despite an energetic attempt to present a united exterior to the world, the home front and maternal values are under siege from within. Although Rilla is dedicated to her works (Junior Red Cross, Baby Jims, writing letters), she cannot knit up her world into a seamless whole as Mrs Lynde, Marilla, and Anne could in *Green Gables.* More than the women in the earlier novel, Rilla sees with great force the inequities and limitations of the prescribed maternal roles.[3] Echoing Nellie McClung, she complains of 'this Great Game which was to be played out on blood-stained fields with empires for stakes – a game in which women-kind could have no part. Women ... just had to sit and cry at home' (35). Rilla longs to be a man and participate in the war. In a mood of romantic exaltation she pens the quotation, '*He goes to do what I had done / Had Douglas's daughter been his son*' (43), and her desire continues to manifest itself in dead earnest after she becomes intimate with the agony of waiting and wondering. When her second brother, Walter, enlists, she tells her mother '*Our* sacrifice is greater than *his* ... Our boys give only *themselves. We* give them' (120).

The ongoing fight for suffrage for women was strengthened by such sentiments, as more women realized that lip-service to female moral superiority and maternal influence must be replaced with legal rights. Rilla is at one with the 'knitting women [who] know now why the militant suffragettes broke windows and destroyed property, and went to jail for it joyously, and without a murmur – it was the protest of brave women against the world's estimate of woman's position' (McClung 25). These women, too, can no longer knit up their world into an integral whole where all is right, and they wish and agitate for change.

The First World War made it painfully clear to an increasing number of Canadian women that the hand that rocked the cradle did not rule the world, but the war also aided the Canadian suffrage movement. The Union government needed to take measures to ensure success in an election fought on the conscription platform, and therefore limited suffrage was granted to Canadian women by the Wartime Elections Act of 1917. Rilla records this event in her diary:

All the women 'who have got de age' – to quote Jo Poirier, and who have husbands, sons, and brothers at the front, can vote. Oh, if I were only twenty-one! Gertrude and Susan are both furious because they can't vote.

'It is not fair,' Gertrude says passionately. 'There is Agnes Carr who can vote because her husband went. She did everything she could to prevent him from going, and she is going to vote *against* the Union Government. Yet *I* have no vote, because my man at the front is only my sweetheart and not my husband!'

As for Susan, when she reflects that *she* cannot vote, while a rank old pacifist like Mr Pryor can – and *will* – her comments are sulphurous. (225)

A woman's need to be granted rights based on her own status and not defined in terms of her relation to men is clearly implied in this passage. Even so, Montgomery does not suggest that there is likely to be unity among women voters: to bring her husband home Agnes Carr will vote against the government, conscription, and the war. Susan, Rilla, and Gertrude, on the other hand, feel the war to be Canada's duty and would vote in favour of the Union government.[4] Clearly, women's limited involvement in politics will not be enough to reweave the tattered Canadian social fabric.

As in *Green Gables*, the continued politicization of the second sex in Canada is most clearly expressed in the older women. Susan Drain has astutely remarked that Rachel Lynde's 'opinions are narrow but her involvement wide,' so that she represents the 'best guide Anne has to what it is to be a fully realized woman' ('Feminine' 47). Likewise, Susan Baker is a central, fully developed character, whose actions are at odds with the conservative opinions she voices. Like Rachel, Susan also becomes a role model for a bright, spirited young woman. Neither is particularly well educated, and each has lived her entire life in a traditional community where women's roles are rigidly defined.[5] Although through what they say Rachel and Susan perpetuate traditional restrictions placed upon women, they strongly oppose these restrictions through their actions. As such, one final similarity can be noted between the two: practise what they do, not necessarily what they preach.

However, Susan's role is more strongly politicized than Rachel Lynde's. Mrs Lynde is no more a suffragist than Susan is, and she abhors women ministers, yet she attends and participates in political rallies and runs all the church charities. Still, her role always remains secondary and domestic, while Susan (at least briefly) takes on a more public, politicized role when she attends a Victory Loan Campaign rally. Speeches are flat and interest is tepid until Susan leaps to her feet and gives a fiery and patriotic speech, which includes a 'trimming down' of the men who taunt her (223). Record sales of Victory Bonds ensue due to her intervention. Susan, Rilla writes, 'always vows she is no suffragette,' but because of the war and her patriotism, Susan has become a political activist, despite feeling afterwards that her behaviour was 'rather unladylike' (223). Through Susan, Montgomery gives a voice to elderly, conservative, uneducated, maternal, hard-working, and resourceful women – those Canadian women who supported the war effort yet were denied political rights and have now moved toward seeking empowerment and recognition.[6]

Simply put, *Rilla* is a novel about transitions on many fronts in Canadian women's lives. Traditional authorities in domestic and economic spheres start to crumble due to the war's influence. Susan begins her pronouncements on the war by quoting the authority of Dr Blythe on international affairs, but through her voracious newspaper reading she learns to advance her own opinions, which do not always agree with the doctor's. Also, with Rilla's help, Miranda Pryor defies the authority of her father and marries the man of her choice before he leaves for the front. These examples are indicative of the lessened submission to male opinion and authority within the domestic sphere. In addition, women also take on new economic roles. Mary Vance puts on overalls and pitches in to help harvest the crop; Rilla takes the place of a male dry goods clerk; and sixty-four-year-old Susan works in the fields with her 'grey hair whipping in the breeze and her skirt kilted up to her knees for safety and convenience' (217).

By the end of the novel, the Canadian woman's home front itself has been irrevocably changed: 'it seems hundreds of years since those Green Gables days,' says Anne Blythe. 'Life has been cut in two by the chasm of the war. What is ahead I don't know – but it can't be a bit like the past.' Anne wonders whether she will really feel wholly at home in the new world. Her foresight is indicative of the trends that emerge in society and literature in the wake of the war and that show a Canadian modernity in which the old maternal values no longer apply.

L.M. Montgomery's Maternal World in Crisis

Critics of children's literature have often noted that it changes in tone and scope after the First World War, which A.A. Milne called 'that nightmare of mental and moral degradation' (Hunt 197). Some authors such as Milne 'turned away from social realism' and returned to a nostalgic portrayal of the child (Hunt 198). Other authors produced works that were darker and more serious, presenting a struggle against forces that increasingly threatened home, tradition, and security. Montgomery's *Jane of Lantern Hill* (1937) incorporates both these patterns. The home and maternal traditions are clearly under attack in *Jane*, yet Montgomery's second-last novel, which lacks the social realism of *Rilla*, also has elements of a nostalgic return to *Green Gables* and Montgomery's early career. Both novels, for example, feature imaginative eleven-year-old female protagonists who have unhappy family backgrounds and whose healing and maturation begin with a journey to the beautiful world of Prince Edward Island in June.

Unlike Anne's world, Jane's is not secure. It is a modern, post-war world that features urban technology and a global outlook, instead of concentrating on one small, rural community. Some of the social changes that are implicitly demanded in *Rilla* have materialized in the Canada of 1937. With the exception of the provincial franchise in Quebec, Canadian women have gained the vote; and a landmark case in 1929 has declared them 'persons' under the constitution;[7] yet things are far from well on the home front. The positive influence that maternalism exercised in *Anne* and the defensive stance it presented in *Rilla* seem to have unravelled, lost influence, and even become debased, reflecting both general post-war malaise and the disillusionment and frustration many Canadian women felt after suffrage was attained and the war won. After the war, many of the freedoms and new rights women had earned underwent a reversal. Women were expected to return to their pre-war status, despite the advances they had made and the rights they had gained.

Even the pioneering Alberta MLA Louise McKinney believed that women who insisted upon trying to consolidate and continue their 'new found liberty and wider sphere' would 'constitute one more of the already numerous after-the-war problems' (n.p.). Suffrage had not provided the solution to women's, or indeed Canada's, social and political challenges. No brave new maternal world materialized. McClung was sadly aware of this phenomenon, for she wrote: 'when all was over, and the smoke of the battle cleared away, something happened to us. Our forces, so well organized for the campaign, began to dwindle. We had no constructive program for making a new world ... So the enfranchised women drifted. Many are still drifting' (Savage 171).

The central mothers in *Jane of Lantern Hill* do not inspire admiration for maternal values as earlier Montgomery characters do: mother figures are repressive and controlling or weak and helpless, suggesting a crisis within maternal feminism. Victoria Kennedy, Jane's grandmother uses her power to ruin the marriage of her daughter, Robin Stuart, and hold her in a sort of thralldom that consists of a meaningless round of teas, bridges, and dinner parties, which make Robin feel 'like something shut up in a cage' (19). Writing in 1930, McClung seems to describe the essence of the life poor Robin is trapped in when she speaks of the new existence of the post-war women, 'foolishly studying ten thousand ways of appearing busy, but not having great success. Bridge absorbs some, but even those who sit in a game five afternoons a week are conscious that bridge does not make a real heart-warming, soul-consuming, life-work ... [A] great many women ... are wandering in a maze of discontent and disillusionment ... Having little to do they do nothing; and doing nothing they miss that sense of work well done which sustained their grandmothers' (Savage 171–2). Robin Stuart, although beautiful, warm, and loving, is also weak, impressionable, and ineffectual. Ironically, even though surrounded by two mothers, Jane is as much without a positive maternal role model as Anne was before arriving at Green Gables.

In the post-war period, Montgomery has moved from reservations and gentle critiques of a generally positive feminine power to portraying its opposite: a maternal force that is either cold, crippling, and repressive or weak and helpless. Such figures do little to nurture individuals or advance necessary social change. Indirectly she agrees with McClung's admission that suffrage has not really brought about positive change for women. Commenting upon the coming of suffrage in her journals, Montgomery declares herself 'glad,' but adds 'I truly doubt whether it will make as much change in things as it advocates hope or its opponents fear' (*SJ* 2: 211).

In critiquing mother-monopolized child rearing, which she feels reinforces society's devaluation of women and the maternal, Nancy Chodorow calls for a 'reorganization of parenting.' Thus, the cause of sexual equality will be furthered by producing women who are able to construct an identity for themselves that is not exclusively bound up in caring for others, and by raising men who are more able to nurture and to value the activity (105). Ironically, Montgomery does present a new scheme of parenting, which features a man who is willing and able to attend to his daughter, as discussed by Diana Chlebek in chapter 10.

Andrew Stuart's nurturing of his daughter, however, is almost at the expense of maternal power and the mother–daughter relationship, although Chlebek's interpretation of this issues draws a different conclusion.

Neither Victoria Kennedy nor Robin Stuart are women who knit.[8] On the Island, the three wise women whom Jane sees knitting are clearly rooted in the virtues and traditions of yesterday, allowing Montgomery to indulge in a nostalgic return to the values and images of the past. The two Miss Tituses live at the end of a treed lane in a hundred-year-old house surrounded by an old garden. When they decide to satisfy their maternal longings by adopting Jane's chum Jody (after a conference that involves interchanging glances while knitting), Justina says that Jody 'must not expect to find here the excitements of the mad welter of modern life,' but that 'wholesome pleasures' await her (195). Crone-like Little Aunt Em also lives apart from the modern world, and Andrew Stuart calls her 'a wise old goblin' who lives on a 'little side-road' and 'does weaving and spinning and dyeing rug rags' (119).

While the old woman knits, Jane asks her about the separation of her parents, a subject over which she has repeatedly agonized, but never spoken of to anyone. Aunt Em's maternal wisdom is crucial to Jane's development, and upon leaving Aunt Em's retreat, Jane is imbued with new confidence that allows her to confront fear and obstacles with increasing courage and confidence. On the way home, she walks bravely through a field filled with cows (earlier she had been deathly afraid of such creatures), and moves on to speak bravely to both her parents about their separation, and, eventually, to defy and flee from her grandmother. Finally, Jane takes charge of her own life. *Jane of Lantern Hill* ends with restoration and healing, and the disparate parts of Jane's family are knit into a whole once more.

Conclusion

The intersections between the works of Montgomery and McClung suggest that Montgomery was an astute social historian and maternal feminist who kept her finger upon the pulse of Canadian women's experiences. She powerfully knit into her fiction the events, circumstances, beliefs, experiences, and realizations that were of moment in the living history of Canadian women. Montgomery knits up her portrayal of the changing status of the mother, recreating the tapestry of maternal feminism in Canada. The strands of her work tell the story of

Canadian women's lives in relation to the changing social and political circumstances of Canadian society in the first half of the twentieth century.

In the pre-war years of *Anne*, maternal values and the home front they help to maintain are strong and serene, and their positive effects are in no hurry for change. In the war years of *Rilla*, these elements are under siege from all sides as women find their lack of rights and freedoms inconsistent with the new roles they fill, the challenges they meet, and the increasingly politicized world they inhabit. Finally, in the post-war years of *Jane*, rights such as suffrage have been attained, but maternal values are fallen and divided, exercising little or purely negative influence. However, with the coming of Jane, who combines traditional nurturing, maternal qualities with new independence and freedom, the community seems to be approaching a renewal.

Jane of Lantern Hill closes with its joyful heroine telling her father 'I know the very house!' (217). The move to this new house parallels a move to a new home front in which both parental forces will be balanced by the interpretive, synthesizing skill of adolescent girls like Jane, and in which perhaps at last a comfortable equilibrium is found.

NOTES

1 Sylvia B. Bashevkin dates the 'formal beginnings of the suffrage movement in English Canada' from the founding of the Toronto Women's Literary Society in 1877 (249). The society disguised its feminist nature until Dr Emily Stowe, with the aid of other activists, founded the Canadian Woman Suffrage Association in 1883. The Dominion Women's Enfranchisement Association was founded in 1889 and the Canadian Suffrage Association in 1906.

2 The novel is 'unique among war novels' in presenting 'the woman's point of view,' as Mary Rubio and Elizabeth Waterston (*Writing* 70), Elizabeth Epperly (*Fragrance* 95–130), and Owen Dudley Edwards point out.

3 Like her heroine, Rilla, Montgomery ran and organized a Red Cross Society, but she does not make any reference to knitting during the war years. However, she clearly recognized its therapeutic value from personal experience. Early in 1914, she writes 'To-day *I began to knit a quilt*. That sounds like an arrant folly in a woman who is as busy as I am. Yet there is a method in my madness ... [K]*nitting* has always had a good effect on me when I am nervous. I was always very fond of knitting and I find that it helps me greatly these bad days (*SJ* 2: 142–3).

4 Montgomery was allowed to vote because her half-brother, Carl

Montgomery, had enlisted and was overseas in France. Due to injuries sustained at Vimy Ridge, Carl lost a leg and returned to Canada late in 1917. She voted for the Union government.

5 In studying suffragism across Canada, Bashevkin notes that 'affiliates in Francophone Quebec and Atlantic Canada were particularly slow to develop, meaning that the organizational strength of the movement existed outside those areas where women's traditional roles were most constraining and, in the view of many activists, most in need of legislative reform' (251). Living in Ontario by 1920, Montgomery, a former Islander, may have intended to reflect the particular conditions of Atlantic Canada in creating the character of Susan.

6 Indeed, Owen Dudley Edwards identifies Susan with 'Canada herself' (132) and suggests that through her character the war is 'portrayed as self-liberation in feminine terms' (133). Susan, therefore, is an expansion and a strengthening of the feminine political voice begun by Mrs Lynde.

7 Alberta, Manitoba, and Saskatchewan granted women suffrage in 1916; British Columbia and Ontario in 1917, Nova Scotia in 1918; New Brunswick in 1919; Prince Edward Island in 1922; Newfoundland in 1925; and Quebec in 1940. The Wartime Elections Act (which Rilla refers to above) granted the national vote to women who were British subjects and who had served in any branch of the military, or who had a close relative serving in the forces of Canada or Britain. Full female enfranchisement for national elections was granted to all Canadian women on 24 May 1918 (Bashevkin 250). The Persons Case arose over the issue of women's eligibility for the Canadian Senate. On 24 April 1928, the Supreme Court declared that 'Women are not "qualified persons" within the meaning of Section 24 of the BNA Act, 1867, and therefore are not eligible for appointment by the Governor General to the Senate of Canada.' Emily Murphy led an appeal to the Judicial Committee of Privy Council in England (then Canada's final court of appeal), which ruled that 'women were indeed persons and thus eligible for appointment to the Senate' (Bashevkin 260).

8 Aunt Irene, who sends Jane a pretty knitted sweater for Christmas, is jealous, conniving, and controlling. Her constant interference in her brother's life is a lesser reflection of Victoria Kennedy's machinations. Irene is, however, an exception, and her knitting is not witnessed by Jane but takes place 'off stage.'

10

The Canadian Family and Female Adolescent Development during the 1930s: *Jane of Lantern Hill*

DIANA ARLENE CHLEBEK

Montgomery wrote *Jane of Lantern Hill* at the end of her career to please herself when the demands of the publishing market made the obligation of churning out more Anne books most disagreeable to her, and the psychological need to portray her spiritual autobiography through the Emily Starr series seemed played out. Through the creation of the character Jane, who was one of her favourite fictional 'children,' Montgomery was able to fulfil her creative desire to write a fantasy about frustrated and reconstructed adolescent development.[1] Most importantly, Montgomery's artistic urge appears to have sprung out of an emotional need to counteract the intense mental depression she suffered because of serious problems in her own family life.

If the novel stands out among Montgomery's works as a modern fairy tale (Epperly, *Fragrance* 221), part of its modernity lies in its focus on the transformation of the family in early-twentieth-century Canada. The novel uses as a theme a fairly sophisticated problem for a children's book – that of marital separation and divorce, a touchy subject even for adult novels in a country where establishment views were still fairly inflexible on the topic. It is the energy of social critique that propels a narrative depiction of an adolescent's development in a world of parental separation, child abuse, and adoption. Like many Canadian novels written in the period after the First World War,[2] Montgomery's book probes the legacy of family tension; as a result, *Jane of Lantern Hill* is a new 'bend in the road' in the author's recreation of the idyllic romance.

The Context for L.M. Montgomery's Family Romance

Many of the works Montgomery wrote after permanently leaving Prince Edward Island are increasingly related to a sense of loss and guilt.

Certainly her series of Emily and Pat of Silver Bush books are structured on tensions that induce despair and on conflicts that tear the novels' heroines between the practical demands of everyday existence and the more soul-satisfying attractions of either an artistic career or a romantic involvement. By contrast, *Jane of Lantern Hill*, published in 1937, late in the author's career and five years before her death, appears to have been a restorative process of creation for her. Given the extremely stressful circumstances in her personal life, especially in her marriage, at this time, the work provided Montgomery with emotional compensation through her spunky heroine's success at restoring her broken family in a way that her creator could not in her own household.

Montgomery's journal entries and her letters to two lifelong friends, Ephraim Weber and George MacMillan, provide an especially illuminating context in which to read the novel. In her correspondence to MacMillan after the book's publication, she describes an almost maternal kinship to her creation, using very personal, emotional terms; the novel is an exception to the economic obligations she was unhappily grinding out to appease publishers: 'But it isn't always easy to spin books wholly "out of my own personality" and sometimes I just have to fall back on my notebook to make the book long enough. In my latest book "Jane of Lantern Hill" ... I think I was not guilty of this fault. I wrote the book because I loved it and its little heroine' (*My Dear* 186). Her husband's mental breakdown, which had begun in 1919, had progressively worsened during the period 1936–7 when Montgomery wrote most of her novel, likely contributing to the author's nervous collapses and illnesses. As the editors of her journals, Rubio and Waterston, have noted, so intense was her depression during this stressful period that she stopped making continuous entries in her diaries, even though this form of writing was usually a therapeutic process for her (*Writing* 109).

The much documented incompatibility between herself and Ewan,[3] combined with the irresponsible behaviour of her son Chester toward his spouse, had soured the author on the whole institution of marriage. Moreover, these were also the years when Canada was rocked by the scandalous affair between Edward VIII, heir to the British throne, and the American socialite Wallis Simpson; for Montgomery, as for many Canadians, the king's abdication to marry a divorcee reinforced the impression that modern society, with its increasingly lax standards, was seriously eroding the structure of the family. Montgomery feared for the fragility of her own marital relationship and that of her son.[4] At home in Canada, a serious economic depression was sapping the vitality of everyday life; abroad in Europe, the threat of yet another apocalyptic world war loomed. More and more, Montgomery had come to regard the twentieth century, in both personal and universal terms, as a 'world turned upside-down,' words she had earlier used in letters to MacMillan (Gillen, *Wheel* 168).

The creation of *Jane of Lantern Hill* presented itself as a chance to rewrite the scenarios of her life-text, including her unhappy upbringing under her rigid grandparents. Through Jane, she could fantasize and concretize the prospect of having another chance at reuniting with the father she felt had abandoned her in her teens when he had moved and settled permanently in Western Canada for new career prospects and a new wife. The novel could allow her to resuscitate the sweet and girlish mother she had lost at birth and whom she felt she had always deserved. The fact that Montgomery had never known her mother, except through some faded mementoes, had often pained her, through the privation of maternal love (*SJ* 3: 205). Best of all, the novel would let her blot out her own unhappy, unromantic marriage and replace it with the fantasy of a love-filled and more sensuously satisfying union that she might have had. Before we examine Montgomery's solutions, the story of the changing perceptions of childhood in early-twentieth-century Canada needs to be told.

Children as a Social Problem

In the early twentieth century, the populations of large urban areas like Toronto began to swell with large numbers of homeless and delinquent juveniles, while orphan agencies frequently placed children as boarded-out servants. As Canadian social historian Mariana Valverde reports,[5] children were increasingly seen as a social problem by the new professional child-savers who styled themselves as overseers of social policy and order and saw poverty increasingly as an inborn trait indicative of personal pathology and inadequacy. In *Jane of Lantern Hill*, the attitudes of professional child-savers are satirized through Grandmother Victoria Kennedy's suspicions of Jane and Jody. By befriending and bringing Jody, the boarding-house servant, into the home, Jane herself is perceived as unwelcome and alien. From Victoria's viewpoint this friendship bolsters her prejudice that Jane's inherent qualities are suspect because of her father's unworthy lineage, including his questionable occupation as a writer and his upbringing on Prince Edward Island, regarded as a paltry backwater by the snobbish Toronto elite. She fears that Jane may contaminate the clan through her 'bad' blood and disruptively liberal actions and ideas; she may be unfit to perpetuate the family line and inheritance.

From these precepts of her narrow moral universe Grandmother Kennedy codifies a form of social control and imposes it upon her granddaughter Jane, whom she treats as an outsider, a foster child to be watched and shaped so as to eliminate her unsuitable inherited tendencies. The girl is overwhelmed by a complex structure of dynastic and class rules that her grandmother enforces with the rigour of criminal law in regard to deportment, dress, table manners, friends, education, reading matter, and so on. Jane's punishment recreates the psychological torture of the child Maud in her grandparents' home: a raking-over-the-coals as the child's sins are catalogued and reviewed by a jury of aunts, uncles, and cousins on their weekly visit (*SJ* 1: 300–1). Moreover, Grandmother Kennedy's judgment that the careful husbandry of money was an index of moral worth reflects a strict Calvinist attitude that Montgomery knew well from her own background. At the same time, Victoria indulges in conspicuous consumption to decorate her daughter and even her despised granddaughter, using them as signposts of her clan's elevated status in the ranks of the city's wealthy establishment.

Jane internalizes her grandmother's message that the prime indices of her undeservedness are, of course, her plainness, her incompetence, and, most of all, her low association with Jody, the waif who lives next door. At the same time, the emotional bridge between the two girls becomes the road to psychic liberation for Jane. The author keeps sentimentality at bay in this story of friendship between the two girls by providing it with a solid texture of social reality. Jody is a physically abused child labourer whose plight was only too common in a large Canadian city like Toronto during the early decades of the century.[6] Montgomery vividly portrays the psychological and emotional credibility of child abuse through a narrative technique of doubling in the characterization of the two girls. Jane and Jody mirror each other in their love of nature, their torment at the hands of cruel adults, and especially in the discovery of caring parental figures on Prince Edward Island. This story of psychological and emotional healing now requires further investigation.

The Canadian Family Romance in Psychology and Myth

By the early 1930s, the study of the psychological life and development of children had come to the attention of psychologists such as Melanie

Klein and Anna Freud, mainly through the analysis of the unconscious in adults.[7] Translations of landmark works on psychoanalysis had become widely available in North America from the early decades of the century, and by 1915 popular articles on Freudian psychology had already reached mass circulation women's magazines.[8] Montgomery's journals are peppered with allusions to psychoanalysis, theories of repression and the sublimation of unconscious impulses, particularly in relation to explanations of her husband's mental illness or accounts of symbolic dreams she had that sprang from her own distraught mental state.[9] Some of her knowledge was based on observations gleaned from the diagnosis and treatment of her husband's neurosis in the Boston clinic where he was sent for help when his mental breakdown began in 1919. In the later years of her life, which were so despairing and stressful, Montgomery came to realize the therapeutic value of conscious, creative fantasizing (*SJ* 3: 243–4). Montgomery's deep interest in the new psychology is particularly striking since Freudian ideas had had a lukewarm or even hostile reception among Canada's conservative medical and intellectual establishment in the early decades of the century.[10]

According to the Freudian critic Bruno Bettelheim (66–70), the child who both loves and hates a parent resolves the conflict by dichotomizing the adult just as the fairy tale form dichotomizes characters. Thus the parent is divided into two opposites: a beautiful and loving version, and an evil and hateful version. In her novel Montgomery does indeed create two contrasting mothers for her heroine: a cruel all-powerful grandmother, and a sweet, but ineffectual, mother who herself needs mothering. At the same time, Montgomery wrestles with restoring a relationship structure not unlike the nuclear family romance often described in psychoanalysis. Until Jane can solve the problem of reuniting her parents, she serves as substitute mother/wife for herself and for her father, thus preparing the domestic path for her mother's arrival. With her new-found competency in domestic skills, she mothers her dad, proves her self-worth, and in this way strikes two blows against her 'bad' mother, Grandmother Kennedy. The old image of the inadequate Victoria is superseded by a new self, 'Superior Jane,' as she is teasingly christened by her father. Montgomery has Jane resolve the question of 'Who am I?' by giving birth to – that is, 'mothering' – a new Jane.

By confronting the reality that her family conceals, Jane simply channels the energy of her anger into constructing her own secret garden of life on the Island. On this site she grows beyond the state of mere psychic defence that protected her against the moral narrowness of her existence with her Toronto relatives. Jane achieves recognition of her heritage and her parents' reconciliation with their past and with each other. A large part of Jane's mission is to free her mother and restore her to an idealized setting like that of the Island in order to bring about the reconciliation and connection between father and mother, the child's ultimate fantasy of power in the nuclear family.

Even while restoring the traditional family romance, the story also expands from the patriarchal fantasy of women saved by a father-figure into a matriarchal vision of Jane's reconstruction of her family within a nurturing environment that is sustained by the closely knit community of Islanders. Jane rescues herself and her mother from the material and psychological entrapment of inhuman values. These forms of deadening oppression are symbolized by the forbidding Kennedy castle in its desolate urban setting with its cruel caretaker, the despotic grandmother. It is she who inhibits Jane's mother from taking full charge of her maternal duties and responsibility for her own daughter. Thus Jane's escape and rescue action come to represent an assertion of the feminine will of a new generation: that of liberating itself from the old Victorian sphere that wishes to enchain the new generations of women in a perpetual state of dependency and immature 'femininity.'

To underscore the role playing in the myth that Jane's story represents, Montgomery invests her novel with a strong network of symbols centred on the heroine. The image of the house both as a metaphor (Epperly, *Fragrance* 223) and as a theme for the decay and integrity of the family becomes central, as the title, *Jane of Lantern Hill* indicates. It is central to the wish-fulfilment process for Jane, who has fantasized owning her own home instead of remaining a 'possession' in her grandmother's mansion household. In contradistinction to the Toronto stronghold of the Kennedys, Jane furbishes the Island house with flowers, shells, and other bounties of nature that the inhabitants of this Eden share or barter in a form of unspoiled pre-capitalist economy. Like the domestic symbols in the novel these products, which spring from the life forces of the earth and the sea, are all associated with the archetype of the mother. Jane's mystical relationship with her home and with her Island frames a longing to return to her family roots, the same desire that Montgomery expressed so often in her journal and, in the end, realized she could never really fulfil.

Jane's aim in healing the breach within her parents' marriage through their relocation to an island Eden also evokes the 'quest for the peaceable kingdom' described by Northrop Frye in the *Bush Garden* (249). Yet the parents' reconciliation significantly requires the near-sacrifice of the heroine herself. Jane's illness, which prompts the mother's arrival on the Island, is symbolic of the psychic pain and desperate measures Jane endures through the divisive choice demanded of her by the Kennedy dynasty: mother or father, Toronto or the Island. It does, however, facilitate the entry of the 'true' mother and wife back into the life of Jane and her father, capped by a realistic solution to the geographical split as well: the family's move to a new kind of home, a cozy but practical house in a suburb of Toronto, Lakeside Gardens, modelled on Montgomery's last home in Swansea, outside downtown Toronto.

Yet this conventional ending is significantly accompanied by another, perhaps more unusual, denouement. When Jane achieves the reconciliation of her mother and father, she also helps Jody get adopted by the two quirky, kindly spinsters, the Titus sisters, and thus rescues her friend from the social and emotional limbo of perpetual orphanhood. This domestic arrangement, based on a mutual decision between Jody and her adoptive parents, presents a more unconventional advance over the repressive Victorian family order that Jody and Jane have escaped. Thus within the family structure an emotional kinship comes to replace bonds of consanguity, which stress hierarchy and possession.

Conclusion

From a critical standpoint, *Jane of Lantern Hill* is probably one of L.M. Montgomery's most underappreciated works.[11] Yet within both the context of Canadian fiction and the corpus of the author's literary achievements, the novel breaks new ground in its exploration of disturbing elements in the reality of the dysfunctional family. The author brings to the novel a modern psychological understanding of the repressions and wish-fulfilments of the un-extraordinary child, the 'plain Jane' who confronts alienation and emotional turbulence in the adult world around her. In this regard, Jane is comparable to the heroine of Frances Hodgson Burnett's ground-breaking children's classic, *The Secret Garden*. Both Mary Lennox of *The Secret Garden* and Montgomery's Jane succeed in outgrowing the narrowness of the adults around them. As a depiction of the Canadian family in the early twentieth century, Montgomery's novel goes well beyond providing a snapshot portrayal. Through the dynamic lens of Jane's viewpoint as a developing adolescent, *Jane of Lantern Hill* renders the full impact of an institution in all its stages of transformation. As a confluence between the social and psychic spheres of a culture, Montgomery's picture becomes emblematic of Canada and its people in a new century, wrenching away from an old order, struggling with new alternatives.

NOTES

1 Both Waterston's ground-breaking early study, 'Lucy Maud Montgomery' (216), and Epperly's *Fragrance of Sweet-Grass* (220) describe the novel as wish-fulfilment for Montgomery.

2 These would include Laura Salverson's *Viking Heart* (1923), Frederick Philip Grove's *Settlers of the Marsh* (1925), and Mazo de la Roche's *Jalna* (1927).

3 See Rubio and Waterston, Introduction (*SJ* 3: xi–xii), and journal entries for 18 February 1923 (*SJ* 3: 114–16) and 16 to 29 March 1924 (*SJ* 3: 169–80); see also the final letter to Macmillan dated 23 December 1941 (*My Dear* 204).

4 See Rubio and Waterston, *Writing* (105), and letter to MacMillan for 23 December 1941.

5 The eugenics movement in Canada and its influence on social and child-welfare policies are discussed in Valverde, ch. 2 and 3; also see Richardson 69–74, 185–92.

6 On the social welfare policy of boarding-out dependent children in Canada, see Rooke and Schnell 273–329.

7 Melanie Klein's influential work *The Psychoanalysis of Children* was published in 1932; in 1938 Anna Freud left Vienna for London, where she continued her work on the application of psychoanalysis to the treatment and education of children.

8 On the dissemination of Freud's publications and the reception of Freudian ideas in North America see Demos 23–7 and also Parkin 20–2.

9 See Montgomery (*SJ* 3: 2), including Rubio and Waterston's Introduction (xi); see especially their notes (*SJ* 3: 402) and the index under 'books,' for the very substantial list of works in psychology and medicine that Montgomery discusses in relation to Ewan's mental illness or to her own interest in psychology.

10 On the resistance in the Canadian medical community to Freudian theories and techniques, and to psychoanalysis in general, see Parkin 35, 39–40, and 48–50.

11 Four studies of substance have been written about the book since it was first published in 1937. These are all recent: Jean Little's journal article (1975), and analyses in books by Epperly (*Fragrance* 220–7, 229), Wiggins (143–8) and by Rubio and Waterston (*Writing* 105–10).

11

Reflection Piece – 'I Wrote Two Hours This Morning and Put Up Grape Juice in the Afternoon': The Conflict between Woman and Writer in L.M. Montgomery's Journals

ROBERTA BUCHANAN

'I wrote two hours this morning and put up grape juice in the afternoon,' L.M. Montgomery wrote in her diary on 2 October 1919 (*SJ* 2: 347) – a sentence that encapsulates her double life as housewife and as writer. Montgomery was proud of her expertise in both fields. One of the strong themes in her journals is what might be called the power politics of the home, where both home and diary become sites of the intersection between the private and public selves. As Felicity Nussbaum points out in 'Toward Conceptualizing Diary,' 'Diary serves the social/historical function of articulating a multiplicity of contestatory selves' (132). The 'contestatory selves' in Montgomery's journals include the public self – at first, the cheerful Maudie of the early Cavendish journals, always ready for some jolly 'racket,' changing in the later journals to the smiling, gracious minister's wife – and the private hidden self, 'growling,' brooding, embittered, angry, sarcastic, often tormented and depressed. Denyse Yeast sees Montgomery's writing as often negotiating 'among several conflictual ideologies to establish a space from which to speak' (116). Diary 'is a way to expose the subject's hidden discourse' (Nussbaum 135).

Even in the present journal's abridged form, several themes emerge strongly as vital to Montgomery: the conflict between woman as writer and homemaker; and her desire to conform to social expectations of femininity. This conflict between woman and writer has been seen as central by twentieth-century 'gynocritics.' Adrienne Rich saw the great poet Emily Dickinson enmeshed in a similar domestic situation: 'writing, *My Life had stood – a Loaded Gun –* / in that Amherst pantry while the jellies boil and scum' ('Snapshots of a Daughter-in-Law' #4). Sara Mills, in her study of British women travel writers in the colonial period, sees them as being pulled 'in different textual directions' so that 'their writing exposes the unsteady foundations on which it is based' (3). Mills comments on the split between expectations of the feminine role and that of the traveller/writer: 'In the colonial context, British women were only allowed to figure as symbols of home and purity; women as active participants can barely be conceived of' (3).

There is a similar conflict in L.M. Montgomery's journals: her attempt to create the ideal post-Victorian home and family, with herself as the exemplary mother and minister's wife, and the cracks in this façade revealed in her journals. She supported the status quo through conscientiously fulfilling her social obligations – 'did all the proper didoes' (*SJ* 2: 195) – while simultaneously attacking and undermining it through her bitter and subversive comments, such as remarking on her disgust at what she called her 'tea-martyrdom' as a minister's wife (*SJ* 2: 120), wasting her time attending boring teas with her husband's parishioners.

Woman and Homemaker

Montgomery's attitude toward housekeeping and homemaking expressed in the journals before her marriage must be seen in the context of the placelessness of an unmarried Canadian woman at the turn of the century, who had no home of her own and was obliged either to live with relatives (as she did with her grandparents) or in a boarding house. In her stint as a 'newspaper woman' in Halifax, the loneliness and rootlessness of an unmarried working woman's life seems to have frightened and depressed her. For a woman to live alone in an apartment or house seems to have been virtually unthinkable at that time. Her remarks on the spinsters of her childhood are often depressing, such as the 'three old maids' whom she had had as Sunday school teachers who were 'neither lovable nor helpful': 'One of them ... became insane ... and drowned herself' (*SJ* 1: 378). The pressure toward marriage must have been relentless. She comments on the plight of the unmarried woman: for example, Tillie McKenzie, once beautiful but degenerating into the 'shopworn' after 'several broken engagements,' and drifting into a bitter 'old maidenhood': 'she had to occupy a home where a married brother and his family lived. She had no recognized place in society. Her beauty faded' (*SJ* 2: 47).

At age thirty-nine, Tillie was obliged to marry beneath her. Her husband, according to Montgomery, did not love her but 'was badly in need of a housekeeper,' and Tillie was 'a pattern housekeeper and a queen of cooks' (*SJ* 2: 48). Marriage changed Tillie into a nicer person. 'She had a nice home and a certain prestige in society as the result of being the mistress of it.' She made her 'cosy house' in North Rustico 'a pretty, dainty place' (*SJ* 2: 48). Montgomery enjoyed visiting Tillie, and having 'a dinner and tea such as only Tillie can set up,' even though she had to fend off the unwanted advances of her husband, Will Houston (*SJ* 2: 50).

The story of Tillie and Will Houston serves as a kind of cautionary tale that works on several levels: being an old maid is a bitter and embittering life – she has 'no recognized place in society;' being 'a pattern housekeeper and a queen of cooks' can get you a husband even at the ripe age of thirty-nine; getting a husband also secures you a cosy home of which you are mistress and gets you prestige and respect. And the spinster (Montgomery) is turned into the 'other woman' in the triangle, the threat to the stability of the marriage, and the object of 'insulting,' 'degrading,' and unwelcome attentions (*SJ* 2: 50).

Montgomery saw marriage as the only way out of her problems: her lack of a home, her marginalization as a spinster, the dread of loneliness. She did not expect 'perfect and rapturous happiness' in marrying Ewan Macdonald (*SJ* 1: 322). 'I wanted a home and companionship; ... I wanted children,' even though 'the life of a country minister's wife' was 'a synonym for respectable slavery' and she would have to 'cloak her real self under an assumed orthodoxy and conventionalism that must prove very stifling at times' (*SJ* 1: 321). She dared not 'keep [her] freedom and trust life' (*SJ* 1: 322); marriage was the lesser evil.

Yet Montgomery was also committed to her vocation as a writer. When her first book, *Anne of Green Gables*, was published, she exulted: '*mine, mine, mine,* – something to which *I* had given birth – something which, but for me, would never have existed' (*SJ* 1: 335). At the same time she complained of 'nervous weakness' and 'nervous ills' (*SJ* 1: 338). She was haunted by a 'reasonless dread' while acting the part of someone who 'must be bright and smiling and cheery' (*SJ* 1: 341), creating a false self of that persona which Virginia Woolf called 'the angel in the house.' As with other women writers – such as Woolf, for example, or Charlotte Perkins Gilman – she was advised to give up writing: 'Ewan is much concerned over my condition and has insisted that I do no writing for a month. I have yielded to please him but I do not think it is a wise thing after all. When I am writing I am happy for I forget all worries and cares' (*SJ* 1: 342).

The post-marriage Leaksdale diaries lovingly describe Montgomery's creation of her new home. Although her first sight of the manse revealed

torn wallpaper hanging in strips from ceiling and walls, Montgomery –
now Mrs Macdonald – was not dismayed. 'It was *our* home and I was its
mistress. No woman ever forgets that delightful sensation – especially if,
like me, she has never lived in any house before where she had any
rights or privileges beyond those of a dependent child' (*SJ* 2: 83). And 'at
last my longed-for home was an accomplished fact – no longer a dream
but a reality' (*SJ* 2: 87). She furnished it 'comfortably' and 'in good taste'
out of her royalties. The furniture included a 'spandy new desk' – 'a desk
where I can keep all the notebooks and "utensils" of my trade together'
(*SJ* 2: 88). She had no intention, in becoming a wife, of giving up her
'trade' as a professional writer. Despite considerable work for the church,
including pastoral visits to parishioners, attending 'deadly dull' mission
meetings, teaching Sunday school, running the Young People's Guild,
her priorities were firm: she had her own 'special work' to do, her writing. 'I am not going to waste my time and strength on work for which I
have no aptitude, to the neglect of my own work which has been as truly
"given" to me to do as any missionary's or minister's' (*SJ* 2: 91).

Household Science

While some other feminists at the time were trying to think of new
solutions to housework so that women could spend more time on other
activities – including political and social activism – Montgomery's journals show that she continued to spend a large amount of her time in
domestic chores. American feminist Charlotte Perkins Gilman was pro-
posing 'alternatives to the traditional domestic workplace,' including
the 'kitchenless house' (Hayden 184). Gilman's friend, Helen Campbell,
in her book *Household Economics*, criticized the 'organized waste and
destruction' in the 'isolated, individual system' of the nuclear household (Hayden 186). Both were enthusiastic supporters of the National
Household Economics Association, founded in 1893 during the Wom-
en's Congress at the World's Columbian Exposition in Chicago (Hayden
186).
   Canadians Alice Chown and Adelaide Hunter Hoodless were among
those feminists promoting home economics in Canada (MacDonald;
Chown; Howes). By the early 1900s, 'advanced training in domestic
science was being provided at the Macdonald Institute in Guelph, and
Macdonald College ... near Montreal'; later it was also offered at the
University of Toronto, and at McGill, Acadia, and Mount Allison (Prentice
et al. 157; *SJ* 2: xiv). Lillian Massey, of the National Council of Women of

Canada, believed that the study of domestic science at the university level would make 'home the centre of moral progress and intellectual growth. When the majority of homes are ideal, many of the present social and economic evils will disappear' (Roberts 22). To that end, she provided funding for the School of Household Science at the University of Toronto (Gillen 134).

Perhaps the most revealing story in the journals concerning Montgomery's attitude to domesticity and the role of woman has to do with Montgomery's cousin, best friend, and spiritual companion, Frederica Campbell. Montgomery wanted Frede to have a 'chance to do something with her brains' (*SJ* 2: 10), and she paid for Frede's higher education, hoping to rescue her from the drudgery and hopelessness of the life of an unmarried schoolteacher in a rural Island community. Montgomery herself had felt fortunate to escape such a life.

Ironically, perhaps, Frede chose not to do an arts degree at McGill (she evidently thought she would feel too old) but embarked on the practical, new 'Household Science' course at the newly created Macdonald College in Montreal. The college had been founded in 1907 and financed by Prince Edward Island–born tobacco millionaire Sir William Christopher Macdonald (Macmillan 259; Collard 129). 'The School of Household Science was included ... as an adjunct to the agricultural program: good farmers, he [Macdonald] recognized, needed good wives and this is what the school set out to produce' (Frost 2: 64).

Frede used her new skills to cater Montgomery's wedding to Ewan Macdonald at Park Corner; she 'had all the latest frills of decoration and serving and it was the smartest repast I have seen anywhere,' Montgomery remarked (*SJ* 2: 67). Frede went on to teach at Macdonald College, as 'Demonstrator to the Home-Makers' Clubs of Quebec' (*SJ* 2: 303), thus becoming part of the trend of professionalizing housework, and raising its status to a 'science.'

But even the raising of domesticity to the status of a science was not going to change the cultural pressures on the unmarried woman. According to Montgomery, Frede became lonely; 'she had begun ... to experience the bitterness in the lot of a woman whose youth is almost gone – the social neglect, the heart's loneliness, amid the crowd of younger girls' (*SJ* 2: 316). She made an imprudent 'war marriage' to a young soldier (*SJ* 2: 316), and in 1919 died tragically of pneumonia following Spanish flu in the infirmary of Macdonald College (*SJ* 2: 287). In reflecting on Frede's marriage, Montgomery saw it as following her own pattern – marrying to avoid loneliness and the stigma of spinsterhood, as with Frede's sister, Stella Campbell: 'Escape from old maiden-hood, a home, support, companionship ' (*SJ* 2: 316).

Montgomery's journals show her juggling her roles as wife, mother, and writer. 'This morning I resumed work on my third *Emily* book and this afternoon I cleaned the horse stable' (*SJ* 3: 184). This should have been Ewan's job, but he often reneged on his chores. As minister's wife, she often presented a false self to the world: 'I force myself to chat and smile ... But I detest it all' (*SJ* 2: 121). Her anger went into the journal. 'It is like lancing a fester and letting out the pus' (*SJ* 1: 341).

When her son Chester was seven years old, Montgomery encouraged him to keep a diary, and commented in hers: 'Dear boy, I hope he will never need a journal for what I have needed mine – the outlet of pain and bitter experiences which none shared with me and which I could tell to no other confidant' (*SJ* 2: 349).

Part 3.
Montgomery and Canadian Iconography:
Consuming the Popular

ANNE AS CULTURAL ICON

12

The Hard-Won Power of Canadian Womanhood: Reading *Anne of Green Gables* Today

FRANK DAVEY

L.M. Montgomery's *Anne of Green Gables* played an ambiguously progressive role in various turn-of-the century ideological conflicts concerning religion, child rearing, and opportunities for women. In its strategic focus on an orphan it linked itself to a textual formation that had already seen such works as Dickens's *Oliver Twist* (1839) and *Great Expectations* (1861), Twain's *Huckleberry Finn* (1885), Kipling's *Kim* (1901), and – in a less complex way – Frank L. Baum's *The Wonderful Wizard of Oz* (1900) deploy this figure to interrogate social practices. In her invocation of the orphan figure, Montgomery, like the nineteenth-century authors who preceded her, was using a sign of considerable psychological and cultural power – including the power to outlast any specific social issue a novel might engage. For orphanhood and feelings of orphanhood, whether caused by separation, migration, family conflict, parental death, or rapid social change, are conditions that cultures repeatedly create, despite and because of changing material circumstances.

In her specific deployment of a female orphan Montgomery was launching a figure that would play a extremely prominent role in Canadian writing later in the century. Montgomery's Anne was both an actual and metaphorical orphan – a young girl who had not only lost her parents but who had come to experience herself as radically estranged from society generally. In compensation, she finds alternate realities – those of nineteenth-century popular and literary romance (including Campbell's 'The Battle of Hohenlinden,' Scott's *The Lady of the Lake* and *Rob Roy*, and Heman's 'The Woman on the Field of Battle') and those she can create herself, at first in her construction of imaginary companions and later in her writing of her own romance narratives.

This pattern of a young girl's social estrangement leading her into fantasy creation and eventually into literary creation has recurred in several of the most important, and popular, works of fiction in recent Canadian literature: Alice Munro's *Lives of Girls and Women,* Margaret Laurence's *A Bird in the House* and *The Diviners,* and Margaret Atwood's *Lady Oracle* and *The Robber Bride.* In somewhat less obvious form it has also appeared in fiction like Daphne Marlatt's *Ana Historic* and Gail Scott's *Heroine.* Undoubtedly there is much more at work here than the continuing influence of a 1908 novel much-read and much-loved by generations of young Canadian women readers, including Munro. In constructing her orphan and this orphan's sense of the oddness of the family, church, and educational institutions she encounters, Montgomery had somewhat vaguely identified a mismatch between the possible dreams of women and the opportunities society would allow them – a mismatch that would become increasingly visible as the century unfolded.

Social Creativity and Social Stability

As Elizabeth Epperly, Genevieve Wiggins, and others have noted, Montgomery's overt ideological emphases in her novel concern social creativity and social stability, and often do not appear to be gender marked. These emphases are signalled by the image of the brook with which the novel opens, by the kinds of characters it gives prominent roles to, and by the numerous dichotomies it develops. The novel begins by presenting a brook that has 'its source away back in the woods of the old Cuthbert place.' This brook 'was reputed to be an intricate, headlong brook in its earlier course through those woods, with dark secrets of pool and cascade; but by the time it reached Lynde's Hollow it was a quiet, well-conducted little stream, for not even a brook could run past Mrs Rachel Lynde's door without due regard for decency and decorum' (7). The image prepares the way for various contrasts that are to follow: between the eccentric Cuthberts, with their farmhouse set an unconventional distance from the road, and relentlessly orthodox Rachel Lynde; between the dark and somewhat secret past of the orphan girl Anne Shirley and the open predictability that most of the villagers in Avonlea prefer; between Anne's complexity and 'headlong' passions and the self-discipline and quietness Avonlea claims to expect of its children; and between Anne's self-celebrated 'imagination' and the rules, dogmas, and authority of church and school.

The major characters the novelist creates for Anne to relate to all play some part in the conflict between convention and spontaneity that the brook image delineates. Good-hearted but verbally inhibited Marilla Cuthbert, unable throughout most of the book to articulate her feelings toward Anne, is moved in the penultimate chapter to declare her love for her openly and explicitly. Her early preference to adopt a child who will be 'useful' to her and her aging brother, Matthew, contrasts with Matthew's quickly developing preference for a child who is 'interesting' (56). Rachel Lynde, who at the opening appears to be a suspicious and mean-spirited busybody, is by the end a kind neighbour who makes clothes for Anne, offers her practical advice, and has totally reversed her opinion on the wisdom of the Cuthberts' adopting her. Her early advice to Marilla to discipline Anne 'with a fair-sized birch switch' (75) contrasts with Marilla's belief that she could not 'whip a child' (76), as well as with Matthew's reluctance to see Anne subject to any form of punishment. Miss Rogerson's rigid style of teaching Sunday school, a style that allows only her to ask questions, contrasts with the approach of her successor, Mrs Allan, of allowing the children to ask any questions they like. Mr Allan's interesting sermons contrast with the long and doctrinaire ones of the previous minister, Mr Bentley. Anne's comment about the latter, 'I didn't think he was a bit interesting,' leads Marilla to the chapter-ending observation that her own 'secret, uncluttered, critical thoughts had suddenly taken visible and accusing shape and form' (93) in a small girl's words. The repetition of 'secret' here from the earlier passage about the brook is only one of numerous devices that serve to foreground the novel's repeated suggestion that a gender-neutral orthodoxy (shared by Mr Bentley, Miss Rogerson, and Mrs Lynde) is being critiqued through a juxtaposition with 'imagination' and complexity.

However, a male–female binary that poses questions of women's social roles is also concurrently developed by Montgomery. Without the mistake in communication that brings the elderly Cuthbert siblings a girl instead of the 'useful' boy they had requested, Anne's story could not begin. 'You don't want me because I'm not a boy! I might have expected it,' exclaims an indignant Anne in the third chapter when a surprised Marilla complains to Matthew about the sex of the child he has brought home (31). This scene poses the issue of a woman's value. Is she to be 'useful' only as domestic labour – a kind of labour of which Marilla has no need – or can she be useful at productive labour outside the home? This question is returned to at numerous points within the narrative, with the argument that women are at best only of domestic use usually associated with Rachel Lynde, and the argument that a girl can be 'fitted to earn her own living' (262) associated with the pragmatic Marilla.[1]

Scandalous Questions

Yet despite the clarity with which Montgomery delineates such gender issues and suggests progressive and perhaps – in her time – 'scandalous' positions on them, the extent of her novel's progressiveness is arguably ambiguous. The novel risks asking 'scandalous' questions such as why women cannot occupy a church minister's position of authority, but carefully qualifies and contains them. This particular question concerning female clergy is placed by Montgomery in the context of Anne's childish garrulousness – a characteristic that can elsewhere produce quite a mixture of naive, mundane, and penetrating observations. Here Anne's simplicity becomes immediately apparent when she follows her question with the suggestion that the dogmatic Rachel Lynde could have been a minister – that Mrs Lynde can pray as well as the school superintendent, Mr Bell, and could likely learn to preach as well.[2]

Moreover, although the novel allows Anne some years of education, and qualification as a public school teacher by the time she is sixteen, in the overall structure of the novel this attainment is not exactly progress. She has done no more than attain the position that her mother had held some twenty years before. If she should eventually marry her suitor, Gilbert Blythe, who has also qualified as a school teacher, she will have replicated her mother and father's status as school teachers, and in a sense returned her family to the occupational standing it had far in the past. The Anne that the novel develops is not someone who necessarily wishes to lead a life greatly different from that enjoyed briefly by her parents, or lived by Marilla. Although she speaks often about her imagination, what she seems to desire most deeply is a home, and people who will want and care for her. Yet on the other hand the issue of textual production by a woman has been broached – an issue that sixty years later will see another literary orphan, Morag Gunn, leave her very conventional husband, Brooke Skelton, for her own career as a novelist.

Another sign of the novel's ambivalence about the women's capabilities is its handling of the competition between Anne and Gilbert Blythe for top academic honours at the village school and later at Queen's school in Charlottetown. In the early stages of this competition the novel repeatedly emphasizes the key role that Gilbert's teasing of Anne (his calling her 'Carrots'), and the rage and bitterness she feels toward him in response, is playing in motivating her to compete. Here Gilbert is often portrayed as not especially motivated, and as earning the high grades he would have earned no matter what the circumstance, while Anne is portrayed as driven by her anger toward him to perform at a level higher than she would have otherwise attained. 'The rivalry between them,' Montgomery's narrator reports when the competition begins, 'was entirely good-natured on Gilbert's side; but it is much to be feared that the same thing cannot be said of Anne, who had certainly an unpraiseworthy tenacity for holding grudges. She was as intense in her hatreds as in her loves' (151). Yet despite this tenacity, Gilbert appears to top the class at least as often as Anne.

Later, as public school graduation nears, the narrator tells us that Anne's anger toward Gilbert has faded, but not her determination to defeat him, and that Gilbert's competitiveness has increased. 'There was open rivalry between Gilbert and Anne now. Previously the rivalry had been rather one-sided, but there was no longer any doubt that Gilbert was as determined to be first in class as Anne was' (264). Throughout their final exams 'Anne had strained every nerve ... So had Gilbert' (280). This is the period in which Anne has the greatest success, tying Gilbert for the highest grades in the province. Toward the novel's end, during their last competition for grades at Queen's, Montgomery suggests that another change has occurred in Anne. 'Her rivalry with Gilbert was as intense as it had ever been ... but somehow the bitterness had gone out of it. Anne no longer wished to win for the sake of defeating Gilbert; rather, for the proud consciousness of a well-won victory over a worthy foeman' (305). Without the bitterness, however, Anne apparently cannot win. Gilbert earns the medal for first place in the class, while Anne wins only the Avery Scholarship for top standing in English.[3]

There are a number of implications here. One is that Anne may have been performing above her abilities when motivated by bitterness. Another is that her talents may be concentrated mostly around 'imagination' – something associated in the novel elsewhere with women and the arts – and may not range, as Gilbert's seem to do, across the more 'useful' areas of history and mathematics. A third – latent in the ease with which Anne and others accept Gilbert's victory – is that it is normal or natural for a male to win. This imbalance between Gilbert and Anne is reinforced by Montgomery when they look for employment. Gilbert is the Avonlea board's first choice to teach at their school. Anne gets this board's position only because Gilbert, conscious that the power he thereby has over her – 'I was pleased to be able to do you some small service' (328) – is also a power to be generous, declines its offer and signs a contract with a nearby district. Interestingly there are few outstanding scholars among the later female Canadian literary 'orphans,' and several who are presented as having their academic work severely compromised by their sex. Munro's Dell Jordan in *Lives of Girls and Women* believes her final high school exams have been 'sabotaged by love' – her brief but ill-fated liaison with Garnet French. Atwood's Joan Delacourt in *Lady Oracle*, writing her final exams while losing more than a hundred pounds and discovering the perils of being an attractive young woman, knows that she's 'failed at least four papers' (135).

Yet another way in which the novel signals its ambivalence about its various progressive propositions is through its gentle characterization of Rachel Lynde, and the credence it assigns to many of her pessimistic or narrow observations. Although the woman who unfeelingly and gratuitously insults a relatively defenceless eleven-year old Anne in the ninth chapter eventually comes to see her as 'a real smart girl' (268) and 'a credit to [her] friends' (283), and to admit that she had made 'a mistake in judging' her (268), she never abandons her conservative views about corporal punishment or women's education. Yet a year after her cruelty to the orphan, when Anne, after engaging in a humiliating classroom altercation with Gilbert, refuses to return to school, it is Rachel whom Montgomery chooses to give Marilla the shrewd advice to allow Anne to stay away from school as long as she wishes. That January, when a tour by the Canadian prime minister increases Avonlea's interest in politics, it is Rachel whom Montgomery chooses to raise the question of women's suffrage; 'Mrs. Lynde,' reports Anne, 'says if women were allowed to vote we would soon see a blessed change' (155). A year later, after being approached by Matthew to help him give Anne a fashionable dress with puff sleeves and having generously volunteered to sew one, Mrs Lynde is shown by Montgomery producing the extremely non-doctrinaire proposition that 'there's no hard and fast method in the world that'll suit every child' (216). As well, on many occasions Rachel's narrower comments are allowed by Montgomery to become touchstone proverbs for Anne. When her teacher Mr Phillips resigns from her school, Anne says to Marilla 'Dear me, there is nothing but meetings and partings in this world, as Mrs. Lynde says' (182). When various candidates for the church ministry are being interviewed, she on several occasions cites the authority of Mrs Lynde's appraisal of the soundness of their theology. She cites Mrs Lynde as an authority of the health of church ministers (187), on the quality of baking powder (188), and on original sin (196). 'We can't have things perfect in this imperfect world, as Mrs. Lynde says' (263), she exclaims in order to comfort herself when she and her best friend Diana Barry are separated in school by their curricular choices. When Anne is nearly fifteen and growing rapidly, she agrees with Mrs Lynde that once she has had to 'put on longer skirts I shall feel that I have to live up to them and be very dignified' (267). When she is nervously awaiting the results of her final school exams she again comforts herself with one of Rachel Lynde's aphorisms, 'If you can't be cheerful, be as cheerful as you can' (276–7).

Montgomery mixes these moments during which something Rachel Lynde has said becomes of use or comfort to Anne with others in which a Rachel Lynde comment disturbs her, as when Rachel criticizes Mr Allan for 'worshipping the ground' his wife 'treads on,' and Anne objects to her friend Diana that 'even ministers are human.' The overall effect of this mixture, however, together with various generous comments by Marilla (such as that although Rachel's nagging of people to do good often makes them wish to rebel, she is nevertheless 'a good Christian woman and she means well. There isn't a kinder soul in Avonlea' [271]), is to blunt the novel's overall criticism of authoritarianism and dogmatism.

In fact, *Anne of Green Gables* is a novel that has no characters of any importance, including Rachel Lynde, who would have been read in 1908, or can be read today, as antagonistic or malevolent. Potential conflicts between good and evil, arrogance and modesty, cruelty and kindness are either dissolved by Montgomery into ambiguities like those of Mrs Lynde's characterization, or allowed to disappear from the novel along with the negatively portrayed character. The two troubled families that take Anne in immediately after the death of her parents indeed abuse her, but occupy little space in the narrative. The 'sharp-faced, sharp-eyed' (53) Mrs Blewett, about whom 'fearsome tales' circulate regarding 'her temper and stinginess' (52), appears only in the sixth chapter. Members of the Pye family, who in Marilla's view 'can't help being disagreeable' (320), serve to annoy or disappoint Anne, but appear infrequently and have little power to distress her. The more prominent characters who react negatively at some point to Anne – Mrs Lynde, Mrs Barry, and the elderly Miss Barry – are all helped by Anne's insouciant hopefulness to reveal themselves as more flexible and more sensitive than they have previously demonstrated. The most potentially unpleasant characters in the novel are presented as changeable or redeemable by the catalyst of Anne's combination of trust and optimism.

If they are not so changeable, they become – like Josie Pye – minor parts of the narrative.

The Orphan as Touchstone Figure

Overall, there is much evidence in *Anne of Green Gables* of a rather delicate negotiation of conflicting ideological positions – a negotiation that results at some times in the excising of problematic characters and issues and at others in a softening of potentially offensive portrayals. There is almost no evidence of poverty, for example, or of the dehumanizing effects of poverty, except in the fifth chapter. Here we learn that after the infant Anne was orphaned, she was taken in by Mrs Thomas, who was 'poor and had a drunken husband' (47). After the latter's death when Anne is eight, she is taken as a servant by Mrs Hammond, the wife of a sawmill worker, who has eight children and lives 'in a little clearing among the stumps' (48). When the millworker dies, the wife is so impoverished that she must '[divide] her children among her relatives' (48). These scenes of abject poverty, however, are contained not only by being confined to two pages of one chapter, but also by being retrospectively narrated by Anne from the Cuthbert buggy amid the 'lovely' and 'wonderful' landscape of Avonlea. In Avonlea itself, there are no further such scenes – the houses Montgomery lets us see are warm and decently furnished, and children comfortably and often fashionably dressed.

Similarly, potentially negative characterizations are softened, sometimes through humour and sometimes through the sudden and heartwarming appearance of redeeming qualities. Anne's first schoolteacher in Avonlea, Mr Phillips, who is careless and unfair in his discipline, and who neglects many of his teaching duties because of his infatuation with the comely sixteen-year-old Prissy Andrews, is constructed by Montgomery as humanized by this infatuation, and forgivable because of it. (A late-twentieth-century reader is more likely to consider him guilty of sexual harassment.) And positive presentations of characters who are sensitive and generous are qualified often in a much different way by Montgomery's pointing out areas in which they are conventional and reliable. Mr Allan, for example, may give 'interesting' sermons and '[pray] as if he meant it' (185), but it is still important to stress that Mrs Lynde considers his theology sound. Convention and authority in the novel can teased and tweaked, but not discredited.

The various narrow or dogmatic characters who are the most softened in the book are the ones who, like Marilla, Mrs Lynde, or old Miss

Barry, are moved by Anne's influence to greater generosity to others and consequently to greater happiness for themselves. What is interesting here is that these are all characters who are materially comfortable, and who have the means to be generous without great inconvenience to themselves. There is a subtle association in the novel of potential personal worth with a level of material security. Marilla, Mrs Lynde, and old Miss Barry are all landowners, with either money or a source of income. This status, it would seem, has something to do with their being redeemable as human beings. There are noticeably no impoverished characters whose lives are improved by Anne's optimism and innocence.

Yet in some sense this emphasis on the comfortable conditions in Avonlea is produced by the structure of the orphan figure. The literary orphan is typically a part of only two situations: one of poverty and abuse (Oliver Twist's life with Bumble); or one of unaccustomed comfort or hopes of wealth (Pip's life as a student in London, and his hopes of Miss Havisham). In Harold Gray's comic strip *Little Orphan Annie*, Annie – another red-headed orphan – bounces forever between periods of comfort with Daddy Warbucks and ones of poverty on the streets. Montgomery's narrative repeatedly emphasizes the refreshingly comfortable side of this figure, and the stability and age of an Avonlea that in the nineteenth century is already old and with history.

When the novel opens, Anne is about to be brought to the 'old Cuthbert place' (7), a farm and house that were built by a Cuthbert who is long dead, and whose children, Matthew and Marilla, are already greying and only a few years away from decline and death. The farm is so old it has been 'embowered' by the shrubbery that has grown around. Nearby, Montgomery writes, are numerous 'snug farmsteads' (28), and 'the "Avenue," ' ... a stretch of road four or five hundred yards long, completely arched over with huge, wide-spreading apple-trees, planted years ago by an eccentric old farmer' (24). It is this long-settled landscape, with its fruit trees in blossom, that so overwhelms Anne with 'beauty' when she first sees it from the front seat of Matthew's buggy – first the tree-lined lane, which she christens 'the White Way of Delight,' and then, situated beside a bridge, the Barry's pond, which she names 'Lake of Shining Waters.'

Montgomery lets the reader see this settled and humanized landscape through the eyes of the orphan girl, and graphically so when she first sees – among more 'snug farmsteads' – Green Gables.

She opened her eyes and looked about her. They were on the crest of a hill. The sun had set some time since, but the landscape was still clear in the mellow afterlight. To the west a dark church spire rose up against a marigold sky. Below was a little valley and beyond a long, gently-rising slope with snug farmsteads scattered along it. From one to another the child's eyes darted, eager and wistful. At last they lingered on one away to the left, far back from the road, dimly white with blossoming trees in the twilight of the surrounding woods. Over it, in the stainless southwest sky, a great crystal-white star was shining like a lamp of guidance and promise. (28)

This Christmas-card scene with its repetitions of warm words – 'mellow,' 'snug,' 'blossoming' – and its guiding star quickly and not unexpectedly evokes from Anne the word 'home' – 'as soon as I saw it,' she tells Matthew, 'I felt it was home' (28). Beauty here is linked to fruitfulness and prosperity – a plausible enough understanding of beauty in an orphan. Later, Anne will reveal herself willing to have her impetuousness and impulsiveness subjected to numerous restraints in order that she can be accepted and approved by this home and its community.

The impression of age and stability in this scene, linked to other signs of duration and permanence – to vegetation, agriculture, and the church – marks the positive extension of the orphan figure, the orphan's relief at the onset of comfort. One could argue the continuing power of this figure on archetypal grounds, positing its source in Biblical stories of exile and promised land. My own inclination is to argue its power in terms of the material uncertainties and insecurities that the novel itself proposes, and in terms of the new or continuing manifestations of these in the late-twentieth-century cultural context in which one now reads Montgomery.

One of these uncertainties is the continuing and unequal conflict between rural and urban, the beginnings of which are evident throughout Montgomery's text, from the building of the new railway line from Carmody to Avonlea midway through the novel, to Anne's exclamation to Marilla on having first visited Charlottetown. 'I came to the conclusion, Marilla, that I wasn't born for city life and that I was glad of it. It's nice to be eating ice cream at brilliant restaurants at eleven o'clock at night once in awhile; but as a regular thing I'd rather be in the east gable at eleven, sound asleep, but kind of knowing even in my sleep that the stars were shining outside and that the wind was blowing in the firs across the brook' (254–5). Throughout, the novel resists the urban, at times linking it to almost apocalyptic images of ugliness, alienation, and estrangement: 'Anne knew [in Charlottetown] that outside her window was a hard street, with a network of telephone wires shutting out the sky, the tramp of alien feet, and a thousand lights gleaming on stranger faces' (299). It resists the urban nowhere more strongly than at the end when Anne chooses to stay at Green Gables, with Marilla, and teach near Avonlea, rather than continue her studies in Halifax. Her budding relationship with Gilbert, with its potential to allow her to recreate her parents' marriage of two rural schoolteachers, serves also as a sign that you can go home again, that what one once had can be regained. Yet the power of the urban at this very point in the novel is also presented as large and irresistible – as large and irresistible as death. For the urban, constituted in terms of banks and investment instruments, has precipitated Matthew's fatal heart attack. In his hand when he collapses is a city newspaper containing 'an account of the failure of the Abbey Bank,' (315), and with it all of his and Marilla's savings (315).

Anne's subsequent rescue of Green Gables from having to be sold, however, together with the promise of her relationship with Gilbert to regain for herself her parents' circumstances before her birth, allows the novel to stand for contemporary readers as a sign that the urban can be resisted. In addition to the nostalgia that the novel's warm descriptions of snug farmsteads produces (or which the lush panoramas of the novel's recent television adaptation produce), the narrative constructs a complex and most likely inaccurate statement that, with the right combination of duty and sensitivity, the rural world and its values can be retained, despite the changes that continue to threaten it.

Another continuing manifestation of uncertainty involves rules and practices – the struggle to get things 'right,' whether in order to pass a nineteenth-century examination or to retrain today in some new 'information technology' skill. One of the strongest features of *Anne of Green Gables* – and this despite its numerous heart-warming scenes – is the high level of anxiety that permeates Anne's speech. It is as if only Anne knows how uncertain life can be, and what unpleasant surprises change can bring. From her recurrent fears during her first years in Avonlea that Marilla may send her back to the orphanage, to her fear that she will fail her examinations and disgrace her adoptive family, Anne is plagued by uncertainty. Her anxiety is signalled in part by the numerous invocations of authority in her speech: phrases like 'as Mrs. Lynde says,' 'as Mrs. Allan says,' 'as Miss Stacy says' at times punctuate every second of her sentences. It is signalled by her terror of not getting things 'right' – her fear that she will break rules of etiquette when she is invited to visit Mrs Allan, or that she will fail to be a 'model student' at school.

The notion of rules and methods and models both terrifies and fasci-

nates Anne – as it does lower-middle-class Avonlea – because it promises both the disaster of failure and the security of getting things punc-
tiliously correct. Her anxiety is signalled most visibly by her
garrulousness, her nervous habit of talking on about a matter by cover-
ing all its possibilities, and all views of it, as if terrified of omitting the
single 'right' one. This anxiety signals the undoubted power of convention and conformity in Avonlea, and the limits these impose on the
power of Anne's energy and so-called imagination.[4] It signals also the
extent to which Anne's desire for the security of 'home' recurrently
overpowers any desire she has for independence and creativity.

A third area of uncertainty and change that has continued from 1908
to the present concerns the situation of women. Almost all of the recent
critical work on Montgomery and *Anne of Green Gables* has been initiated by women – by Elizabeth Epperly, Genevieve Wiggins, Elizabeth
Waterston, Mary Rubio, and Mavis Reimer. Much of this work has
focused on contextualizing Montgomery's writing within turn-of-the-
century writing by women and on relating it to the difficulties her sex
brought to her own life. Much has focused also on the preponderance of
women speakers in *Anne of Green Gables*, on the particular discourses
available to them, and on the young Anne's infatuation with the discourses of popular and literary romance. Here the nineteenth-century
women's issues of employment and suffrage have segued into a late-
twentieth-century feminist effort to revise understandings of the literary canon and of literary issues in order to give greater prominence to
writers such as Montgomery within literary history. The women scholars who write on Montgomery in the 1990s are in a sense Anne's inheri-
tors, most of them having made in their own lives bargains with
institutional orthodoxy similar to those made by Anne in her journey
from orphan to schoolteacher. In fact, because Montgomery has Marilla
insist that Anne become 'fitted' to earn her own living, the novel has
become increasingly relevant to Canadian women's lives as the percentage of women in the Canadian workforce has risen.

Anne and Personal Identity

A fourth area in which uncertainties evident in *Anne of Green Gables*
engage those of the present is that of personal identity. The late twentieth century has made identity one of its major cultural issues – particularly through various feminist and right-wing resistances to
post-structuralist theories of the role of cultural construction in indi-

vidual identity. For example, proponents of charter schools and home-education have attempted not only to 'take charge' of their own lives but to diminish the cultural influence of public education on their children. From very different ideological positions, advocates of various 'consciousness-raising' techniques to diminish the effects of sexist, racist, or other ideologies have extended the hope that individuals can re-shape who they are and thus gradually change society.

Anne of Green Gables is above all else a story about identity. Anne comes to Avonlea not liking who she is – her thinness, her freckles, her grey eyes, or her red hair. 'I'm so homely nobody will ever want to marry me,' she tells Matthew when they first meet (20). She has learned to accept accusations that she is 'wicked,' and despairs of ever being 'divinely beautiful' or 'angelically good' (24). She particularly does not like her identity as an orphan, nor the name that reminds her of her orphanhood. When Marilla asks her for her name, she replies 'Will you please call me Cordelia?'(32). Marilla responds by suggesting that she should not be 'ashamed' of her own name.

'Oh, I'm not ashamed of it,' explained Anne, 'only I like Cordelia better. I've always imagined that my name was Cordelia – at least, I always have of late years. When I was young I used to imagine it was Geraldine, but I like Cordelia better now. But if you call me Anne please call me Anne spelled with an *e*.'

'What difference does it make how it's spelled?' asked Marilla ...

'Oh, it makes *such* a difference. It *looks* so much nicer ... A-n-n looks dreadful, but A-n-n-e looks so much more distinguished.' (33)

Anne's sense that 'Ann' looks dreadful echoes her belief that her appearance – her freckles, grey eyes, and red hair – is dreadful. She is determined to change herself by renaming herself – a reader never learns in fact whether her birth name was Ann or Anne and whether or not she may be renaming herself at that very moment. Her preference here for the Shakespearean name of Cordelia seems on the surface an attempt to counter her orphanhood by linking herself to social and literary history. But it also, with some irony, reasserts the issues of orphans and parents and parental responsibility: in Shakespeare's play Lear's disowning of Cordelia leads both to her death and to his reacceptance of her, and in a general way highlights the precariousness of the orphaned child.[5]

Two chapters after her exchange with Marilla over her name, Anne will clearly rename herself. After attempting to imagine that her name is

'Lady Cordelia Fitzgerald,' she goes to the mirror and looks at her 'pointed freckled face and solemn gray eyes' (69). Although Montgomery casts this moment as one in which Anne gives up some of her fantasies in order to connect herself to actuality, it is also readable as a moment in which Anne manages to acknowledge actuality without giving up her desire for upper-class identity and standing. '"You're only Anne of Green Gables," she said earnestly, "and I see you just as you are looking now whenever I try to imagine I'm the Lady Cordelia. But it's a million times nicer to be Anne of Green Gables than Anne of nowhere in particular, isn't it?"' (69). Anne's desire to be something other than she has been born to (the orphan state of being from 'nowhere in particular') is paralleled in the novel by Marilla's desire to change her – to 'train' her out of having 'too much to say' (50), to train her to be 'useful' (56), and to teach her to pray devoutly and appropriately.

Yet when Anne does appear to have greatly changed, Marilla experiences nostalgia for the insouciant child she first took in. 'The child she had learned to love had vanished somehow and here was this tall, serious-eyed girl of fifteen, with the thoughtful brows and the proudly poised little head, in her place. Marilla loved the girl as much as she had loved the child, but she was conscious of a queer sorrowful sense of loss' (273). When she expresses these feelings to Anne, however, Anne protests that her identity is still the same: 'I'm not a bit changed – not really. I'm only just pruned down and branched out. The real *me* – back here – is just the same. It won't make a bit of difference where I go or how much I change outwardly; at heart I shall always be your little Anne, who will love you and Matthew and dear Green Gables more and better every day of her life' (296). Interestingly, the stable identity that Anne rather unconvincingly asserts here – or that Montgomery unconvincingly asserts through her – is not necessarily the one she brought to Avonlea. The identity she claims is an Anne defined by her relationship to the Cuthberts and Green Gables. But it is also not necessarily an Anne formed by Marilla, who has in this formulation contributed mostly by 'pruning.'

Overall, there is a extremely strong argument in the novel that Anne discovers who she is, or can be, at the Cuthbert farm, and that she – through her earnestness and optimism – changes Marilla, and influences Marilla's parenting, at least as much as Marilla changes and influences Anne. The novel also implies that Marilla's eventual mellowness ('Marilla Cuthbert has got *mellow*,' announces Mrs Lynde in the last chapter [327]) has also been latent within her since the opening chapters when she first experiences sympathy for Anne or finds herself amused by her naive candour. Ideologically, the novel's claim that Anne is 'not a bit changed' asserts that the wild brook of the opening paragraph has not been channelled, that Anne's impetuous imagination has continued to triumph over social orthodoxy. But of course this is not the case. In the unfolding of the novel Anne has learned many times over not only to reconcile herself with social orthodoxy but on occasion to embrace enthusiastically its practices and genres.

Anne and Kim Campbell

In my 1993 book on then Prime Minister Kim Campbell, *Reading 'KIM' Right*, I suggested that it was Anne's authority-challenging candour, her attempts to control and name her own identity, and the impression of unconventionality her orphanhood gave her, that most connected the public image of the once red-haired, self-renamed, and mother-deserted Campbell to the little girl in Montgomery's novel. Perhaps most important of these to Campbell's public image were the images of independence and convention-disturbing candour – images disastrously subverted when, as the 1993 election campaign unfolded, she seemed increasingly to resemble other politicians. Many of the difficulties Campbell faced in the campaign paralleled those encountered by Montgomery's Anne. In *Fragrance of Sweet-Grass* Epperly observes how the entertainment value of Anne's various confessions and apologies on several occasions leads to her being forgiven because she has been 'interesting' or charming, but how later in the novel the need to prove herself a serious person causes her to adopt a direct and less endearing way of speaking (*Fragrance* 17–38). Campbell, like many contemporary women, found herself in a society that similarly enjoyed viewing the melodramatic self-exhibiting woman, but mistrusted her seriousness. Her quick evolution in public perception from 'candid Kim' to merely another Tory politician – 'a Mulroney in skirts,' as Sheila Copps quipped – closely parallels Anne's evolution from 'original, fiercely independent' orphan (Epperly, *Fragrance* 18) to hard-working and conforming student. Campbell's unsuccessful struggle in the 1993 campaign for a stable and complex image that contained both fierce independence and institutional credibility suggests that the contradiction in Anne of Green Gables' world between 'interesting' women and trustworthy women remains very much with us.

Part of Kim Campbell's difficulties arose from her relationship to the institutional history and practices of the Conservative Party and the recent history of the Mulroney government in which she had served. The conventionality of such institutions can offer a useful backdrop to the unconventionality of the disruptive individual (as when Campbell marched into the 1986 British Columbia Social Credit leadership convention behind a lone piper), but ultimately imposes upon anyone who seeks institutional success. For a woman, a good deal of this conventionality consists of the norms of patriarchy, where even to be female constitutes departure or disruption. In *Anne of Green Gables* this disruption begins when Anne arrives as a girl occupying a space on the Carmody railway platform which the Cuthberts expected would be occupied by a boy.

Anne's complex relationship to institutional practices is apparent in the way in which her early lack of schooling and discipline has helped make her different from other children, and for the most part has given her a potential advantage over them. But this advantage can only be realized within the containment of conventions and education offered by Avonlea and the Cuthbert home. Anne's red hair, passionate temper, and unquenchable hopefulness all represent entertaining and at times even socially useful disruptions of the routines of Avonlea, but are nevertheless presented by Montgomery as needing the discipline of regular bedtimes, curfews, and schedules, sound theology, and conventions of etiquette in order to be productive. Matthew and Marilla's sedate and narrow lives are enriched by this disturbing child, as they acknowledge, but the child herself would have had little chance of happiness or success without them. Similarly, Kim Campbell's refreshing difference from other politicians could be productive only within male-dominated political institutions that valued predictability and sameness. She successively joined the Social Credit government of Bill Bennett in British Columbia and the Conservative government of Brian Mulroney in Ottawa and constructed herself as an irreverent and unpredictable voice within those parties.

Also implicit, but difficult to notice, in the novel is the role that the rigidity of society plays in Anne's early difficulties, and the extent to which she must adjust to its expectations and hypocrisies in order to receive its approbation. The extent of this adjustment, and Anne's awareness of it, is signalled by the prominence the novel gives to the theme of performance. Very early on, Anne learns the usefulness of melodrama, and of people's willingness to accept its fulfilment of social norms. She masters the genres of confession and apology, impressing even Marilla with her invented confession of having lost the amethyst brooch, and triumphing in her apologies to Rachel Lynde and Miss Barry, largely through her grasp of what the genres require. She experiences the same challenge with praying, having to learn the genre in order to avoid scandalizing Marilla and, presumably, God. Her early schooling, done largely on her own, has consisted mostly of memorizing poems, including most of Thomson's *The Seasons*. This learning of other people's scripts continues at school, where she must eventually master the genre conventions of final examinations and produce acceptable answers. Her major triumph at Avonlea before leaving for college is a recitation, 'The Maiden's Vow,' that she gives at the hotel concert. The genre of recitation – so important to the culture of this time – can be read as a metaphor for what has been demanded of Anne since her arrival in Avonlea: the mastery of scripts and roles, including apologizing, confessing, praying, cooking, studying, and entertaining. Far from resisting the mastery of these and other genres, Anne eagerly acquires them, as part of the bargain she wishes to make for acceptance in a home. Interestingly, in investigating Kim Campbell's early life, I found a similar passion for theatrical production. In her history were stories of her having staged impromptu can-cans for her grade 8 classmates, organizing skits for high-school assemblies, and, during her first marriage, taking the female lead in impromptu performances of Gilbert and Sullivan operettas.

In nineteenth-century Avonlea society, of course, someone like Anne would indeed be unlikely to survive unless she had the ability to learn, recite, and mimic such scripts. In our own time women have numerous scripts to master in order to produce identities acceptable to the various parts of society they encounter, a requirement foregrounded in contemporary fiction such as Gail Scott's *Heroine* or Margaret Atwood's *Lady Oracle*. Anne's growing success at performing a variety of scripts – and the way in which the novel, through Marilla's, Matthew's, Mrs Lynde's, and Anne's own expressions of pleasure at these accomplishments, leads a reader to interpret this success as a good thing – masks the extent to which the scripts are coming to control her disruptive and 'imaginative' aspects.[6] Anne may claim that her identity is unchanged, but by the end of the novel she has become a trusted agent of the society that her red hair and passions once disrupted. In effect, the novel that appeared to have been endorsing the 'headlong' brook of its opening paragraph concludes by implying that the brook could survive only in the decorous channels of the Lynde farm.

Conclusion

In the final chapters Anne makes two decisions that further clarify the novel's ideological emphases and further modify the meaning of the image of the headlong brook. One is to give up her scholarship to Redmond College in order to stay at Green Gables with the rapidly aging Marilla. While this is readable as a choice of the rural over the urban, and of gratitude over ambition, the novel also suggests two other readings. One is that it is a choice of security and 'home' over opportunities for change and adventure. By her decision Anne's Avonlea home, the farm of Green Gables, will be saved from having to be sold. Her announcement of this decision to Marilla continues the 'snug farmstead' image of home and links it to family companionship and happiness: 'You sha'n't be dull or lonesome. And we'll be real cozy and happy' (324). The narrator's comment that 'Anne's horizons have closed in' and that 'the path set before her' was now 'to be narrow' but bordered by 'flowers of quiet happiness' (330) suggests that the once headlong brook may be better off in narrower and more decorous channels.

Her second decision is to make peace with Gilbert, extending her hand to him, thanking him for having given up the Avonlea school position, and offering a 'complete confession' of her regret that she had not made peace with him long ago. As well as reinvoking the genres of apology and confession, ones Anne has learned well, this scene, with its distant echoes of Austen's *Pride and Prejudice,* reverses the relationship between passion and decorum offered at the novel's beginning. It is by giving up her passion – her passionate indignation toward Gilbert – and by approaching him with the conventions of good manners that Anne opens the way to a relationship with him.

Anne's last words in the novel reassert the security and stability her recent actions have moved her toward. 'God's in his heaven, all's right with the world,' she cites Browning's song from *Pippa Passes* 'softly' (330). Perhaps all is right, from her sixteen-year-old perspective, and on this particular night, with her world – although I suspect that few contemporary teenage readers, in this time of shrinking employment and ecological decay, would be as sanguine about theirs. Anne is again safely in the home she has wanted since first seeing Green Gables from beside Matthew in his buggy, and with reasonable expectation of being able to continue living in it. Oh that the rest of us should be similarly fortunate. The narrator clearly intends some irony here, as Browning did in *Pippa,* but one that appears directed more against a young woman's continuing optimism than against the stability for which she yearns.

NOTES

1 Mrs Lynde believes that the appointment of the first female teacher in Avonlea, Miss Muriel Stacy, may be 'a dangerous innovation' (197), and later condemns Miss Stacy's introduction of physical culture exercises as the 'goings-on' that come 'of having a lady teacher' (205). She is especially upset when Anne asks why a woman cannot be a church minister, replying that such would be 'a scandalous thing' (270), and later expresses relief when Anne decides not to attend college. 'You've got as much education now as a woman can be comfortable with. I don't believe in girls going to college with the men and cramming their heads full of Latin and Greek and all that nonsense' (325).

2 Perhaps not yet knowing how well the job of minister can be done (Mr Allan has only recently been hired), Anne unwittingly produces a double-edged praise of Mrs Lynde. Her example of a woman who might do the job appropriately is also an example of one who might do so only because her talents resemble those of Mr Bell, someone whom Anne has already appraised as long-winded and uninteresting (91). The irony of this is evident to Marilla, who then undercuts Anne's suggestion by remarking 'drily' that Mrs Lynde could indeed learn to preach. 'She does plenty of unofficial preaching as it is. Nobody has much of a chance to go wrong in Avonlea with Rachel to oversee them' (270).

3 While Montgomery *seems* to have arranged events here once again to balance Anne and Gilbert's accomplishments, as she did before when arranging for them to tie for the highest public school grades in the province, and indeed presents Anne and the Cuthberts as being as pleased by the scholarship as they would have been by the medal, the suggestion of equivalent performance is illusory. Gilbert has received the higher honour, for grades across the curriculum, while Anne has excelled only in English.

4 Even Anne's 'imagination,' however, as a possible ground of her independence and creativity, is suspect in the novel. Almost all of its images are taken from the clichés of gothic romance. The conflict that Montgomery appears to characterize initially as one between Anne's imagination and Rachel Lynde's orthodoxy is textually a conflict between two sets of conventions – those of popular romantic literature and those of a nineteenth-century Prince Edward Island village.

5 Anne's final attempt to imagine Cordelia and Geraldine may have served as a basis for one of the central episodes of Margaret Atwood's novel *Cat's Eye*. This is Anne's fantasy story in which Cordelia, spurned by Bertram de Vere in favour of Geraldine, pushes the latter off a bridge into a stream, causing both her death and that of Bertram, who drowns in an attempt to save her. Afterward 'Cordelia ... went insane with remorse and was shut up in an insane asylum' (210). In *Cat's Eye*, Elaine's friend Cordelia pushes her into a stream below a bridge, and she is 'rescued' by her vision of a madonna-like woman on the bridge. Years later she finds Cordelia confined to an insane asylum.

6 In this regard it is noteworthy that the several crises of the novel, in which a reader is led to fear that Anne may be rejected by the community she so wishes to belong to, all involve incidents in which the community may come to believe that Anne has not truly exchanged her impetuousness for the community's conventions of honesty, politeness, and thoughtfulness. On each occasion – Anne's talking back to Rachel Lynde, Marilla's loss of her brooch, Diana's accidental drunkenness, and Anne and Diana's disturbing of Miss Barry's sleep – Anne must demonstrate that she indeed has accepted the community's conventions.

13

Anne in Hollywood: The Americanization of a Canadian Icon

THEODORE F. SHECKELS

The 1934 motion picture version of *Anne of Green Gables* – screenplay by Sam Mintz and direction by Walter Nicholls, Jr – debuted for Christmas and was very well received, both in the United States and in Canada, as holiday season entertainment. The seventy-nine-minute RKO movie follows Montgomery's novel rather closely during the first third. During the second, major departures in plot are noticeable; and, during the final third, the novel is simply discarded in order, one supposes, to give the motion picture audience the happy ending they escaped to the theatre for. This translation from novel to film has important implications, reducing the novel's proto-feminism, as well as diminishing Anne's subversiveness. A comparison between Montgomery's novel and the 1934 movie offers us a lens through which we can see both what characterizes the American culture reflected in the film and the Canadian culture reflected in the book.

For Better or for Worse? Anne as Hollywood Star

Anne of Green Gables, as has been noted by many commentators, places the story of an orphan girl in a female-gendered context. The 1934 motion picture virtually eliminates this context. The film de-emphasizes the community of women the novel depicts as well as the concept of community itself. Although this arguably feminist characteristic of Montgomery's writing is more apparent in *Anne of Avonlea* (1910) than in her first book, it is nonetheless there. But it is gone from the movie in which Marilla Cuthbert talks with Rachel Barry (a composite character) only three times and Mrs Spencer and Mrs Blewett once. Gone are the references to community activities and organizations, which in the novel are directed by women. Also gone is the sense of 'gossip,' a term that Åhmansson has rehabilitated and used critically and which, she argues, informs the Avonlea community (*A Life* 37–44).

Quite frequently, as Joseph M. Boggs notes in his *The Art of Watching Films*, the cutting of characters as well as the creation of composite characters (thus, Rachel Barry in the movie) are necessary in adaptations from novel to film. What is deemed expendable, however, speaks loudly of cultural biases and preferences. The cuts can be seen as a cultural subconscious, which constitutes the forgotten, the repressed. In the 1934 motion picture of *Anne of Green Gables*, the cuts in characters and conversations have the crucial effect of de-emphasizing friendship among women and girls. Although the novel does not quite give us the friendship between Marilla and Rachel Lynde that Kevin Sullivan's more recent telefilms do, it goes far beyond the brief, stiff encounters of the 1934 movie. Perhaps more tellingly, the movie offers an abbreviated view of the relationship between Anne and Diana Barry, one that does not permit either the personality of Diana or the girls' close relationship to emerge. Among other scenes cut are the afternoon during which Anne inadvertently got Diana drunk; Anne's request to her 'bosom friend' for 'a lock of [her] raven tresses'; Anne and Diana's 'attack' on Miss Barry in the guestroom bed; and the many ways the two girls communicate with each other as kindred spirits. Equally important in a study of the movie's repression is its systematic elimination of several of Anne's female role models – Anne's beloved teacher Miss Stacy, Diana's Aunt Josephine Barry, and the Sunday school teacher Mrs Allan – all of whom are an important part of the gendered context the novel creates. With them disappears both the concept of women mentoring women *and* the validity two of these women give to the single life.

Within the female-gendered context, the novel offers the story of Anne's growth into what Davey in the preceding chapter calls 'the hard-won power of Canadian womanhood.' The motion picture strategically recentres the story on Anne and Gilbert's courtship from very early in the film, when Anne flirtatiously pursues Gilbert and Gilbert earnestly pursues Anne. With this recentring, Anne's quest for beauty, achievement, and independent worth recedes and her character changes significantly: in the movie she brags to Diana that she can wrap Gilbert around her little finger; she is motivated to confess to losing Marilla's brooch because she wants to go on the hay ride in order to 'make Gilbert Blythe eat right out of [her] hand'; and she invites Gilbert to kiss her after he saves her from drowning. She even invents a rival beau to make Gil jealous.

Having so recentred the story, the motion picture must follow the new story to its logical conclusion. The motion picture ends by joining Anne and Gilbert in what we presume will be marriage, while the novel ends with Anne and Gilbert – especially Anne – talking about their friendship, not their wedding, and merely hints at the possibility of their union at some future point. Male–female friendship, then, is – maybe – possible in the novel; however, that possibility is lost in the movie because of the changes the RKO team made in the plot. The film also changes the background story to a family feud initiated when John Blythe stole away Matthew Cuthbert's intended bride. Not only does this change privilege the actions of male characters by making the story that of the rivalry in romance between John Blythe and Matthew Cuthbert for an unnamed bride instead of that of an ill-fated romance between John Blythe and Marilla Cuthbert, but the change alters the force blocking Anne and Gilbert's relationship from one within Anne to one external to her/them. In short, the movie's plot becomes *Romeo and Juliet* superimposed upon *Anne of Green Gables*, thereby marginalizing Anne as the passive victim of circumstances. The movie eliminates the parallel between Anne and Marilla as proud, independent women, while also reducing Anne's heroism to the sacrificial.

L.M. Montgomery and the Reception of the Movie

RKO was trying to turn a profit with a Christmas-time 'feel good' movie that mixes several tried formulae. Therefore, *Anne* was packaged for the holidays as a combination of plots: young lovers overcoming feuding families; orphan winning love; gallant young hero saving the day. The studio's desire probably was to make the novel fit the formulae. If damage was done to the novel in the process, it mattered little: after all, the novel was merely a 'children's book.' Reviews were positive, welcoming the film as the holiday fare RKO intended it to be.

Montgomery's own reaction to the 1934 film is best characterized as mixed. 'I don't know why I keep on going to see my favourite books screened. The result is always a disappointment,' writes Maud in her diaries in 1922, after watching *Quo Vadis* (*SJ* 3: 26). In the recently published fourth volume of her *Selected Journals*, she expressed some satisfaction at seeing her story showcased in the very glamorous medium of the Hollywood film: 'on the whole, the picture was a thousand-fold better than the silent film in 1921,' Maud writes, before adding. 'The whole picture was so entirely different from *my* vision of the scenes and the people that it did not seem *my* book at all. It was just a pleasant, well-directed little play by somebody else' (*SJ* 4: 326). Montgomery was alert to the changes that RKO or Sam Mintz or Walter Nicholls, Jr, had made: 'Gilbert was much too crude' and 'Diana was a complete wash-out,' she writes (*SJ* 4: 326). She seems especially alert to the changes in the film's final third: as she noted in 4 November 1939 letter to a Mrs Aiken, 'As for the movie, I liked the first two-thirds of it reasonably well but the last third I did not care for' (*Road* 11). Her objections were not, however, sufficient for her to be concerned over what the same studio, screenwriter, and director were going to do to *Anne of Windy Poplars*. In that same letter, she looked forward to the 1940 film on the later Anne book.

Why Montgomery and her fans did not protest more forcefully at the distortions is a question worth considering. The most compelling answers are related to the powerful concept of genre, which is doubly at work in this case, because the movie was viewed and the book was read within distinct generic constraints operating on viewer and reader. There are many motion picture formulae, as Thomas Schatz notes in *Hollywood Genres*, the most well-defined American film genre being the Western. Since audiences view cinema through a generic lens, directors can either conform to the definition or go beyond it. As Stanley J. Solomon notes in *Beyond Formula*, directors as auteurs tended to take the latter course. The studios of the 1930s, however, which churned out movie after movie, were not the place for auteurs. The studio directors frequently tended to conform and, thereby, give the audience what they had come to expect.

Viewers were enthralled by the glamour of Hollywood; the filmmaking technology impressed in a time before television. They, therefore, beatified the motion picture itself. It was a wonderful tribute to L.M. Montgomery and her novel that a Hollywood studio wanted to make *Anne of Green Gables* into a movie. To audiences enthralled by the ability to lose oneself in the magic of film, the motion picture of *Anne* offered just such an experience. Even Montgomery, who was well-aware of the inaccuracies, spoke in terms of liking or disliking the movie as an entirely separate artefact.

To what extent were viewers aware of the inaccuracies? Many had never read the novel, because it was 'for' adolescent girls, but what about those who came to the film with some familiarity with Montgomery's book? The answer to this question returns us to the question of genre and to Janice Radway's important study of the romance genre and how women construct the meanings of members of the genre. In

Reading the Romance, Radway rejects the New Critical assumption that a text has a meaning that 'good' readers (such as critics with advanced degrees) can decipher. Texts, rather, have the many meanings the many readers construct from them. Readers, however, do not read in a cultural vacuum. One reason why graduate school–trained critics read in similar ways is that they have become acculturated in ways of reading through that shared training. Women who read popular romances are similarly acculturated in ways – very different ways – of reading. As a discourse community, these women, their ways of reading, and the meanings they make can be studied empirically. And Radway sets out to do just that.

Romance readers construct two meanings. The overt one confronts the patriarchy; its construction is 'cathartic in the sense that it allows the reader[s] to express in the imagination anger at men that [they] would otherwise censor or deny' (Radway 215). However, readers simultaneously construct a covert meaning based on their acquired understanding of that offensive patriarchal behaviour. The romance teaches that the male behaviour, if read 'correctly,' is really an expression of men's love. Not only does this covert meaning thwart the rebellion of the overt, but it discourages the future construction of the overt in so far as the readers are taught, through reading, to be 'correct' readers from the outset. Thus, what seems as if it might be a liberating experience is actually an act that confirms the patriarchy and the gender relations allowed within it.

If readers, especially early ones, of Montgomery's novel read it in a manner similar to that which Radway describes, they might well applaud Anne's challenges to the patriarchy, embodied largely by Gilbert Blythe, only to realize that his affronts are inspired by his love of Anne. Once Gilbert (and the patriarchy) are 'correctly' read, the diegesis may well shift from one focused on Anne's subversion of the patriarchy to one focused on Anne and Gilbert's courtship. Within such a diegesis, certain episodes – for example, most of Anne's heroic triumphs – become expendable. Such a diegesis is very much in line with the story the 1934 motion picture offers. Therefore, female readers may not have found the movie to be a significant distortion of the book.

The Movie and Canadian Culture

The changes that the RKO team made when they transformed *Anne of Green Gables* into a movie nonetheless may have to do with the novel's female authorship and the motion picture's male production team, which privileged different elements in the novel. However, I would like to suggest that the translation reflects a further difference, one that is connected to the cultural differences between the United States and Canada, a difference that emerges clearly from a feminist and post-colonial perspective.

The comparison between the movie and the novel alerts us to how Montgomery's novel offers a text that privileges community, especially that formed by women, and friendship among girls and among women, including intergenerational ones such as that between mother and daughter. The novel furthermore offers strong role models for adolescent girls, including ones that do not include marriage. The novel offers the story of a girl seeking beauty, achievement, and independent self-worth rather than a beau or husband. As it traces this story and, in conjunction with it, offers us glimpses of other women's life stories, the novel validates the actions of women, whether the consequences be good or ill, rather than their reactions or their passive victimization. Insofar as the novel postpones marriage, it marginalizes it as a defining moment in a woman's life: rather than focusing on what happens to a woman, the novel focuses on what she does. Thus, Montgomery's book portrays female heroism in active, consequential terms. Within this definition of heroism, sacrifice plays a part rather than being the essence. And male heroes also make sacrifices, implying an androgynous definition of the term 'heroic.'

Montgomery's novel, so described, is certainly proto-feminist. The movie, by contrast, is a different text. Community and the relationships among women and girls within it are suppressed. Rather, the individual is stressed, with the male individual (Gilbert) acting and the female individual (Anne) largely reacting. Within the movie, marriage is *the* goal: no other roles – no other ways to define one's self – are valued. Gilbert overcomes the family feud that stands in the way of his relationship with Anne; he does so by heroically (although indirectly) saving Matthew Cuthbert's life. Anne all the while waits. She remains passive, while the male acts heroically.

The movie reflects a very male culture, oriented toward the individual and emphasizing male action and female passivity. In effect, the film suggests the dominance of male cultural values in the United States at the time the motion picture was made. The book reflects a female culture. *Anne* was written by a woman for a predominantly female readership. One, however, is tempted to push the analysis further and explore the extent to which the culture implicit within *Anne* is a reflection of Canada. As a popular icon within the national culture, Anne Shirley ranks right up there with the moose, the beaver, the Mountie, and the Habs. What is it then that marks Anne as Canadian?

The answer to this question is implicit in the extent to which feminism and post-colonial thinking have common ground. Many have noted the similarities between the oppressed position of women and the oppressed position of post-colonial nations and have noted the double colonization of women in such nations. Many, such as Kirsten Holst Petersen and Gayatri Spivak, have also noted how double colonization puts women in a bind, for fighting against post-colonial oppression can result in an uneasy alliance with the oppressing patriarchy in the colonized nations. Others, notably Ketu H. Katrak and Trinh T. Minh-Ha, have attempted to revise both critical discourses to achieve a rapprochement between these two positions.

We can acquire some sense of what that loosely defined common ground might be if we embrace the values implicit in the description of the feminine culture implicit in *Anne of Green Gables* and use those values within a post-colonial context. If we do so, we arrive at a post-colonial culture that recognizes the community and its history, that privileges the actions of those within the culture rather than chronicling their reactions, and that provides self-worth by exorcizing the patriarchal or colonial view of self as 'other.' The common ground also is subversive. Within post-colonial theory, the target of the subversion is frequently the dominant discourse itself. Critics as varied in background as Linda Hutcheon ('Circling'), Helen Tiffin, Abdul R. JanMohamed, and Homi K. Bhabha ('Signs') have demonstrated how the master's discourse can be subverted. Although subversion may well be far from the Canadian cultural stereotype, the number of writers, primarily women, who use their work to subvert has been chronicled by Lorna Irvine, Patricia Smart, and others. The list includes writers such as Nicole Brossard, France Théoret, Yolande Villemarie, and Madeleine Gagnon from the French tradition and Marian Engel, Margaret Laurence, Alice Munro, and Margaret Atwood from the English.

I list Atwood last because she has a place in both the use of subversive strategies and the theorizing about them in her 1972 *Survival*. Although Atwood's work has been critiqued by some – for example, Russell Brown, Frank Davey, Robert Kroetsch, and B.W. Powe – her analysis of what some have dismissively called 'victim-lit' is indeed relevant to a conception of Canadian culture as post-colonial. Atwood traces several stages of consciousness: in the early stage, one survives. In the second stage one goes beyond surviving. One, I would suggest, begins to act subversively. In the third, one refuses to accept victimization, and, in the fourth and last, one becomes 'a creative non-victim' (38). Atwood focuses her attention on the liberation one achieves in this last stage. A superimposition of post-colonial theory onto Atwood's thoughts shifts the focus from survival as a theme to the subversive strategies that inform the liberation from victimization.

Anne Shirley is iconic within the post-colonial Canadian culture because she is subversive. Anne survives her victimization, rejects it, and then passes beyond the third victim position to the prized 'creative' fourth. At the novel's beginning, she blames fate for her being an orphan and having red hair. Once she gains acceptance in the Cuthbert home, she begins combatting all of the assumptions that might hold her back. On the surface, she challenges those who would oppress her as orphan or woman; just beneath the surface, she offers to her community and her readers a set of values that one finds compelling, as one reads, and 'feminine,' if one takes the time to scrutinize them.

The difference between the experience of reading the novel and the experience of studying the novel takes us to the second way the novel is subversive. Reading the novel has, since its original publication in 1908, been a delightful experience – for children and for adults, for women and men. Anne, who she is and what values she stands for, has been joyfully embraced by generations. If one were to tell these readers that Anne or the book was subversive, some consumers of the Anne novels might react with surprise. Some might, upon reflection, recognize the rebel in her breaking her slate over Gilbert Blythe's head or the undaunted in her walking the ridgepole at the Andrews farm, but neither Anne the rebel nor Anne the undaunted would necessarily strike these readers as subversive. She is simply too young and too charming to be subversive. However, when one recognizes through the lens provided by contrasting film and novel what Anne truly represents, her – and Montgomery's – deeply subversive nature becomes apparent.

The novel has a doubled voice that makes possible multiple readings: one speaks to the reader immediately; the other delivers its subversive message subtly but nonetheless powerfully. This doubled-voicedness – something Mikhail Bakhtin finds in works, be they by Rabelais or Dostoevsky, that challenge hegemonic discourse – is among the strategies critics often ascribe to post-colonial writers. Elaine Showalter, in 'Women's Time,' identifies this strategy within the discourse of feminist criticism; Linda Hutcheon, in *The Canadian Postmodern*, identifies this strategy within the discourse of Canadian women writers; Ashcroft, Griffiths, and Tiffin, focusing more on the level of words, identify this strategy as part of the subversive appropriation of the centre on the part of post-colonial writers from Canada, the Caribbean, Africa, India, and Australia. This subversive strategy then takes us again to the common ground between the feminist and post-colonial agenda.

Conclusion

Anne of Green Gables may have conquered Hollywood, but at a costly price. The critical elements that made the novel a distinctly Canadian and feminist work were sacrificed in the process of translation. The comparison of movie and novel in turn highlights the Canadian novel's, and the Canadian culture's, subversive components. As George Bluestone noted back in 1957 in his classic study *Novels into Film*, cuts are the most striking characteristic when directors or screenplay writers translate a novel into a movie. The episodic nature of the excised scenes that were noted in this essay facilitated their deletion. Nonetheless, the 1934 motion picture adaptation of *Anne of Green Gables* reveals much that is interesting about Hollywood, audiences in the mid 1930s, and Canada. The adaptation points to ways in which the motion picture industry was hegemonic, while also highlighting that Hollywood was ultimately inspired by the profit motive. The absence of a negative response to the adaptation reveals interesting dimensions of how viewers viewed films as glamorous entertainment within expected generic categories. Finally, both the subversive qualities of Anne and the subversive way she and Montgomery celebrate these qualities – dimensions of the 1908 book highlighted by the movie's distortions – reveal something of the nature of the culture or identity of Canada that the nation shares with its icon Anne.

14

Reflection Piece –
Anne Shirley and the Power of Literacy

SHARON J. HAMILTON
Interviewed by DIANNE HICKS MORROW

Every summer thousands of girls and women make the pilgrimage to Green Gables, the home of that fictional icon of Canadian culture, Anne Shirley. On a muddy April day in 1997 a fifty-two-year-old Winnipeg-born woman made hers. In the nineteenth-century kitchen of Green Gables, she proudly autographed her own book for the site director, who had opened the out-of-season Green Gables for her. Sharon J. Hamilton, now living in the United States and teaching at Indiana University, is the author of *My Name's Not Susie: A Life Transformed by Literacy* (1995), an autobiographical account of the author's childhood in Canadian foster homes – and a work in which Anne figures prominently.

My Name's Not Susie chronicles how Hamilton slowly found a positive sense of identity through the pages of books – such as *Anne of Green Gables*, where she met another misunderstood young girl. As the following interview reveals, Anne's story as an orphan not only paralleled Sharon Hamilton's childhood experience, but, more importantly, Anne's survival strategies, the power of words and literacy, became an inspiration for Sharon Hamilton, the child and the adult writer. Like Anne, Sharon Hamilton as a child intuitively understood the power of naming. When one of her foster mothers, Mrs Simmons, wished to rename her, Sharon told her, 'I'm not Susie Simmons,' and insisted on being called by her own name (Hamilton 13). It is her connection with Anne that forms the basis for my interview, which explores the links between her reading of Montgomery's fiction and her own self-constructions in writing, as well as between her modelling on a fictional character and her growth and development through the power of words.

DIANNE: Sharon, you grew up in urban Manitoba, whereas Anne Shirley lived in rural Nova Scotia and Prince Edward Island. Yet as a child, you

r identified with this character, as you detail in your book. Would
escribe the connections you detected as a child?

: We both lost our parents at an early age (although I was taken
ine because they did not look after me, whereas Anne's loved her
d of fever). We each lived in many foster homes where there was
no love or nurturing. The expectations of society for Anne were
ı; nor were they for me. However, Anne's expectations for her
were very high; so were mine. We were both adopted by a family
ected some other kind of person – Anne's family wanted a boy;
ly wanted a compliant and grateful little girl to be quiet and
ıe's first rewarding experiences were to be good in school, and
she always came either first or second in class. My first rewarding experiences were also in school, and I was among the top three in class up
until high school. We both went to teacher's college and began teaching
in a one-room eight-grade schoolhouse. Anne enjoyed writing, and
used writing as a means of coping with her world. So did I. Anne thought
herself unattractive. So did I.

DIANNE: You certainly identified with Anne. In what ways did she become
a role model for you?

SHARON: Possibly the strongest way Anne was a role model was in the
area of ethics and values. She would not lie or steal. I did. But I wanted
so much to be like Anne that I would imagine her watching over me
when I was tempted to lie or steal. Increasingly her 'presence' began to
have a stronger effect on these impulses, and I began to take more
control over my ethical and moral behaviour, in order to be worthy of
Anne, in order to be more like her. But her optimism was also infectious,
and gave me strategies for buoying myself up when circumstances were
pulling me down. And, since she always got into trouble when she lost
her temper, I tried to go her one better and control my temper (that was
uphill work!). She grew up to be the kind of woman I wanted to be: kind,
generous to others, intelligent, loving and loved, hard working, consci-
entious, lovely, at home and at ease in her community.

DIANNE: Could you describe Anne's effect on your sense of health and
well-being?

SHARON: Anne made me feel less alone in being unwanted and lonely. Her
story offered me hope for the possibility of a better life in terms of

having my parents and my school chums eventually like me better. She had her imaginary friends, just as I had mine, and so I felt less abnormal to realize that others made up friends too. Trying to be good, she often ended up in trouble inadvertently. So did I. I felt less 'bad,' or rather that other people who did not want to do bad things or get into trouble managed to do so, just as I did.

When things went wrong, she always held her head high rather than ranting and raving as I often did. From her I learned more sense of dignity; learned how to honour my efforts even when the results did not go as I had hoped. I had a tendency to feel sorry for myself. Anne did not. She used her imagination to transport her beyond the circumstances that made her unhappy. I followed her imaginative lead, and learned to cope more effectively when things did not go well. Anne gave me hope for a better life, and several strategies to work toward achieving that life.

DIANNE: When Marilla forces Anne to tell the truth about her past, Anne admits that she was orphaned at three months when her parents died of fever. She lived with Mrs Thomas, a scrubwoman with a drunken husband and four children to look after, until she was eight. When Mrs Thomas was widowed, Mrs Hammond from up the river took Anne because she needed help with her eight children. When he died, ten-year-old Anne ended up in the asylum for four months until Mrs Spencer came to send her to Avonlea. When Anne tells Marilla she's sure the folks she lived with meant to be good to her, Montgomery writes, 'What a starved, unloved life she had had – a life of drudgery and poverty and neglect; for Marilla was shrewd enough to read between the lines of Anne's history to divine the truth' (49). How does your experience of foster homes compare with Anne's?

SHARON: I had already been in eighteen foster homes by the time I was adopted at three years of age. I had been labelled a borderline autistic, a potential sociopath, and a bad apple by the Winnipeg Children's Aid Society before I was three. Then there were the abusive homes, such as I describe in *Susie*, where the foster father molested me and then threw me down the basements stairs, reporting to the hospital that I had ridden my trike down the basement stairs. The record showed no police follow-up of that, but then I was not allowed to read the record, since I had been a ward of the court at that time. When a Children's Aid Society staff person read parts of the record to me when I was doing research for *Susie*, that is where I learned about my saying 'I'm not Susie Simmons,' the comment that led to the title of my book. The similarities with Anne are that we were both 'social problems' that needed to be solved and resolved rather than young human beings who needed to be loved.

DIANNE: Have L.M. Montgomery and Anne influenced your writing style and/or your personal style? I can't help but notice a similar flare for the dramatic in Anne and you.

SHARON: Right from the moment that Anne responded to Rachel Lynde's greeting, 'How are you?' with 'I'm very fine in body, though considerably rumpled in spirit, thank you,' I was charmed by Anne's style. In fact, I even answered that question myself with the same phrase a few times, but never found a response any more welcoming than Rachel Lynde's bemused frostiness. But I would say that I mirrored Anne's romance with words, her love of polysyllabic words that filled the mouth and danced a romantic harmony of sound and imagination.

Of course, L.M. Montgomery controls Anne's style, as well as the more severe style of Marilla and gossipy style of Rachel Lynde, all of whom nonetheless exude human values of warmth and caring. It's a style that bespeaks a kinder, gentler time, an intention not to wound too caustically, even when language is used as a control or a come-uppance. And I do believe I use language similarly, with similar values as the motivating force behind lexical choices.

On a more personal level, Anne's 'style' of responding to situations with a knee-jerk over-the-top worst possible interpretation of others' intentions is very similar to me. I don't think she influenced me in this, because it is the way I have always been, though I have tried for many years (decades even) to grow out of it. Style is so close to character, is, I suppose, the external expression of character. Yet the aspects of Anne's style (or character) that were already similar are the characteristics that got her and me both into trouble. The aspects of her character or style that I tried to emulate (honesty, sincerity, integrity) were aspects of Anne's way of being that took a lot more struggle and time to achieve.

DIANNE: Please talk about how the subtitle of your book, *A Life Transformed by Literacy*, is a theme in both Anne's life and yours.

SHARON: In Anne's life, reading was both a solace from the pain of her real world and a pathway to other (im)possible worlds; so it was with me. Reading both inspired and fed her imagination, whether she was floating down the Lake of Shining Waters as a tragic heroine from Tennyson or figuring out beautiful names for herself, such as Cordelia. In both these instances, literature was shaping her notion of the ideal identity for herself while the practicalities of her existence were shaping other aspects of her identity. And reading also shaped her writing, which propelled her into public acknowledgment of her abilities, and began to carve a whole new existence for her (much like L.M. Montgomery, I assume).

Literacy transformed my life on several levels. First it provided an escape into a more pleasant and more predictable literary world, where, in most instances, the good were rewarded and the bad were punished, and children were, by and large, appreciated and loved, though not always. None of the people in the books and stories I read seemed to live lives possible to me, but I was fascinated by them anyway.

However, with Anne, there were so many points of similarity that I began to see her way of living as a possible way. And the core of that seemed to be her absolute honesty (which got her into trouble more often than out of trouble during her early days). Anne would not lie and she would not steal, and I did both. But if I wanted to live the possible life held out to me in her fictive world (a world that became less fictive and more possible the more I identified with Anne), I had to stop lying and stealing. It was not easy, and it took not several months but several years, but the turning point came when I would say to myself: Anne would not lie about this; Anne would not steal this. Sometimes it worked; sometimes it only delayed the act; but eventually, once I progressed from imitating Anne's actions and decisions to understanding the reason and necessity for honesty, the transformation occurred. I moved from pretending to behave the way I wanted to behave, to reasoning out each decision, to actually, automatically, behaving honestly. So the ethical transformation was the second, and the most significant, literacy transformation that occurred as a result of reading *Anne*. But other transformations occurred as well.

The third was an enhanced acknowledgment of myself as a human being who, while different from others, should have some access to love and affection. I thought I was out of the running for that. Anne never thought she was out of the running. She just thought her time hadn't come yet, but that the time was right around the corner. Her 'right around the corner' philosophy became part of my philosophy, and, with it, a slightly better sense of well-being.

But while literacy was providing paths of escape in an existential and then ethical sense, it was also building up my abilities to engineer a more powerful kind of 'escape' because it was enabling me to think in increasingly diverse ways. My thinking capacities had been shaped by foster homes that did nothing to foster cognitive abilities and by an adoptive home that, while introducing me to literacy, still believed that children should be seen and not heard and that a difference of opinion was a contradiction. Under those circumstances, it is extraordinarily difficult to develop the kind of scholarly scepticism and modes of inquiry that are essential for critical thinking. However, as my reading became more sophisticated, and I began to encounter a wide variety of ways in which people with different perspectives discussed and came to deeper understanding and some kind of resolution, I learned not just thinking, but ways of thinking, ways of negotiating difference, ways of understanding untenable positions, ways of seeking alternative approaches. This new understanding had a powerful impact on my social as well as intellectual life, as I became able to appreciate those whom I did not understand, and became able to appreciate those who did not understand me. Tolerance, civility, responsibility, inquiry: all moved from abstract nouns to behaviour, and from behaviour into my evolving understanding of what kind of a person I was – and am – becoming (because the process continues).

DIANNE: Thank you, Sharon.

Sharon Hamilton's muddy April visit to Prince Edward Island included her courageous and riveting talk to over one hundred literacy workers and learners at the PEI Literacy Alliance conference. She received a standing ovation – additional proof, if she needed it, that she had indeed achieved her goals by taking the personal risk to write her own painful story. She is asked to speak all over the United States and Canada. Sharon Hamilton now does for thousands of adults what Anne Shirley did for her: she inspires them to recreate themselves and their lives, thus exemplifying, like the fictional Anne, the transformative power of literacy.

15

Japanese Readings of *Anne of Green Gables*

YOSHIKO AKAMATSU

In recent years in Japan, L.M. Montgomery's *Anne of Green Gables* has established the image of the Canadian who lives with nature and is considerate of others. With almost all of Montgomery's works of fiction available in translation, it is no wonder that so many Japanese people have been able to encounter Canadian culture through her books. Besides, there are so many Anne-goods made in Japan that many Japanese, both children and adults, have heard of *Akage no An*, Red-haired Anne, even if they have never read any of the books. Some scholars lament the lack of knowledge in Japan about other Canadian authors, some critics complain of the unpopularity of modern realistic works of children's literature, and some professors despise *Anne of Green Gables* for the very reason of its popularity, but they cannot stop the readers from loving Anne. The popularity of Anne shows Japanese interest in Western culture. As good readers, the Japanese have found diverse meanings in this novel. This paper will analyse how Japanese readers have reread *Anne of Green Gables*, in the modern, post-war society.

Akage no An, *Wakakusa Monogatari*, and *Haiji*

Let me begin by considering *Anne of Green Gables* in the history of Japanese children's literature, comparing it with *Little Women* and *Heidi*, all of which are considered classics of children's literature in the West. I will examine three points: the time of translation, the meaning of the Japanese title, and the present status of publication. It is worth noting that the modern history of Japanese children's literature began in the late nineteenth century, during the Meiji Restoration, when Western children's literature was often translated into Japanese. 'Learn about the

West' was one of the policies of the Japanese government, and learning from written texts was the first step of westernization in the educational system. As a result of this policy, *Little Women, Heidi,* and *Anne of Green Gables* were first introduced to Japanese readers in translation and were included in various collections of famous stories for boys and girls.

First, Louisa May Alcott's *Little Women* (1868) was introduced by Syuho Kitada in 1906, during the Meiji period (1868–1912), which was some time after the opening of Japan in the 1850s. Second, a famous woman writer, Yaeko Nogami, translated *Heidi* (1880) by Johanna Spyri in 1920, in the middle of the Taisho period (1912–26), when so-called Taisho-democracy flourished. Third and last, L.M. Montgomery's *Anne of Green Gables* (1908) was translated by Hanako Muraoka and published in 1952, during the period of Showa (1926–89) and the last year of occupation by the U.S. Army after Japan's defeat in the Second World War.

The translation process from one language into another yields some transformation. Sometimes the translators change the titles based on their, or the publishers', beliefs about and prejudices toward the young readers of the day. This was the case when *Little Women, Heidi,* and *Anne of Green Gables* were translated into Japanese. The Japanese titles of these books reflect the adult co-readers' interpretation of the text and show the tastes of the Japanese. When *Little Women* was first translated by Kitada, his title was *Sho Fujin* (which means both 'A Little Woman' and 'Little Women' because there is no distinction between singular and plural in Japanese). In later translations, Kenji Uchiyama's title was *Yon Shojyo* (*Four Girls*) in 1923, and Sakiko Nakamura's was *Yon Shimai* (*Four Sisters*) in 1932. Although I am not sure who first used it, the title *Wakakusa Monogatari* (*The Story of Young Grass*) was used in Katsue Yoshida's translation in 1958, and it is the accepted title to this day.

The original English title comes from a letter Mr March writes his wife early in the novel: 'I know they [my girls] will remember all I said to them, that they will be loving children to you, will do their duty faithfully, fight their bosom enemies bravely, and conquer themselves so beautifully that when I come back to them I may be fonder and prouder than ever of my *little women*' (11; my italics). It is clear that, though they are still young, Mr March wants his daughters to be independent young women. The title itself symbolizes the American spirit. In contrast, the established Japanese title, *The Story of Young Grass*, emphasizes the tender freshness of youth and appeals to readers with its lyricism. The focus has been shifted from the independent female protagonists to the romantic ambiguous story of youth.

As for *Heidi*, the first translator, Nogami, named the book *Haiji*, which is almost the same as the original title and has a similar pronunciation in Japanese phonetics. Later, in 1950, Nogami called the book *Arupusu no Yama no Otome* (*A Damsel of the Alpine Mountains*), and Yoshio Minami used the title *Arupusu no Shojyo* (*An Alpine Girl*) in 1954. *Haiji* and *An Alpine Girl* are both still used in Japanese translation. The two Japanese titles make the readers imagine an innocent girl who lives on a beautiful Alpine mountain.

Anne of Green Gables has been published in Japanese as *Akage no An* (*Red-haired Anne*) since Muraoka's first translation. Interestingly, Muraoka herself had thought the title would be *Madobe ni yoru Shojyo* (*A Girl Standing beside a Window*) or *Yume miru Shojyo* (*A Dreaming Girl*). As she did not know which was better, she listened to her family's opinions and followed her daughter Midori's suggestion (Miki 93). This anecdote shows that Muraoka had interpreted the text as the story of a lonely girl or a girl who loves to imagine, while her daughter was impressed with the protagonist's physical appearance, which is the cause of an inferiority complex and a series of amusing predicaments in the text. In the end, *Red-haired Anne* has been accepted as the title. Few young Japanese readers understand what green gables are, but everyone understands the nuances of a red-haired girl. It provides a vivid image and evokes the curiosity of the Japanese, who have dark eyes and black hair. In addition, the Japanese title has the effect of assonance (*Akage no An*) and is easy to remember. However, it detracts from the connection made in the original title between the heroine and the nineteenth-century Canadian farmhouse symbolic of home. It also loses the effect of the original title being 'a combination of a name and an epithet' (Nikolajeva 85).

As both *Little Women* and *Anne of Green Gables* have sequels, it is interesting to see their Japanese titles. The sequels of *Little Women* are simply called as *The Second Story of Young Grass* and *The Third ...* and *The Fourth ...*, which seem to show the translators' lack of enthusiasm for Jo's married life. In the case of the Anne series, the changed titles reflect the translators' or the publishers' manipulation of the young readers. *Anne of Avonlea* was called *An no Seisyun* (*Anne's Adolescence*) by Muraoka in 1954 and was finally literally translated as *Avonri no An* by Sumiko Ishikawa in 1990. *Anne of the Island* was named *An no Aijyo* (*Anne's Affection*) by Muraoka in 1954, *An no Konyaku* (*Anne's Engagement*) by Sakiko Nakamura in 1959 and *Daigakusei An* (*A University Student, Anne*) by Ishikawa in 1991. *Anne of Windy Poplars* was titled *An no Kofuku* (*Anne's Happiness*) by Muraoka in 1957 and *An no Ai no Tegami* (*Anne's Love Letters*) by Nakamura in 1961. *Anne's House of*

Dreams has been exactly translated as *An no Yume no Ie* by Muraoka in 1958, still the only title in translation. *Anne of Ingleside* has both a direct translation, *Rohenso no An* (*Rohen* literally means Ingleside), and an adapted title, *An no Ai no Katei* (*Anne's Beloved Family*), both by Muraoka in 1958. Interestingly, later books have kept the primary identification with Anne even after Montgomery had abandoned it: *Rainbow Valley* was called *Niji no Tani no An* (*Anne of Rainbow Valley*); and *Rilla of Ingleside* was named *An no Musume Rira* (*Anne's Daughter, Rilla*) by Muraoka in 1959. Although all the titles are recognized among readers, Muraoka's titles are the most widely used and clarify that the protagonist is always Anne, while the original English titles suggest that Anne is becoming a member of a larger community and moving on to a new life.

In this way, all three of the books – *Little Women*, *Heidi*, and *Anne of Green Gables* – were given titles that would appeal to Japanese readers. The works have had many translators, but Muraoka's translation of *Anne of Green Gables* is the most unforgettable, in spite of her omission of some parts of the original text.[1] Her style of translation still influences new translators, who have continued to work since her death in 1968. Almost all of them imitate Muraoka's translation when they translate Anne's 'handles' (43) such as 'the Lake of Shining Waters' (27) and 'Lovers' Lane' (118) as well as the titles. Those nicknames, created by Anne and used by her kindred spirits in the original book, stimulate the readers' sensitivity to words and draw the readers into Anne's world. As Sho Hara says, 'Muraoka's style is sensitive, and, especially, girls' conversations are natural and vivid' (210; my translation). In other words, her style has a so-called Tokyo–Yamanote accent, which is the speech style of high-class ladies and sounds very feminine. Considering that it is Anne's voice that continues page after page, Muraoka's colloquial style certainly influences the readers' understanding of Anne's character. Muraoka's Anne sometimes uses words that are *too* proper, but they effectively show her trait of imagining herself as a noble heroine, and emphasize that she is 'feminine to the core' (122).

There are great differences in the present publication status of *Heidi*, *Little Women*, and *Anne of Green Gables*, though all of them have been classics for many years, and animated versions were broadcast on television in the 1970s and 1980s. *Heidi* is included in only a few series of Collections of World-Famous Stories for Children, and other books of Spyri that once were translated are out of print. *Little Women* can be found in both Collections for Children and the pocket-sized *bunko-bon* books for adults, but the sequels are not as popular as the first book, in spite of being reprinted after years of being out of print. In contrast, *Anne of Green Gables* has been perennially popular among both children and adults. It has never been out of print, nor have its sequels; and new editions for children and adults are set to be published.

In the 1980s and 1990s new complete translations of *Anne of Green Gables* appeared by Midori Chino, Sumiko Ishikawa, Noriko Tanizume, Yasuko Kakegawa, Yumiko Taniguchi, and Yuko Matsumoto. Tanizume's and Matsumoto's translations are for adult readers; Matsumoto's particularly is conscious of cultivating a new readership of *Anne*, with the notes emphasizing the parodies within the novel of English and American literature. Chino, Ishikawa, and Kakegawa also translated the sequels, focusing on children as their main readers, and Kakegawa has completed the ten volumes of the Anne series, illustrated by the popular artist Yoko Yamamoto, with an afterword full of pictures and new information. It should be mentioned here that from February 1995 to June 1996, a translation contest for *Red-haired Anne* appeared serially in *Honyaku no Sekai* (*The World of Translation*), a magazine for prospective translators.[2] Translation is a way of interpretation and should change with the times. *Anne of Green Gables* still holds good prospects of new interpretation with each translation.

The popularity of the Anne series among both children and adults continues to outweigh that of *Heidi* and *Little Women*. This popularity may account for the increased interest in Canadian life and culture among Japanese today.

Anne of Green Gables and Japanese Pop Culture

The integration into Japanese pop culture of *Anne of Green Gables*, including its translation in the 1990s, has resulted in a myriad of Anne-related cultural products. In addition to the many translations, there are countless Anne-related books devoted to pot-pourri, herbs, quilting, sewing, Western cuisine, gardening, and photographs of Prince Edward Island. There are Anne-related guidebooks for 'country life,' informing the reader about accommodations and restaurants in Japan that are like those on Prince Edward Island. In addition to the immensely popular Anne animations, there are Canadian telefilms as well as translated and Japanese Anne musicals and five volumes of comic books newly published in 1998. Anne aficionados are invited to join fan clubs with names such as *An wo shiru Ichizoku* (the Tribe of Anne), Buttercups, Anne Academy, and so on. Until it was closed because of economic depression, they could enjoy Anne-related activities in the Anne Theme Park, founded by the Canadian World in Hokkaido in 1990.[3] The more academically minded will find Anne stories in numerous English textbooks. In addition a nursing school founded in Okayama City in 1992 was granted permission by the Prince Edward Island government to call itself the 'The School of Green Gables.' Such a variety cannot be seen in the cases of *Little Women* and *Heidi*, except for some photograph books, cartoons, and movies. *Anne of Green Gables* has been interpreted practically and spiritually by the Japanese culture, especially mass culture.

As Edwin O. Reischauer writes in *The Japanese Today* (1988), 'in Japan, the high culture seems to have been absorbed much more fully into mass culture' (216). He argues persuasively that the relative homogeneity of Japanese mass culture can be attributed to two factors: a standardized educational system and the development of the mass media (217–18, 223). Yet he also reminds his readers that much more significant than the uniformity of Japan's mass culture is 'its tremendous vitality, creativity, and variety (226–7).' The integration of *Anne of Green Gables* provides examples for both tendencies. The homogeneity can be seen in the rapid acceptance of Muraoka's Japanese-titled *Red-haired Anne* and in the new translators' reluctance to change it. The popularity of Anne has been supported by the growth of readership based on the two factors noted by Reischauser – standardization of education and the glut of television programs, movies, magazines, and other publications. The vitality and creativity of mass culture can be seen in the various ways in which Anne has been adapted into Japanese pop culture. *Anne of Green Gables* has stimulated the imagination of Japanese readers, both on personal and community levels. It has produced new businesses whose product is Anne. Why is the image of Anne that Japanese readers understand through translation still appealing in present-day Japanese society? This will be understood by considering how the Japanese reread the text.

The Image of Anne in Japanese Society

An Orphan Story and a Family Story

Both Anne and Heidi are orphan girls. According to Jerry Griswold (5), the March sisters can be called 'virtual orphans' because father is away and their mother soon departs. If this is the case, why has Anne attracted Japanese readers more than the other heroines have? Timing may be a significant factor: Anne was welcomed by Japanese children when she appeared in 1952 in a society full of war orphans. In the 1950s and 1960s, the Japanese were struggling to live their impoverished lives in communities in which, like Avonlea, everyone knew everyone else. Anne, who never loses hope, overcomes her hardships by changing the adults' feelings. The message is that if one cherishes sincere hopes and continues to try to pursue them, those hopes will surely be fulfilled. Anne has such a positive attitude toward life that has been regarded as a role model for Japanese children. But one of her characteristics, continual chatter, must have been quite new to those first readers. Since the Japanese value silence, children were not allowed to talk freely in the presence of adults. The talkative Anne became a new heroine symbolizing the democratic world after the war.

Unlike Heidi, who is guarded by her grandfather, and the March sisters, who have their parents and a rich aunt, Anne is totally alone and has to find a way to live with people who are not blood relations. It is Anne's personality that won the sympathy of Matthew and Marilla and formed a family. In this point, this novel is different from family stories like *Heidi* and *Little Women*, in which the characters are bound by blood relations. Anne has garnered the sympathy of those people who regard themselves as spiritual orphans, those that feel they are different from other people who belong to one community. Anne gives them a hope that, despite their uniqueness of character, some day they will be accepted by their own community. As long as there are people who consider themselves as outsiders, *Anne of Green Gables* will be read.

A School Story

Education and child rearing are common issues in *Heidi, Little Women,* and *Anne of Green Gables.* Unlike Heidi, who learns to read for the first time at Mr Sesemann's house and then goes to a school in Dörfli during winter, and Jo, who has finished her schooling, Anne learns a lot from school life, teachers, and friends. Actually, education at school is very important in *Anne of Green Gables.* Marilla advises Anne to go to Queen's Academy in order to get a teacher's licence, saying 'I believe in a girl being fitted to earn her own living whether she ever has to or not ... [N]obody knows what is going to happen in this uncertain world, and it's just as well to be prepared' (261–2). Her speech 'may sound like radical feminism to some, but in fact it is just a sample of Maritime self-reliance,' according to Margaret Atwood (see chapter 17). Whether it is typical Maritime self-reliance or not, to be a teacher is a noble profession for women in many countries, including Japan. It is one of the ways for women to be economically independent. Anne is a role model for girls who are striving to get the training to earn their own living.

According to Reischauer, education has shaped national uniformity in modern Japan: 'All Japanese experience nine years (and 94 [now 96.7] percent of them twelve years) of virtually identical education, which is not greatly diversified by the higher education approximately a third [now 45 percent] of them receive' (218).[4] As the Japanese phenomenon of 'examination hell' shows, Japanese children have to study for entrance examinations with the same pressures that Anne feels when confronting the Queen's Academy exams. In short, the Japanese readers can easily relate to Anne's feelings toward education.

It is said that 'the term "school story" is generally used to describe a story in which most of the action centres on a school, usually a single-sex boarding school,' though 'the [school] story for girls usually reflects close links between home and school' (Ray 348). *Anne of Green Gables* has some mutual elements of the school story, showing those close links, which are familiar to the Japanese.

Fiction for Girls

Because Anne, Heidi, and Jo and her sisters are girls, their stories have been categorized as fiction for girls. Housekeeping and clothing for girls are often mentioned in all three books, but *Anne of Green Gables* is peculiar compared with the other two stories. Little Heidi shows no interest in girls' possessions, even after the city life in Frankfurt. For instance, when she comes back to Dörfli at the age of about nine, she easily gives her hat with a feather, which has been given to her by Clara, to Peter's mother, Bridget, as a present (161). She is satisfied with her old battered hat, and she declares to her grandfather, 'Clara gave me so many clothes I'm sure I shall never want any more' (163). Fifteen-year-old Jo in *Little Women* likes 'boys' games and work and manners ... [and she] can't get over [her] disappointment in not being a boy' (4). She does not care if she has to wear her poplin dress with 'the burn and the tear' (33) when she is invited to a party with Meg. In contrast, Anne likes pretty dresses; she seems to be sensitive about fashion and enjoys being a girl. Her longing for puffed sleeves is understandable to Japanese girls, especially when Anne insists that 'Puffed sleeves are so fashionable now. It would give me such a thrill, Marilla, just to wear a dress with puffed sleeves ... I'd rather look ridiculous when everybody else does than plain and sensible all by myself' (88). In a sense, Anne is just an ordinary girl who wants to show herself off, and she appeals to Japanese girls who live in a society that aggressively promotes fashionable things.

A Guidebook for Life

Unlike *Heidi* and *Little Women*, *Anne of Green Gables* has been regarded by the Japanese as a guidebook for life, both spiritually and practically. It shows, not didactically but enjoyably, a better way of life for people. As a book that displays its philosophy of life, it represents a positive way of thinking. As a book that advocates developing cultural life, it provides the way to make life more beautiful. This way of reading is related to the rapid recovery of economy and society of post-war Japan. Until the end of the 1970s, information on Montgomery and Prince Edward Island was so limited that Japanese readers read the translation of *Anne of Green Gables* closely as their only source about life in turn-of-the-century Canada. Many girls and women regarded it as a guide for life, because Anne is a girl who always finds some joy in everyday activities. They share with Anne the positive themes of imagination, a love for nature, and a desire for study.

The close description of the interior of houses, cooking, gardening, and sewing evoked the yearning for Western culture. Akiko Kumai wrote in one of her essays, *Akage no An no Jinsei Noto* (*Life Book of 'Red-haired Anne'*), that it was in Muraoka's translation of *Anne of Green Gables* and in 'Aunt Olivia's Beau' from *Chronicles of Avonlea* that she first encountered the words 'patchwork' and 'pot-pourri (Kumai 171–4, 130–3). She was impressed with Anne's words, 'I do *not* like patchwork, ... there's no scope for imagination in patchwork' (103) and in Aunt Olivia's preparation of picking 'late roses for pot-pourri' (107). It is ironic that Kumai developed a keen interest in patchwork, which Anne does not like: for Kumai there was a lot of scope for imagination in the unfamiliar patchwork. In 1968, Kumai first wrote an essay on patchwork and quilting for a magazine, *Kurashi no Techyo* (*Notebook of Life*); and in 1979, she published the first introductory book of pot-pourri in Japan, *Ai no Popuri* (*Pot-pourri for Love*). Studying Western women's work and hobbies through the Anne books, Kumai became a pioneer in both fields, leading her readers to regard *Anne of Green Gables* as a textbook for those Japanese women who long for an enjoyable, Western cultural life.

By the 1980s Canadian culture started to be more clearly understood by the Japanese, owing to the mass media and the popularity of the animated television program *Anne of Green Gables*. It is said that the animation staff went to Prince Edward Island in order to view its beautiful scenery for the first time. The 1980s was a decade in which Anne's publishers and readers helped each other. Some publishers sponsored essay contests on *Anne of Green Gables*, the first prize of which was a trip to PEI; and other publishers even sponsored tours to the province. The island was a beautiful place that did not betray Japanese Anne fans' expectations, and fan clubs and private schools devoted to Montgomery's works were formed in 1980s. Anne's spirit toward life is the bond that connects them. This tendency has continued into the 1990s, when a theme park and a school were established. Since the 1980s, some readers have regarded *Anne* as a guidebook for 'country life,' a life that values handmade natural products. Moreover, the readers' interest has been focused on the Canadian life and culture that Anne symbolizes. The most widespread influence occurred when Kevin Sullivan's film of *Anne of Green Gables* opened in 1989 in Japan. The popularity of this film and its sequel in 1990 directed the Japanese readers' attention more to the life in Prince Edward Island itself, and homestay programs to the Island have increased.

In English-speaking countries, especially Canada, the publication of L.M. Montgomery's *Selected Journals* has changed the estimation of her and her works. Unfortunately, there are still not many Japanese who know and understand the new wave, as only parts of the first volume of her journals have been published in Japanese translation.[5] The feminist approach to reading *Anne of Green Gables* is not especially popular in Japan. By contrast, an academic work such as Terry Kamikawa's *Akage no An no Seikatsu Jiten* (*A Dictionary of Red-haired Anne's Daily Life*), whose subtitle is *A Guide to the Good Old Days*, has been well read in Japan. Living on Prince Edward Island, Kamikawa researched the daily life in 'the good old days' around 1900 in order to understand the culture in the Anne series.

An English Textbook

For a long time, Japanese readers have been satisfied with reading the translations of *Anne of Green Gables*. It is said that in the 1960s, Muraoka's translations of chapter 9, 'Mrs. Rachel Lynde Is Properly Horrified,' and chapter 10, 'Anne's Apology' were used in a Japanese Language textbook for first-year junior high school students (Matsumoto 32–3). In the

1990s English textbooks of *Anne of Green Gables* with Japanese notes are published for college students by various Japanese publishers, although most of them are abridgements of the original text. As some professors, such as myself, use the Bantam edition or the Penguin edition at college, the number of Japanese students who encounter Anne and Montgomery in English lessons has increased rapidly, while *Heidi* and *Little Women* rarely appear in language textbooks. Also, since 1994, in an English textbook for high school students, there has been a chapter titled 'The Birth of Anne Shirley,' which includes an introduction of Anne, Montgomery, and Prince Edward Island.[6] Considering that language itself is the product of one's culture, I would like to say that the Japanese have finally begun to realize Canadian culture through English.

Conclusion

The Japanese integration of *Anne of Green Gables* is supported by the translation and diverse readings of the text. All of them coexist and have stimulated an interest in Canada and Canadian culture. As Miss Barry says, 'That Anne-girl improves all the time ... and [she] has as many shades as a rainbow and every shade is the prettiest while it lasts ... [S]he makes me love her' (306). With her diverse charms, Anne casts a spell over Japanese readers, and they cannot help but love her. As Anne herself admits, 'There's such a lot of different Annes in me' (176), and she shows how to love and accept people who have characteristics different from her own. It is wonderful that a fictional character like Anne has become a model who leads us to a better understanding of others. She has been and will be a symbol who links Canadian and Japanese cultures.

NOTES

1 Cf. Yuko Katsura, 'The Reception,' 42.
2 *Honyaku no Sekai* Vols. 20–1 (Tokyo: Babel Press, 1995–6). The contest was held in fourteen series. The instructor of the contest, Mariko Kono, is a professional translator who later published *Akage no An no Honyaku Ressun* (*Red-haired Anne's Translation Lesson*) (Tokyo: Babel Press, 1997).
3 When Green Gables in Prince Edward Island was damaged by fire in 1997, the Canadian World helped the Canadians to restore it, sending the blue prints used to build the exact replica of the Green Gables house in Japan.

4 The adjustments are taken from *Japanese Youth Today, 1996* (Tokyo: Center of International Youth Exchange, 1997), 42–4.
5 The latest publication is translated by Yuko Katsura and is entitled *Mongomeri-Nikki: Ai sono Hikari to Kage (The Selected Journals of L.M. Montgomery [1897–1900]: Love, Its Light and Shadow)* (Tokyo: Rippu Shobo, 1997).
6 *Powwow: English Course I* (Kyoto: Bun-eido, 1993), 31–9.

16

Anne of Red Hair:
What Do the Japanese See in
Anne of Green Gables?

CALVIN TRILLIN

I can't say that when I heard about the Japanese infatuation with *Anne of Green Gables* a simple explanation came to mind. It was not immediately clear to me why, for instance, some Japanese couples would travel to Prince Edward Island, the bucolic Canadian province that was the setting for the Anne stories, in order to have a wedding ceremony in the parlor where Lucy Maud Montgomery, the creator of Anne, herself got married, in 1911. Even with reasonably good airline connections, after all, the journey from Tokyo to Charlottetown, P.E.I., takes about twenty hours. Of course, it is well known that the Japanese are regularly gripped with intense enthusiasm for any number of things that Westerners think of as distinctly non-Japanese – fifties doo-wop or bluejeans or Peter Rabbit. On a trip to Japan awhile back, I saw a somewhat frayed jean jacket in a shopwindow priced at the equivalent of three hundred and fifty dollars. I also noticed that during any stroll through a Japanese flea market I spotted at least one framed picture of Audrey Hepburn. A friend of mine who lives in Tokyo told me that someone who gets the sudden urge to see *Love in the Afternoon* can count on finding it playing somewhere in the city. Apparently, the Japanese are gaga for Audrey Hepburn. I have no trouble at all understanding that. I wouldn't call my own feeling for Audrey Hepburn infatuation, but it is, at the least, deep respect.

It's possible that an interest in Anne was less understandable to me partly because my exposure to *Anne of Green Gables* has been much less extensive than my exposure to, say, *Sabrina* or *Breakfast at Tiffany's*. In the United States, the series of books that L.M. Montgomery wrote about Anne is popular mainly with girls of ten or twelve. I do have two daughters, both of whom read *Anne of Green Gables*, the first and most popular of Montgomery's books, at the usual age. Because we happen to live in the Canadian Maritimes in the summer, we even took a trip to Prince Edward Island one August so that the girls could see the musical version of *Anne of Green Gables*, which has been playing in Charlottetown in the summers since 1965. From that trip, I knew roughly what *Anne of Green Gables* is about: a brother and sister named Matthew and Marilla Cuthbert, both unmarried and both getting on in years, intend to adopt (if that's the word) an orphan boy from Nova Scotia to help with the chores on the family farm near Avonlea, and are sent instead a spunky, independent-minded, determined, romantic, imaginative girl named Anne Shirley. It doesn't take much more than superficial exposure to *Anne of Green Gables* to understand why it has been an enormously popular book from the time it was published, in 1908. I don't know if Anne is actually, as the cover of our paperback copy of *Anne of Green Gables* claims, 'the most beloved, beguiling and timeless heroine in all of fiction,' but she is a terrifically appealing character.

As an orphan girl in a family-oriented farming community, she is, of course, an underdog from the start. Like a lot of girls her age, she finds her looks disappointing – she's a skinny redhead who wears her hair in braids that her handsome classmate Gilbert Blythe refers to as 'carrots' – but the reader knows better. Marilla – a high-minded but stern farm woman who thinks of herself as someone who has no time for frivolous nonsense – grows to love Anne despite being in an almost constant state of exasperation with her; Matthew, Marilla's shy brother, adores Anne almost from the moment he spots her at the train station, sitting forlornly on a pile of shingles. The plot of *Anne of Green Gables* consists largely of Anne's getting herself in scrapes that then have to be sorted out – getting her friend Diana drunk by mistaking currant wine for raspberry cordial, for instance, or talking back to a local busybody who calls her skinny and homely. ('How would you like to have such things said about you? How would you like to be told that you are fat and clumsy and probably hadn't a spark of imagination in you?' [74].)

Anne's independence and her curiosity and her outspokenness – what Marilla sums up as her 'queer ways' – sometimes shock the conventional ladies of the Church Aid Society and Foreign Missions Auxiliary and often get her sent to her room. But it's clear that some sort of accommodation with Prince Edward Island ways is going to be worked out before anything frightening or dangerous happens. In the final accommodation, after Matthew dies and it becomes obvious that Marilla's sight is failing, Anne puts off her dreams of college to remain on the farm and care for Marilla. Anne sometimes displays a sort of innocent wisdom ('Saying one's prayers isn't exactly the same thing as praying'), and she always has a dramatic way of talking, whether she's being punished ('[P]lease don't ask me to eat anything, especially boiled pork and greens. Boiled pork and greens are so unromantic when one is in affliction' [113]), or engaging in an act of derring-do ('I shall walk that ridge-pole, Diana, or perish in the attempt. If I am killed you are to have my pearl bead ring' [201]). Thinking about Anne's charm and insouciance, it occurred to me that she might have been played perfectly by a very young Audrey Hepburn.

When we took our family trip to P.E.I. – this was at the beginning of the eighties – Anne seemed to be an added attraction for touring families that had been drawn from eastern Canada and New England principally by the beaches and the pastoral landscape and the lobster suppers. If there were any Japanese Anne fans there, we didn't notice them. Around that time, though, Anne tourism was getting a start in Japan. *Anne of Green Gables* had been popular with young Japanese readers since 1952, when a noted translator did a translation that carried the title still used for Anne in Japan – *Anne of Red Hair*. The straitened circumstances that most Japanese found themselves in during the early fifties may have made it easier for them to identify with a penniless orphan, but those circumstances also put travel to exotic destinations beyond their dreams. Thirty years later, Japan seemed to be exporting even more tourists than automobiles or television sets. A Tokyo publisher, alerted by the reader-comment cards that are customarily included in Japanese books, organized a tour of Prince Edward Island for people who longed to see the places described by L.M. Montgomery.

From what I could gather, the arrival of Japanese tourists took just about everyone on Prince Edward Island by surprise. P.E.I. people would presumably have taken it for granted that Anne was popular in Japan – Anne is popular in Poland; she's popular in Taiwan – but nobody on the Island could imagine that Japanese Anne fans would fly to Toronto or Vancouver and then to Halifax and then to Charlottetown in order to inspect the presumed setting of what was, after all, a work of fiction. Around the time our family went to P.E.I., a well-dressed Japanese gentleman came to the old house, in the Park Corner section of the Island, that is now called the Anne of Green Gables Museum at Silver Bush. It's a house whose strongest connection to Lucy Maud Montgomery is that it was the scene of her wedding, but, like the other Anne sites, it also features a sort of blurb from the author on how much the place meant to her ('The wonder castle of my childhood'). The proprietor – a collateral descendant of L.M. Montgomery named George Campbell, who grew up in the house – assumed that the visitor was a businessman who happened to be on the Island to buy tuna and had found himself with a spare hour or two. Not at all. The man said that he had come from Japan to see the Anne sites. Campbell found that cheering news, and he was cheered even more when, a couple of years later, the first Japanese tourists in an organized group showed up at Silver Bush. They cleaned out his souvenir shop.

The Japanese visitors did not include many businessmen or many families with ten-year-old girls. They were (and still are) mainly single women in their late teens and twenties who are doing office work for a few years before they marry and begin a family – women who are sometimes referred to in Japan as Young Office Ladies. The Japanese still represent only a tiny percentage of the tourists who come to Prince Edward Island every year. From what I could see on a return visit to P.E.I. this summer, though, they often seem to be in the majority at the places important to Anne fans – the green-gabled house of L.M. Montgomery's cousins, which gave the first novel its title, the tiny house where the author was born, the Park Corner house where she was married, her paternal grandfather's house, the foundation and gardens of the house where she was reared. In tourist promotion, I was told by a provincial tourist official while I was on the Island, P.E.I. markets relaxation to Ontario, beaches and scenery and seafood to Quebec, and history and culture to New England. To Japan, it markets Anne.

Guestbooks at the Anne sites are full of Japanese script. Japanese appears on signs and in restaurant advertisements. The Prince Edward, in Charlottetown, which is the largest hotel on the Island, now has six Japanese-speaking employees and, with advance notice, can provide such amenities as lobster sashimi or a special Anne dinner, which features a Japanese-language video of P.E.I. scenery and what is described as 'enjoyable time with "ANNE."' One of the two tour companies that offer Anne wedding packages sold forty-three last season and nearly seventy this season.

In Japan, Anne remains the heroine of books and television shows and books from the television shows and cartoons from the books and comic books from the cartoons. Apparently, Japanese who are oblivious of the Royal Canadian Mounted Police, say, or ice hockey identify Anne with Canada. In an article in 1993 for the *Journal of Canadian Studies* on Anne's Japanese connection, a historian named Douglas Baldwin included a couple of stunning statistics. One was that out of a hundred and fifty young Japanese women interviewed for guide positions in the Canadian pavilion at the 1970 World's Fair, near Osaka, a hundred and forty-nine were familiar with *Anne of Green Gables*. Another was that a survey taken by a Japanese travel magazine in 1992 listed the places its readers most wanted to visit as New York, Paris, London, and Prince Edward Island. In Japan, the Anne image – usually depicted simply by red braids and Anne's characteristic straw bonnet – is considered so powerful that it has been used as the logo and principal attraction for a sort of theme park in Hokkaido whose name does not strike an American as one that would cause intense excitement among potential fun-lovers: Canadian World.

The Author as Tourist Attraction

Normally, I think, exploiting an author as a tourist attraction presents a problem that also crops up in writing an author's biography: What's to see? The labor that makes a world-famous novelist worth writing about was almost certainly done while he was sitting all by himself in a quiet room. The raw material was probably invisible to everyone but him. A visitor to Herman Melville's study couldn't expect to find any whales. What exactly would the tourist-development director of Samuel Beckett's home town display? Prince Edward Island does have some advantages in making a tourist attraction of what L.M. Montgomery created in her books about Anne, almost all of which were set in Avonlea, a fictionalized version of Cavendish, P.E.I. Only a few years after *Anne of Green Gables* was published, L.M. Montgomery married a Presbyterian minister and moved to Ontario, where she lived for the rest of her life. But even her later books are so imbued with the look and feel of Prince Edward Island that the province itself practically qualifies as one of the characters. Also, apart from Charlottetown and some commercial development near Cavendish that amounts to Anne-sprawl, most of P.E.I. looks remarkably like the picturesque farmland that was described by L.M. Montgomery in the first decades of the century. P.E.I. is still mainly agricultural – it is a speck of an island that produces a significant percentage of the potatoes grown in the second-largest county in the world – and a lot of its farmers still seem to live in the houses their parents and grandparents and great-grandparents lived in. The houses visited by Anne fans look pretty much the way they did when L.M. Montgomery was visiting them, and they also look like the houses down the road. All this may make it somewhat less likely that somebody who is shown 'Matthew's room' at one of the Anne sights will respond by saying, 'Matthew was imaginary. He didn't have a room.'

Also, L.M. Montgomery's early life was so close to Anne's that the real haunts of her childhood are easy to accept as the settings of the novels. Maud, as she was called on P.E.I., was virtually an orphan herself: from the age of two, when her mother died and her father moved west, she was reared by her maternal grandparents – severe and occasionally difficult people, by all accounts, who had little interest in children. Like Anne, she later sacrificed her own ambitions to care for the person who had cared for her: returning from Halifax, where she had started working for a newspaper, she spent thirteen years caring for her aged grandmother. Like Anne in the later books, she taught school for a while. '"Is Anne a real person?" was a question often asked of L.M. Montgomery,' Professor Elizabeth Waterston writes in *Kindling Spirit: L.M. Montgomery's 'Anne of Green Gables,'* a volume that is part of a series on important works of Canadian literature. 'In her Journal she gives a tantalizing answer: "I always answer 'no' with an odd reluctance and an uncomfortable feeling of not telling the truth" ... Anne seemed to have her own existence: "If I turned my head quickly should I not see her?"'

The fact that L.M. Montgomery is sometimes difficult to distinguish from her heroine adds to the commingling of fiction and reality which is part of celebrating Anne on Prince Edward Island, so that being married in the parlor where Maud was married almost seems to put a couple into the book. One of the first people I talked to on my latest visit to Prince Edward Island was George Campbell, who has found himself in the business of staging weddings for Japanese couples – most of whom are there without family or friends and many of whom use the 'free day' of a three-day group tour of the Island to tie the knot. Since Campbell didn't happen to have any weddings scheduled during my visit, I asked him exactly how the ceremony worked. Our conversation went roughly like this:

'So who's in the parlor – the bride and the groom?'

'Well, the groom. The bride is going to come down the stairs, on the arm of her father.'

'I thought you said that the bride and the groom usually didn't have any family with them.'

'The driver plays the father. The one who drove them out from Charlottetown.'

'And there's a minister?'

'Yes, a regular United Church of Canada minister.'

'But is that legal in Japan?'

'Oh, they're married before they come. This is just for the ceremony.'

'And who else is in the parlor?'

'Well, the organist. My wife. She plays "The Voice That Breathed o'er Eden" – the same song that was played at Lucy Maud Montgomery's wedding. Also, there's sometimes a soloist to sing the song.'

'And you're there.'

'No, I'm not there. I'm outside with the horse.'

'What horse? You didn't say anything about a horse.'

'After Lucy Maud was married, my grandfather drove her and her husband to the station. So we have a horse and buggy, and the bride and the groom drive around the Lake of Shining Waters and have their picture taken.'

'You do the driving?'

'Unless it's a de-luxe wedding. Then they get Matthew to drive them. I just hold the horse's head and help them into the buggy.'

'And then they have a sort of reception in the tearoom?'

'Right.'

'Biscuits and things?'

'Right. Except if it's a de-luxe. Then they have a cake that's precisely the sort of cake Lucy Maud had. Also, if it's a de-luxe Anne comes to the reception. Someone playing Anne, of course.'

But Why? Theories Explaining the Anne Phenomenon

Douglas Baldwin, in his article on the Anne phenomenon in Japan, lists any number of theories propounded by experts on Japanese culture to explain Anne's appeal: the Japanese devotion to innocence, their traditional love of nature, the admiration that people in a repressed society have for someone who can be frank and spontaneous, the Japanese sympathy for a poor protagonist who triumphs over long odds. (Several people I mentioned Anne to in Japan said that both Anne and the rags-to-riches heroine of an astonishingly popular Japanese soap opera called *Oshin* have a much admired characteristic known as *gambaru*, which means pluck or perseverance.) Baldwin adds some theories of his own. Despite the decades and air miles separating the two settings, he believes that 'in many ways, the Japan of 1993 is similar to Prince Edward Island in 1900,' and that 'the "Anne" novels are a subtle condemnation of the restrictive nature of Avonlea society, where convention and custom rule everyone's conduct.'

In talking to Japanese people about *Anne of Green Gables*, I did find that what they mentioned as appealing was often something in short supply in modern Japan. The Japanese are known for their love of beautiful scenery, but most of them now live in cities – a string of crowded cities, which tends to strike a Western visitor as one unrelievedly ugly splotch of urban sprawl. When I asked a young Japanese woman who works in the P.E.I. tourist industry about Anne's appeal, she said, 'I think it's the free spirit of Anne. In Japan, everything is so strict. You're not allowed to be different. Having a different personality is not respected.' It is, of course, particularly difficult for a woman in Japan to have a different personality. My business in Japan brought me into contact with a number of Japanese women, many of them highly accomplished in their fields, and they tended to have had mixed success in liberating themselves from the traditional female role of being deferential or cute, or both.

You might conclude that Japanese women see Anne as a sort of idealization of what they'd like to be if they could. 'Anne is just a wonderful person for us Japanese because women feel trapped,' I was told in Japan by Kiyomi Matsufuji, who has been involved with Anne and P.E.I. for years. 'She can do anything, which is what we want to do.' That view, I suspect, would be considered romantic by Clare Fawcett, an anthropologist who speaks Japanese and runs the summer English-language school sponsored by the L.M. Montgomery Institute at the University of Prince Edward Island. After interviews with a number of students at the language school, which so far is all female and all Japanese, she concluded that 'Montgomery's characters and plots reconfirm rather than question traditional definitions of the role of Japanese society.' The Japanese women who had come to the English-language school, she discovered, 'could not imagine themselves having or developing the characteristics which distinguish Anne from the image of the ideal Japanese women,' such as her feistiness and her willingness to speak her mind. Instead, they identified with Anne as a cheerful and loyal member of her family – someone who was willing to give up her opportunity to go to college because Marilla needed her, someone who always comes around in the end. In the later books, Fawcett points out, 'Anne grows up and shuts up just as Japanese women retire to the kitchen.'

To people in the tourist trade, why Anne is a marketable commodity in Japan is less important than, say, whether she might also be a marketable commodity in Korea, where interest in the stories is apparently widespread but somewhat less intense. When I asked Les Miller, who works in tourism marketing for Prince Edward Island, what he thought Anne's appeal was for the Japanese, he listed a few possibilities – the fact that *Anne of Green Gables* was for awhile part of the school curriculum, for instance, and the fact that there were a lot of orphans in Japan when this story of a perky orphan was translated. Then he mentioned Anne clubs in Japan, whose most enthusiastic members tend to be women old enough to have children of their own, or even grandchildren. He said that the feeling the Japanese have for Anne is of a different order from the feeling that my daughters had when they were ten or twelve. 'I've seen people get off the bus at Green Gables and cry,' he said. He paused, and shook his head. Then he said, 'We don't fully understand this phenomenon.'

17

Reflection Piece – Revisiting Anne

MARGARET ATWOOD

Anne of Green Gables is one of those books you feel almost guilty liking, because so many other people seem to like it as well. If it's that popular, you feel, it can't possibly be good, or good for you.

Like many others, I read this book as a child, and absorbed it so thoroughly that I can't even remember when. I read it to my own daughter when she was eight, and she read it again to herself later, and acquired all the sequels – which she, like everyone else including the author, realized were not on quite the same level as the original. I saw the television series too, and, despite rewrites and excisions, the central story was as strong and as appealing as ever.

And several summers ago, when my family and I were spending some time on Prince Edward Island, I even saw the musical. The theatre gift-store was offering Anne dolls, an Anne cookbook, and Anne parapher-nalia of all kinds. The theatre itself was large but crowded; in front of us was a long row of Japanese tourists. During one especially culture-specific moment – a dance in which a horde of people leapt around holding eggs glued on to spoons clenched between their teeth – I won-dered what the Japanese tourists could possibly be making of it. Then I took to wondering what they could be making of the whole phenom-enon. What did they make of the *Anne* dolls, the *Anne* knick-knacks, the *Anne* books themselves? Why was Anne Shirley, the talkative red-haired orphan, so astonishingly popular among them?

Possibly it was the red hair: that must be exotic, I thought. Or possibly Japanese women and girls found Anne encouraging: in danger of rejec-tion because she is not the desired and valued boy, she manages to win over the hearts of her adoptive parents and to end the book with a great deal of social approval. But she triumphs without sacrificing her sense of herself: she will not tolerate insult, she defends herself, she even loses her temper and gets away with it. She breaks taboos. On a more conventional level, she studies hard at school and wins a scholarship, she respects her elders, or at least some of them, and she has a great love of Nature (although it is Nature in its more subdued aspect: hers is a pastoral world of gardens and blossoming trees, not mountains and hurricanes).

It was helpful for me to try looking at *Anne*'s virtues through other eyes, because for a Canadian woman – once a Canadian girl – *Anne* is a truism. Readers of my generation, and of several generations before and since, do not think of *Anne* as 'written.' It has simply always been there. It is difficult not to take the book for granted, and almost impossible to see it fresh, to realize what an impact it must have had when it first appeared.

It is tempting to think of *Anne* as just a very good 'girls' book,' about – and intended for – pre-adolescents. And on one level, it is just that. Anne's intense friendship with the ever-faithful Diana Barry, the hatefulness of Josie Pye, the schoolroom politics, the tempest-in-a-teapot 'scrapes,' Anne's overdone vanity and her consciousness of fashion in clothes and bookmarks – all are familiar to us, both from our own observation and experience and from other 'girls' books.'

But *Anne* draws on a darker, and, some would say, a more respectable literary lineage. Anne Shirley is, after all, an orphan, and the opening chapters of *Jane Eyre* and *Oliver Twist* and *Great Expectations*, and, later and closer to Anne, the bad-tempered, unhappy, sallow-faced little Mary of *The Secret Garden*, have all contributed both to Anne Shirley's formation as orphan-heroine and to the reader's understanding of the perils of orphanhood in the nineteenth and early twentieth centuries. Unless she had been allowed to stay at Green Gables, Anne's fate would have been to be passed around as a cheap drudge from one set of uncaring adults to another. In the real world, as opposed to the literary one, she would have been in great danger of ending up pregnant and disgraced, raped – like many of the Barnardo Homes female orphans – by the men in the families in which they had been 'placed.' We have forgotten, by now, that orphans were once despised, exploited, and feared, considered to be the offspring of criminals or the products of immoral sex. Rachel Lynde, in her tales of orphans who have poisoned and set fire to the families who have taken them in, is merely voicing received opinion. No wonder Anne cries so much when she thinks she will be 'returned,' and no wonder Marilla and Matthew are considered 'odd' for keeping her!

But Anne partakes of another 'orphan' tradition as well: the folk-tale orphan who wins despite everything, the magic child who appears, as it seems, from nowhere – like King Arthur – and proves to have qualities far superior to anyone around her.

Such literary echoes may form the structural underpinnings of Anne's tale, but the texture is relentlessly local. L.M. Montgomery stays within the parameters of the conventions available to her: nobody goes to the bathroom in this book, and although we are in the country, no pigs are visibly slaughtered. But, that said, she remains faithful to her own aesthetic credo, as set forth by Anne's beloved schoolteacher Miss Stacy, who 'won't let us write anything but what might happen in Avonlea in our own lives.' Part of the current interest in 'Avonlea' is that it appears to be a 'jollier,' more innocent world, long-gone and very different from our own; but for Montgomery, 'Avonlea' was simply reality edited. She was determined to write from what she knew: not the whole truth, perhaps, but not a total romanticization either. Rooms and clothes and malicious gossip are described much as they were, and people talk in the vernacular, minus the swear words – but then, the people we hear speaking are mostly 'respectable' women, who would not have sworn anyway. This world was familiar to me through the stories told to me by my Maritime parents and aunts: the sense of community and 'family,' the horror of being 'talked about,' the smug rectitude, the distrust of outsiders, the sharp division between what was 'respectable' and what was not, as well as the pride in hard work and the respect for achievement, all are faithfully depicted by Montgomery. Marilla's speech to Anne – 'I believe in a girl being fitted to earn her own living whether she ever has to or not' – may sound like radical feminism to some, but in fact it is just a sample of Maritime self-reliance. My mother was brought up like that; consequently, so was I.

Montgomery wrote from her own experience in another and more profound way as well. Knowing what we now know about her life, we realize that Anne's story was a mirror-image of her own, and gathers much of its force and poignancy from thwarted wish-fulfilment. Montgomery, too, was virtually an orphan, abandoned by her father after her mother's death to a set of strict, judgmental grandparents, but she never gained the love she grants so lavishly to Anne. Anne's experience of exclusion was undoubtedly hers; the longing for acceptance must have been hers as well. So was the lyricism; so was the sense of injustice; so was the rebellious rage.

Children identify with Anne because she is what they often feel themselves to be – powerless and scorned and misunderstood. She revolts as they would like to revolt, she gets what they would like to have, and she is cherished as they themselves would like to be. When I was a child, I thought – as all children do – that Anne was the centre of the book. I cheered her on, and applauded her victories over the adults, her thwartings of their wills. But there is another perspective.

Although *Anne* is about childhood, it is also very much centred on the difficult and sometimes heartbreaking relationship between children and adults. Anne seems to have no power, but in reality she has the vast though unconscious power of a beloved child. Although she changes in the book – she grows up – her main transformation is physical. Like the Ugly Duckling, she becomes a swan; but the inner Anne – her moral essence – remains much what it has always been. Matthew, too, begins as he means to go on: he is one of those shy, child-like men who delight Montgomery's heart (like Cousin Jimmy in the *Emily* books), he loves Anne from the first moment he sees her, and he takes her part in every way and on every occasion.

The only character who goes through any sort of essential transformation is Marilla. *Anne of Green Gables* is not about Anne becoming a good little girl: it is about Marilla Cuthbert becoming a good – and more complete – woman. At the book's beginning, she is hardly even alive; as Rachel Lynde, the common-sense voice of the community, puts it, Marilla is not *living*, just *staying*. Marilla takes Anne on, not out of love as Matthew does, but out of a cold sense of duty. It is only in the course of the book that we realize there is a strong family resemblance between the two. Matthew, as we have always known, is a 'kindred spirit' for Anne, but the kinship with Marilla goes deeper: Marilla, too, has been 'odd,' ugly, unloved. She, too, has been the victim of fate and injustice.

Anne without Marilla would – admit it – be sadly one-dimensional, an overtalkative child whose precocious cuteness might very easily pall. Marilla adds the saving touch of lemon juice. On the other hand, Anne acts out a great many of Marilla's concealed wishes, thoughts, and desires, which is the key to their relationship. And, in her battles of will with Anne, Marilla is forced to confront herself, and to regain what she has lost or repressed: her capacity to love, the full range of her emotions. Underneath her painful cleanliness and practicality, she is a passionate woman, as her outpouring of grief at Matthew's death testifies. The most moving declaration of love in the book has nothing to do with Gilbert Blythe: it is Marilla's wrenching confession in the penultimate chapter: 'Oh, Anne, I know I've been kind of strict and harsh with you maybe – but you mustn't think I didn't love you as well as Matthew did, for all that. I want to tell you now when I can. It's never been easy for me to say things out of my heart, but at times like this it's easier. I love you as dear as if you were my own flesh and blood and you've been my joy and comfort ever since you came to Green Gables' (317).

The Marilla we first meet could never have laid herself bare like this. Only when she has recovered – painfully enough, awkwardly enough – her capacity to feel and express, can she become what Anne herself has lost long ago, and truly wants: a mother. But to love is to become vulnerable. At the beginning of the book, Marilla is all-powerful, but by the end, the structure has been reversed, and Anne has much more to offer Marilla than the other way around.

It may be the ludicrous escapades of Anne that render the book so attractive to children, but it is the struggles of Marilla that give it resonance for adults. Anne may be the orphan in all of us, but then, so is Marilla. Anne is the fairy-tale wish-fulfilment version, what Montgomery longed for. Marilla is, more likely, what she feared she might become: joyless, bereft, trapped, hopeless, unloved. Each of them saves the other. It is the neatness of their psychological fit – as well as the invention, humour, and fidelity of the writing – that makes *Anne* such a satisfying and enduring fable.

EPILOGUE

L.M. Montgomery and the Creation of Prince Edward Island

DEIRDRE KESSLER

When Prince Edward Island became fixed in time, it was the Island Montgomery constructed in *Anne of Green Gables* and then made fast in the mind's eye of the world with all the novels that tumbled after *Anne*. The fixed time was that romantic touchstone of an era before automobiles altered the look and speed of things. There are hollows in the old clay Princetown–Warburton Road in Central Queens County, for example, where raspberry canes dripping blood-red fruit reach out from sunny patches under a bower of hardwoods unaltered from the days when Montgomery's Grandmother Macneill travelled the road in a horse-drawn carriage. There are similar warps and offerings everywhere, found poking up in the gaps of late-twentieth-century Prince Edward Island, in corners of farms and farmhouses, in speech and song, in gesture, and in the mantle of expectation of community and appreciation of home.

The template of the world's idea of Prince Edward Island, complete with details of flora and fauna, ebb and flow of tide and season, was placed over this island by a million resonant readers – a Swedish girl and her grandmother, a Polish soldier far from home, a Japanese family before the advent of the hearth of television. In dozens of languages, one by one, hundred by hundred, million by million, readers imagined Prince Edward Island as they deciphered L.M. Montgomery's words and partook of the images and sensory experiences trapped in those words. They inhaled the scent of apple blossoms, for instance, and located in themselves the 'irresistible temptation' of picking them (68); heard the sound of the big bee that tumbles out of one apple blossom in the jugful decorating Marilla's dinner table. 'Fancy going to sleep in it when the wind was rocking it,' says Anne. 'If I wasn't a human girl I think I'd like to be a bee and live among the flowers' (67).

Here, as throughout her works, Montgomery presents both fragrance and vision of flower and bee *and* a profound reverence for them. In a lightning-quick shift of point of view – 'Fancy going to sleep' in a blossom – she undoes what is for most people a reflex response to a bee tumbling face-close onto a table. Anne's sensual and spiritual ecstacy in this scene is juxtaposed with her being admonished by Marilla to learn by rote the prayer 'Our Father.'

Seven years before Montgomery wrote the apple blossom and bee scene in *Anne of Green Gables*, she made the following entry in her journal.

Sunday, July 26, 1896
I suppose I must go and get ready for evening service – somewhat against my inclination for I was out this morning and I honestly think once is enough to go to church on any Sunday.

Sunday is supposed to be a day of rest but in reality it is as hard worked a day as any in the week. We cook, eat, and wash dishes galore. We dress with weariness to the flesh and tramp to church in the heat, sit a long and mostly very dull sermon out in a stuffy pew and come home again not a whit better than we went – not as good indeed for we have got a headache and feel very vicious for our pains.

I have an ideal Sunday in my mind. Only, I am such a coward that I cannot translate it into the real, but must drift on with the current of conventionality. And I would stay there for hours alone with nature and my own soul. I think that would really do me great good. But how dreadfully unorthodox and *odd* it would be. The local spinsters would die of horror. (*SJ* 1: 162–3)

It seems to me that Montgomery gave her fictional children and us, her readers, freedom from dreaded orthodoxy; she gave us permission to go against the 'current of conventionality' while she paid with her too-short life, a life filled with the cowardice of dressing 'to the flesh' and sitting out dull sermons on hard pews, a life filled with the laws of church and husband and the dicta of the guardians of the status quo.

From 1908 to the present time, millions of people have been imagining Prince Edward Island. These individual visions have been guided by Montgomery – she might as well have written *A Field Guide to Prince Edward Island*. The reality of place altered by time has been tempered by a parallel and potent reality generated by Montgomery readers for now almost a century. We all know that landscape has more dimensions than the physical.

A few years ago, when I was reading all of the late Geoff Hogan's garden notes and journals in preparation for writing the script and treatment for the video, *Like the Back of My Hand: Journal of Prince Edward Island Naturalist Geoff Hogan (1953–1992)*, I came upon the following passage:

January 26, 1987
I was telling K & S about my interest in L.M. Montgomery. It's funny, but I feel a bond with her. We are alike in many ways, in our love of nature and the Island, gardening, and probably, most importantly, in a belief in ourselves. I know what it is like being away from the Island, missing it terribly – so terribly at times I didn't think I could take it any longer. At least I knew that someday I was coming home to stay. So we've shared that experience too. And we are both spiritual, not religious, but spiritual. We are alike in other ways too, some good and some not so good. Sometimes I wonder if I have a bond with this person, even though she's been dead for 45 years? If common sensibilities in some of your deepest, inner feelings have anything to do with it, then it may be possible ... It all sounds quite ridiculous – I know this better than anyone, but it still doesn't change anything.

Many years ago I was living in a house overlooking the Kennebecasis River and teaching high school English in Saint John, New Brunswick. My neighbour was born and raised in Montague, down east on the Island. I'd never met an Islander before. I was fresh from the United States. I thought this neighbour's Island dialect was charming, and I liked her indescribable but sure sense of self and the way her identity was linked with her place of birth. We got to know each other over the course of the year. When I decided to move to Toronto to be close to my sister and her new daughter, this Montague-born neighbour said, 'You should go to Prince Edward Island. It would suit you.' What did that mean, a place would suit me? No place suited me – I had learned to suit places. No one had ever said such a thing to me before.

I recalled those words two years later when I returned to the Maritimes in search of a teaching position. After exhausting all possibilities in New Brunswick and Nova Scotia, I took the Caribou–Wood Islands ferry to Prince Edward Island. It was a last hope. I would return to Toronto if no job were available on the Island.

It was 15 May 1970. The sun was shining. The Northumberland Strait was bluer than I'd ever seen water except in paintings. And from a distance, the patchwork of red soil and green fields against that Northumberland blue took my breath away. As a child I had fallen in love with the prairie described by Laura Ingalls Wilder. The prairie, a literary landscape, had been my imagination's home, the resting place of my spirit. But here was a real place, a real paradise. I stayed.

As a child, I did not dream of becoming a writer. I wanted only to be with animals in the prairie Laura Ingalls described, to be where, 'Only the tall wild grass covered the endless empty land and a great empty sky arched over it' (26), where the songs of meadowlarks 'came down from the great clear sky like a rain of music' (107).

The place I discovered that showed me I was a writer was Prince Edward Island. I have not recovered from the initial enchantment with this little red-clay island in the Gulf of St Lawrence. It is my home, and it is the home of many of my characters: Lena in *Lena and the Whale*; Ella in *Home for Christmas*; Lee in *Lobster in My Pocket*; and Brupp, an Island cat who sets out to see the world.

In this passage from *Brupp Rides Again*, the fourth and final novel of the series, Brupp returns from his year-long journey across Canada: 'Brupp stood at the prow of the ferry. He filled his eyes with the blue Northumberland Strait and breathed in the moist salt air of home' (140). Brupp has hitched a ride in the back of a pickup truck, which disembarks from the ferry and takes him to a place not far from the farm from which he set out.

Brupp travelled all day and all night until he came to the edge of Aurora's property, and there he sat. Across the field were the familiar barns and house nestled in a grove of spruce trees ... Brupp inhaled the fragrance of late summer and his heart swelled with happiness.

'I shall write in my diary,' he thought, '*In a cat's wide life there is a time for high adventure and a time for coming home.*' (141)

Although I did not read the works of Montgomery as a child, my first experience with her writing was through the eyes of children when I read aloud *Anne of Green Gables* to my grade 3 class at a rural consolidated school where I taught for seven years. It was our scheme, the unspoken agreement between these twenty-seven children and me, to complete all of the curriculum material as quickly as we could so that we could huddle together by the one window and read. The school was one of those wretched open-area designs with little natural light and no circulation of fresh air. I read my own favourite stories to the children – *Charlotte's Web, Stuart Little, Tom Sawyer, Heidi*. But because of all the fuss made about Montgomery in my new home province, one spring I picked out *Anne of Green Gables* from the school library. I did not read the novel to myself before reading it aloud to the children. One day we came to the penultimate chapter, 'The Reaper Whose Name Is Death.' Montgomery writes:

'Matthew – Matthew – what is the matter? Matthew, are you sick?'
  It was Marilla who spoke, alarm in every jerky word. Anne came through the hall, her hands full of white narcissus, – it was long before Anne could love the sight or odour of white narcissus again, – in time to hear her and to see Matthew standing in the porch doorway, a folded paper in his hand, and his face strangely drawn and gray. Anne dropped her flowers and sprang across the kitchen to him at the same moment as Marilla. They were both too late; before they could reach him Matthew had fallen across the threshold. (314)

My throat thickened. Tears filled my eyes. I stopped reading and just sat on the chair by the window. At my feet on the floor and in little chairs in a tight semi-circle were all of the children I had come to love. This was my second year with the same children – I'd been hired as a grade 2 teacher and had requested to follow my class to grade 3. The next year I was their grade 4 teacher, so we came to know each other very well. Gregory Mowery sat at my knee, the way he often did. He had his hand on my foot. In those days I used to wear clogs, brown tights, and the same brown corduroy skirt and jacket nearly every day. Gregory plucked at the ankles of my brown tights, staring at me. I closed the book. I couldn't read any further, couldn't stand the sorrow of Matthew's death. All of the children were completely still and silent. Then Gregory said, 'I didn't know a teacher could cry.'
  The next day we finished the chapter and the book. I did not read another Montgomery novel until after I had published five picture books and five novels of my own. But my life as a writer began in earnest the moment I was caught in the web of real landscape and the landscape described by Montgomery and imagined by all of her readers. Montgomery created a place where there is now licence to write and greater freedom just to be. She longed for such a place herself and found it in the 'solemn wood ... among the ferns,' though, in her own words, she had not the courage to stay there for as long as she would have liked. Her yearning was for the freedom to celebrate life 'with only the companionship of the trees and the wood-winds echoing through the dim, moss-hung aisles like the strains of some vast cathedral anthem' (*SJ* 1: 162).

Montgomery spun her lifelong yearning into words. Tangled in these words were her impressions, emotions, and spiritual understandings inspired in the cathedral of nature. Imagine my delight in discovering a place to call home where the key public figure is a woman and her fictional heroines, where there is not only an unspoken reign of the feminine, but also an articulated and much-demonstrated honouring of a writer, her craft, and her source of inspiration.

Montgomery's work embodies a gaian dimension, a deep cherishing of the earth, as well as a numinous, profoundly spiritual dimension. This work of hers has created a literary landscape that transcends the literary and returns itself again and again to the source. Montgomery's theme and variations and the further variations of her readers have intertwined with this geologic, physical crescent of red clay in the Gulf of St Lawrence until it is impossible to separate the strata of writer, landscape, and writing – person, place, and thing – impossible to un-couple the parallel stories, impossible to unwind Montgomery and a century of readers from the double helix of art and place.

Works Cited

Åhmansson, Gabriella. *A Life and Its Mirrors: A Feminist Reading of L.M. Montgomery's Fiction.* Vol. 1. Uppsala, Swed.: Almquist and Wiksell International, 1991.

– '"Mayflowers Grow in Sweden Too": L.M. Montgomery, Astrid Lindgren and the Swedish Literary Consciousness.' *Harvesting Thistles: The Textual Garden of L.M. Montgomery.* Ed. Mary Henley Rubio. 14–22.

Alcott, Louisa May. *Little Women.* 1868. Harmondsworth: Puffin, 1994.

Allan, David. *Virtue, Learning and the Scottish Enlightenment: Ideas of Scholarship in Early Modern History.* Edinburgh: Edinburgh UP, 1993.

Anderson, Robert David. *Education and Opportunity in Victorian Scotland.* London: Oxford UP, 1983.

Ashcroft, Bill, Gareth Griffiths, and Helen Tiffin. *The Empire Writes Back: Theory and Practice in Post-Colonial Literatures.* London: Routledge, 1989.

Atwood, Margaret. *Bodily Harm.* New York: Simon and Schuster, 1982.

– *Survival: A Thematic Guide to Canadian Literature.* Toronto: Anansi, 1972.

Avery, Donald H. *Reluctant Host: Canada's Response to Immigrant Workers, 1896–1994.* Toronto: McClelland and Stewart, 1995.

Bailey, Rosamond. 'Little Orphan Mary: Anne's Hoydenish Double.' *Canadian Children's Literature* 55 (1989): 8–17.

Bakhtin, Mikhail. *Problems of Dostoevsky's Poetics.* Trans. and ed. Caryl Emerson. Minneapolis: U of Minnesota P, 1984.

– *Rabelais and His World.* Trans. Helene Iswolsky. Bloomington: Indiana UP, 1984.

Baldwin, Douglas. 'L.M. Montgomery's *Anne of Green Gables*: The Japanese Connection.' *Journal of Canadian Studies* 28.3 (1993): 123–33.

Balibar, Etienne. 'The Nation Form: History and Ideology.' *Race, Nation, Class:*

Ambiguous Identities. Ed. Etienne Balibar and Immanuel Wallerstein. Trans. Chris Turner. London: Verso, 1991. 86–106.

Barrett, Michèle, and Mary McIntosh. *The Anti-social Family.* London: Verso, 1982.

Bashevkin, Sylvia B. 'Independence versus Partisanship: Dilemmas in the Political History of Women in English Canada.' *Rethinking Canada: The Promise of Women's History.* Ed. Veronica Strong-Boag and Anita Clair Fellman. Toronto: Copp Clark Pitman, 1986. 246–75.

Becket, Margaret, and Theodora Mills. 'L.C. Page and Company.' *Dictionary of Literary Biography* 49 (1986): 349–51.

Berger, Michael L. *The Devil Wagon in God's Country: The Automobile and Social Change in Rural America, 1893–1929.* Hamdon, CT: Archon Books, 1979.

Berton, Pierre. *Hollywood's Canada: The Americanization of Our National Image.* Toronto: McClelland and Stewart, 1975.

Bettelheim, Bruno. *The Uses of Enchantment: The Meaning and Importance of Fairy Tales.* New York: Vintage, 1975.

Bhabha, Homi K. 'DissemiNation: Time, Narrative, and the Margins of the Modern Nation.' *Nation and Narration.* Ed. Homi K. Bhabha. London: Routledge, 1990. 291–322.

– 'Signs Taken for Wonders: Questions of Ambivalence and Authority Under a Tree Outside Delhi, May 1817.' *Critical Inquiry* 12.1 (1985): 144–65.

Bluestone, George. *Novels into Film: The Metamorphosis of Fiction into Cinema.* Baltimore: Johns Hopkins UP, 1957.

Boggs, Joseph M. *The Art of Watching Films.* 4th ed. Mountain View, CA: Mayfield, 1996.

Bolger, Francis W.P. *Prince Edward Island and Confederation, 1863–1873.* Charlottetown: St Dunstan's UP, 1964.

– *The Years Before 'Anne.'* Charlottetown: Prince Edward Island Heritage Foundation, 1974.

Bone, T.R. *Studies in the History of Scottish Education, 1872–1939.* London: U of London P, 1967.

Boone, Laurel, ed. *The Collected Letters of Charles G.D. Roberts.* Fredericton: Goose Lane, 1989.

Brehaut, W. 'Some Landmarks in Prince Edward Island's Educational History.' Conference paper presented at the Canadian Association of Professors of Education. Charlottetown, 8 June 1964.

Broadie, Alexander. 'A Nation of Philosophers.' *Scotland: A Concise Cultural History.* Ed. Paul H. Scott. Edinburgh: Mainstream, 1993. 61–76.

Brouwer, Ruth Compton. *New Women for God: Canadian Presbyterian Women and India Missions, 1876–1914.* Toronto: U of Toronto P, 1990.

Brown, Russell M. 'Critic, Culture, Text: Beyond Thematics.' *Essays on Canadian Writing* 11 (1978): 151–83.

Budd, Louis. 'Mark Twain as an American Icon.' *The Cambridge Companion to Mark Twain.* Ed. Forrest G. Robinson. Cambridge: Cambridge UP, 1995. 1–26.

Buss, Helen M. 'Decoding L.M. Montgomery's Journals/ Encoding a Critical Practice for Women's Private Literature.' *Essays on Canadian Writing* 54 (Winter 1994): 80–100.

Campbell, Charles J. 'School Consolidation: Seventy Years of Evolution.' *Abegweit Review* 2 (1975): 1–11.

Canada Year Book. Ottawa: Dominion Bureau of Statistics, 1930.

Careless, Virginia. 'The Hijacking of Anne.' *Canadian Children's Literature* 67 (1992): 48–56.

Castle, Terry. *Masquerade and Civilization: The Carnivalesque in Eighteenth-Century Culture and Fiction.* Stanford: Stanford UP, 1986.

Child, Lydia Maria. *The Mother's Book.* Boston: Carter, Hendee, and Babcock, 1831.

Chodorow, Nancy. *The Reproduction of Mothering.* Los Angeles: U of California P, 1978.

Chown, Diana. Introduction. *The Stairway.* By Alice A. Chown. Toronto: U of Toronto P, 1988.

Cleverdon, Catherine Lyle. *The Woman Suffrage Movement in Canada.* Intro. Ramsay Cook. Toronto: U of Toronto P, 1970.

Cochrane, Jean. *The One-Room School in Canada.* Toronto: Fitzhenry and Whiteside, 1981.

Collard, Edgar Andrew. *Oldest McGill.* Toronto: Macmillan, 1946.

Colley, Linda. *Britons: Forging the Nation, 1707–1837.* New Haven: Yale UP, 1992.

The Confession of Faith/ The Larger Catechism/ The Shorter Catechism/ The Directory for Public Workshop/ The Form of Presbyterian Church Government. Edinburgh: William Blackwood, 1966.

Corr, Helen. 'An Exploration into Scottish Education.' *People and Society in Scotland.* Vol. 2. Ed. W. Hamish Fraser and R.J. Morris. Edinburgh: John Donald Publishers in association with the Economic and Social Society of Scotland, 1990. 290–309

Corse, Sarah M. *Nationalism and Literature: The Politics of Culture in Canada and the United States.* Cambridge: Cambridge UP, 1997.

Cowan, Ann S. 'Canadian Writers: Lucy Maud and Emily Byrd.' *Canadian Children's Literature* 1.3 (Autumn 1975): 42–9.

Cowan, Ruth. *More Work for Mother: The Ironies of Household Technology from the Open Hearth to the Microwave.* New York: Basic Books, 1983.

Davey, Frank. *Surviving the Paraphrase: Eleven Essays on Canadian Literature.* Winnipeg: Turnstone P, 1983.

Davie, George. *The Democratic Intellect: Scotland and Her Universities in the Nineteenth Century.* Edinburgh: Edinburgh UP, 1961.

– *A Passion for Ideas: Essays on the Scottish Enlightenment.* Vol. 2. Edinburgh: Polygon, 1994.

– *The Scottish Enlightenment and Other Essays.* Edinburgh: Polygon, 1991.

Davis, Donald. 'Dependent Motorization: Canada and the Automobile to the 1930s.' *Journal of Canadian Studies* (1986): 106–32.

Daymond, Douglas M., and Leslie G. Monkman, eds. *Towards a Canadian Literature: Essays, Editorials and Manifestos.* Vol. 1. *1752–1940.* Ottawa: Tecumseh P, 1984.

Demos, John. 'Oedipus and America: Historical Perspectives on the Reception of Psychoanalysis in the United States.' *Annual of Psychoanalysis* 6 (1978): 23–39.

Doody Jones, Mary E. 'Education on P.E.I.' *The Annotated Anne of Green Gables.* By L.M. Montgomery. Ed. Wendy E. Barry et al. New York: Oxford UP, 1997. 430–4.

Drain, Susan. 'Community and the Individual in *Anne of Green Gables*: The Meaning of Belonging.' *Children's Literature Association Quarterly* 11 (1986): 15–19.

– 'Feminine Convention and Female Identity: The Persistent Challenge of *Anne of Green Gables.*' *Canadian Children's Literature* 65 (1992): 40–7.

– '"Too Much Love-making": *Anne of Green Gables* on Television.' *The Lion and the Unicorn* 11.2 (1987): 63–72.

Duncan, Sara Jeannette. 'American Influence on Canadian Thought.' *The Week* 7 July 1887: 518.

Edwards, Owen Dudley. 'L.M. Montgomery's *Rilla of Ingleside*: Intention, Inclusion, Implosion.' *Harvesting Thistles: The Textual Garden of L.M. Montgomery.* Ed. Mary Henley Rubio. 126–36.

Egoff, Sheila A. 'Children's Literature (to 1960).' *Literary History of Canada.* Vol. 2. Ed. Carl F. Klinck. Toronto: U of Toronto P, 1976. 134–42.

Epperly, Elizabeth R. 'Approaching the Montgomery Manuscripts.' *Harvesting Thistles: The Textual Garden of L.M. Montgomery.* Ed. Mary Henley Rubio. 74–83.

– 'Chivalry and Romance: L.M. Montgomery's Re-vision of the Great War in *Rainbow Valley.*' *Myth and Milieu: Atlantic Literature and Culture, 1918–1939.* Ed. Gwendolyn Davies. Fredericton: Acadiensis P, 1993.

– *The Fragrance of Sweet-Grass: L.M. Montgomery's Heroines and the Pursuit of Romance.* Toronto: U of Toronto P, 1992.

Farr, Marie T. 'Freedom and Control: Automobiles in American Fiction of the 70s and 80s.' *Journal of Popular Culture* (Fall 1995): 137–70.

Feltes, Norman. *Literary Capital and the Late Victorian Novel.* Madison: U of Wisconsin P, 1993.

– *Modes of Production of Victorian Fiction.* Chicago: U of Chicago P, 1986.

Fitzgerald, F. Scott. *The Great Gatsby.* New York: Scribner's, 1925.

Flink, James J. *The Car Culture.* Cambridge: MIT P, 1975.

Freud, Sigmund. 'Family Romances (1908).' *The Standard Edition of the Complete Works of Sigmund Freud.* Ed. and trans. James Strachey. Vol. 9. London: Hogarth, 1953. 237–41.

Frost, Stanley Brice. *McGill University for the Advancement of Learning.* Vol. 2. *1895–1971.* Montreal: McGill-Queen's UP, 1984.

Frye, Northrop. *Anatomy of Criticism: Four Essays.* Princeton: Princeton UP, 1973.

– *The Bush Garden: Essays on the Canadian Imagination.* Toronto: Anansi, 1971.

Fussell, Paul. *The Great War and Modern Memory.* London: Oxford UP, 1975.

Galbraith, John Kenneth. *The Scotch.* Toronto: Macmillan, 1964.

Garvin, John, ed. *Canadian Poets.* Toronto: McClelland, Goodchild and Stewart, 1916.

Gay, Carol. '"Kindred Spirits" All: Green Gables Revisited.' *Children's Literature Association Quarterly* 11 (1986): 9–12.

Gerson, Carole. 'Canadian Women Writers and American Markets, 1880–1940.' *Context North America: Canadian/U.S. Literary Relations.* Ed. Camille La Bossière. Ottawa: U of Ottawa P, 1994. 106–18.

– 'The Canon between the Wars: Field-notes of a Feminist Literary Archaeologist.' *Canadian Canons: Essays in Literary Value.* Ed. Robert Lecker. Toronto: U of Toronto P, 1991. 46–56.

– 'The Changing Contours of a National Literature.' *College English* 50.8 (Dec. 1988): 888–95.

– '"Fitted to Earn Her Own Living": Figures of the New Woman in the Writing of L.M. Montgomery.' *Children's Voices in Atlantic Literature and Culture: Essays on Childhood.* Ed. Hilary Thompson. Guelph, ON: Canadian Children's P, 1995. 24–34.

– *A Purer Taste: The Writing and Reading of Fiction in English in Nineteenth-Century Canada.* Toronto: U of Toronto P, 1989.

Gibson, Ian. *The English Vice: Beating, Sex, and Shame in Victorian England and After.* London: Duckworth, 1978.

Gillen, Mollie. *The Masseys: Founding Family.* Toronto: Ryerson, 1965.

– *The Wheel of Things: A Biography of L.M. Montgomery.* Don Mills, ON: Fitzhenry and Whiteside, 1975.

Godwin, Gail. 'A Diarist on Diarists.' *Antaeus* 21/22 (1976): 50–6.

Gramsci, Antonio. *Selections from the Prison Notebooks*. Ed. Quintin Hoare and Geoffrey Nowell Smith. New York: International Publishers, 1971.

Granatstein, J.L., et al. *Twentieth Century Canada*. 2nd ed. Toronto: McGraw-Hill Ryerson, 1986.

Grant, Nigel, and Walter Humes. 'Scottish Education, 1700–2000.' *Scotland: A Concise Cultural History*. Ed. Paul H. Scott. Edinburgh: Mainstream, 1993. 357–72.

Greven, Philip. *Spare the Child: The Religious Roots of Punishment and the Psychological Impact of Physical Abuse*. New York: Knopf, 1990.

Griswold, Jerry. *Audacious Kids: Coming of Age in America's Classic Children's Books*. New York: Oxford UP, 1992.

Hall, C. Wayne. 'It Was a Long, Uneasy Alliance.' *The McGill You Knew: An Anthology of Memories, 1920–1960*. Ed. Edgar Andrew Collard. Don Mills, ON: Longman, 1975. 207–10.

Hamilton, Sharon Jean. *My Name's Not Susie: A Life Transformed by Literacy*. Portsmouth, NH: Boynton/Cook, 1995.

Hathaway, R.H. 'An Appreciation.' *Later Poems*. By Bliss Casman. Toronto: McClelland and Stewart, 1921. vii–xxii.

Hayden, Delores. *The Grand Domestic Revolution: A History of Feminist Designs for American Homes, Neighborhoods, and Cities*. Cambridge: MIT P, 1982.

Henderson, Hamish. 'The Oral Tradition.' *Scotland: A Concise Cultural History*. Ed. Paul H. Scott. Edinburgh: Mainstream, 1993. 159–71.

Howes, Ruth. 'Adelaide Hunter Hoodless, 1857–1910.' *The Clear Spirit: Twenty Canadian Women and Their Times*. Ed. Mary Quayle Innis. Toronto: U of Toronto P, 1966. 103–19.

Huaco, George. *The Sociology of Film Art*. New York: Basic Books, 1965.

Humes, Walter M., and Hamish Paterson. *Scottish Culture and Scottish Education, 1800–1980*. Edinburgh: John Donald, 1983.

Hunt, Peter. 'Retreatism and Advance.' *Children's Literature: An Illustrated History*. Oxford: Oxford UP, 1995. 195–224.

Hutcheon, Linda. *The Canadian Postmodern: A Study of Contemporary English-Canadian Fiction*. Toronto: Oxford UP, 1988.

– 'Circling the Downspout of Empire.' *Ariel* 20.4 (1989): 149–75.

Hyman, Irwin. *Reading, Writing, and the Hickory Stick: The Appalling Story of Physical and Psychological Abuse in American Schools*. Lexington, MA: Lexington Books, 1990.

Insch, George Pratt. *School Life in Old Scotland: From Contemporary Sources*. Edinburgh: Educational Institute of Scotland, 1925.

Irvine, Lorna. *Sub/version*. Toronto: ECW, 1986.

JanMohamed, Abdul R. 'The Economy of Manichean Allegory: The Function of Racial Difference.' *Critical Inquiry* 12.1 (1985): 59–87.

Jellison, Katherine. *Entitled to Power: Farm Women and Technology, 1913–1963.* Chapel Hill: U of North Carolina P, 1993.

Kalback, Warren E. *The Effect of Immigration on Population.* Ottawa: Department of Manpower and Immigration, 1974.

Kamikawa, Terry. *Akage no An no Seikatsu Jiten.* (*A Dictionary of Red-haired Anne's Daily Life: A Guide to the Good Old Days*) Tokyo: Koudansya, 1997.

Katrak, Ketu H. 'Decolonizing Culture: Toward a Theory for Post-Colonial Women's Texts.' *Modern Fiction Studies* 35.1 (1989): 157–79.

Katsura, Yuko. 'The Reception of *Anne of Green Gables* and Its Popularity in Japan.' *Okayama Prefectural College: Design Department Kiyo* 2.1 (1995): 39–44.

– 'Red-Haired Anne in Japan.' *Canadian Children's Literature* 34 (1984): 57–60.

Kennedy, Mike. 'Is Leis an Tighearna An Talamh Agus An Lan (The Earth and All It Contains Belongs to God): The Scottish Gaelic Settlement History of Prince Edward Island.' PhD diss., U Edinburgh, 1995.

Kensinger, Faye. *Children of the Series and How They Grew.* Bowling Green, OH: Bowling Green State U Popular P, 1987.

Kessler, Deirdre. *Brupp Rides Again.* Charlottetown: Indigo P, 1995.

Klinck, Carl F., ed. *Literary History of Canada.* Vols. 1 and 2. 2nd ed. Toronto: U of Toronto P, 1976.

Kline, Ronald, and Trevor Pinch. 'Users as Agents of Technological Change: The Social Construction of the Automobile in the Rural United States.' *Technology and Culture* (Oct. 1996): 763–95.

Kornfeld, Eva, and Susan Jackson. 'The Female Bildungsroman in Nineteenth-Century America: Parameters of a Vision.' *Journal of American Culture* 10.4 (1987): 69–75.

Kroetsch, Robert. 'Unhiding the Hidden: Recent Canadian Fiction.' *Open Letter* 5.4 (1983): 43–5.

Kumai, Akiko. *Akage no An no Jinsei Noto.* (Life Book of 'Red-Haired Anne') Tokyo: Daiwa Shuppan, 1992.

Laird, David. 'Versions of Eden: The Automobile and the American Novel.' *The Automobile and American Culture.* Ed. David Lewis and Laurence Golstein. Ann Arbor: U of Michigan P, 1983.

Leacock, Stephen. *The Iron Man and the Tin Woman: With Other Such Futurities.* New York: Dodd, Mead, 1929.

– *Winnowed Wisdom.* New York: Dodd, Mead, 1926.

Lecker, Robert. *Making It Real: The Canonization of English-Canadian Literature.* Concord, ON: Anansi, 1995.

Lifshin, Lyn, ed. *Ariadne's Thread: A Collection of Contemporary Women's Journals.* New York: Harper and Row, 1982.

Little, Jean. 'But What About Jane?' *Canadian Children's Literature* 3 (1975): 71–82.

Logan, John D. *Highways of Canadian Literature.* Toronto: McClelland and Stewart, 1924.

Luxton, Meg, Harriet Rosenberg, and Sedaf Arat-Koc. *Through the Kitchen Window: The Politics of Home and Family.* 2nd ed. Toronto: Garamond, 1990.

Lynch, Michael. *Edinburgh and the Reformation.* Edinburgh: John Donald, 1981.

– *Scotland: A New History.* London: Pimlico, 1997.

– 'Scottish Culture in Its Historical Perspective.' *Scotland: A Concise Cultural History.* Ed. Paul H. Scott. Edinburgh: Mainstream, 1993. 15–45.

MacDonald, Cheryl. *Adelaide Hoodless, Domestic Crusader.* Toronto: Dundurn, 1986.

MacLulich, T.D. 'L.M. Montgomery's Portraits of the Artist: Realism, Idealism, and the Domestic Imagination.' *English Studies in Canada* 11.4 (Dec. 1985): 459–73.

MacMechan, Archibald. *Headwaters of Canadian Literature.* 1924. Toronto: McClelland and Stewart, 1974.

Macmillan, Cyrus. *McGill and Its Story, 1821–1921.* London: John Lane, 1921.

Matsumoto, Syoji, and Kaori. *Yappari Akage no An ga Suki (I Like Red-haired Anne After All)* Tokyo: Sekaibunkasha, 1994.

Matthews, William. 'The Diary: A Neglected Genre.' *Sewanee Review* 85.1 (1977): 286–300.

May, Henry F. *The End of American Innocence, 1912–1917.* New York: Knopf, 1959.

McCarthy, Dermot. 'Early Canadian Literary Histories and the Function of a Canon.' *Canadian Canons: Essays in Literary Value.* Ed. Robert Lecker. Toronto: U of Toronto P, 1991. 30–45.

McClung, Nellie. *In Times Like These.* 1915. Intro. Veronica Strong-Boag. Toronto: U of Toronto P, 1983.

McKinney, Louise. 'Editorial.' *Canadian Home Journal* Aug. 1919: n.p.

McNaught, Kenneth. *The Penguin History of Canada.* Harmondsworth: Penguin, 1976.

McNeill, John. School Visitor's Report for the Year 1845. Public Archives and Records Office. Charlottetown, P.E.I., n.d.

Miki, Mie. 'Sobo no Omoi wo Tadotte (Tracing My Grandmother's [Hanako Muraoka's] Thinking.' *Akage no An: Yumekiko (Red-haired Anne: A Dream Journey.* Ed. N.H.K. Shuzaihan. Tokyo: Nippon Hosokyokai, 1989.

Miller, Alice. *For Your Own Good: Hidden Cruelty in Child-Rearing and the*

Roots of Violence. Trans. Hildegarde and Hunter Hannum. New York: Farrar, Straus, and Giroux, 1983.

Miller, Judith. 'Montgomery's Emily: Voices and Silences.' *Studies in Canadian Literature* 9.2 (1984): 158–68.

– 'The-Writer-as-a-Young-Woman and Her Family: Montgomery and Emily.' *New Quarterly* 7.1–2 (1987): 301–19.

Miller, Muriel. *Bliss Carman: Quest and Revolt*. St. John's: Jesperson, 1985.

Mills, Sara. *Discourses of Difference: An Analysis of Women's Travel Writing and Colonialism*. London: Routledge, 1991.

Minh-ha, Trinh T. *Woman, Native, Other: Postcoloniality and Feminism*. Bloomington: Indiana UP, 1989.

Montgomery, L.M. *Along the Shore: Tales by the Sea*. Ed. Rea Wilmshurst. Toronto: McClelland and Stewart, 1989.

– *The Alpine Path: The Story of My Career*, 1917. Markham, ON: Fitzhenry and Whiteside, 1997.

– *Anne of Avonlea*. 1909. Toronto: McClelland-Bantam, 1992.

– *Anne of Green Gables*. 1908. Toronto: McClelland and Stewart, 1992.

– *Anne of Ingleside*. 1939. Toronto: McClelland-Bantam, 1983.

– *Anne of the Island*. 1915. Toronto: McClelland-Bantam, 1992.

– *Anne's House of Dreams*. 1917. Toronto: McClelland-Bantam, 1992.

– *The Blue Castle*. 1926. Toronto: McClelland-Bantam, 1988.

– *Chronicles of Avonlea*. 1912. Toronto: McClelland-Bantam, 1987.

– *The Doctor's Sweetheart and Other Stories*. Ed. Catherine McLay. Toronto: McGraw-Hill Ryerson, 1979.

– *Emily Climbs*. 1925. Toronto: McClelland and Stewart, 1989.

– *Emily of New Moon*. 1923. Toronto: McClelland and Stewart, 1989.

– *Emily's Quest*. 1927. Toronto: McClelland and Stewart, 1989.

– *The Green Gables Letters from L.M. Montgomery to Ephraim Weber, 1905–1909*. Ed. Wilfrid Eggleston. Toronto: Ryerson, 1960.

– *The Golden Road*. Boston: Page, 1913.

– *Jane of Lantern Hill*. 1937. Toronto: McClelland-Bantam, 1989.

– *Kilmeny of the Orchard*. Boston: Page, 1910.

– *Magic for Marigold*. 1929. Toronto: McClelland-Bantam, 1992.

– *Mongomeri-Nikki: Ai, sono Hikari to Kage (The Selected Journals of L.M. Montgomery, 1897–1900: Love, Its Light and Shadow)*. Trans. Yuko Katsura. Tokyo: Rippu Shobo, 1997.

– *My Dear Mr. M: Letters to G.B. MacMillan from L.M. Montgomery*. Ed. Francis W.P. Bolger and Elizabeth R. Epperly. Toronto: Oxford UP, 1992.

– 'Penelope Struts Her Theories.' *The Road to Yesterday*. 1974. Toronto: McClelland-Bantam, 1993. 131–74.

- *The Poetry of Lucy Maud Montgomery.* Selected and intro. by John Ferns and Kevin McCabe. Markham, ON: Fitzhenry and Whiteside, 1987.
- *Rainbow Valley.* 1919. Toronto: McClelland and Stewart-Bantam, 1987.
- *Rilla of Ingleside.* 1920. Toronto: McClelland-Bantam, 1992.
- *The Road to Yesterday.* Toronto: McGraw-Hill Ryerson, 1974.
- *The Selected Journals of L.M. Montgomery.* Vol. 1. *1889–1910.* Ed. Mary Rubio and Elizabeth Waterston. Toronto: Oxford UP, 1985.
- *The Selected Journals of L.M. Montgomery.* Vol. 2. *1910–1921.* Ed. Mary Rubio and Elizabeth Waterston. Toronto: Oxford UP, 1987.
- *The Selected Journals of L.M. Montgomery.* Vol. 3. *1921–1929.* Ed. Mary Rubio and Elizabeth Waterston. Toronto: Oxford UP, 1992.
- *The Selected Journals of L.M. Montgomery.* Vol. 4. *1929–1935.* Ed. Mary Rubio and Elizabeth Waterston. Toronto: Oxford UP, 1998.
- *The Story Girl.* 1911. Toronto: McClelland-Bantam, 1993.
- *A Tangled Web.* 1931. Toronto: McClelland-Bantam, 1989.
- Unpublished Journals, 1929–1942, L.M. Montgomery Papers, U of Guelph Archives.
Montgomery, L.M., Marian Keith, and Mabel Burns McKinley. *Courageous Women.* Toronto: McClelland, 1934.
Morrow, Dianne. 'A Little Learning: Early Education on Prince Edward Island.' *The Island Magazine* 26 (1989): 27–34.
Mott, Frank. *Golden Multitudes.* New York: Bowker, 1947.
Neilson, Helen R. '"Clan Macdonald": Life at Macdonald College.' *The McGill You Knew: An Anthology of Memories, 1920–1960.* Ed. Edgar Andrew Collard. Don Mills, ON: Longman, 1975. 202–7.
Neth, Mary. *Preserving the Family Farm: Women, Community, and the Foundation of Agribusiness in the Midwest, 1900–1940.* Baltimore: Johns Hopkins UP, 1995.
Nikolajeva, Maria. 'Reflection of Change in Children's Book Titles.' *Reflections of Change: Children's Literature since 1945.* Ed. Sandra L. Beckett. Westport, CT: Greenwood Press, 1997.
Nodelman, Perry. 'Progressive Utopia: Or, How to Grow Up Without Growing Up.' *Such a Simple Little Tale: Critical Responses to L.M. Montgomery's 'Anne of Green Gables.'* Ed. Mavis Reimer. 29–38.
Nussbaum, Felicity A. 'Toward Conceptualizing Diary.' *Studies in Autobiography.* Ed. James Olney. New York: Oxford UP, 1988. 128–40.
Pacey, Desmond. *Creative Writing in Canada.* Rev. ed. Toronto: McGraw-Hill Ryerson, 1961.
- 'Fiction (1920–1940).' *Literary History of Canada.* Vol. 2. Ed. Carl F. Klinck. Toronto: U of Toronto P, 1976. 168–204.

Parkin, Alan. *A History of Psychoanalysis in Canada.* Toronto: Toronto Psycho-
analytic Society, 1987.

Parks, M.G. Preface. *Headwaters of Canadian Literature.* 1924. Toronto:
McClelland and Stewart, 1974.

Peabody, George. *School Days: The One-Room School of Maritime Canada.*
Fredericton: Goose Lane, 1992.

Petersen, Kirsten Holst. 'First Things First: Problems of a Feminist Approach to
African Literature.' *Kunapipi* 6.3 (1984): 35–47.

Pierce, Lorne. *Marjorie Pickthall: A Book of Remembrance.* Toronto: Ryerson,
1925.

Ponsonby, Arthur. *English Diaries: A Review of English Diaries from the
Sixteenth to the Twentieth Century with an Introduction on Diary Writing.*
2nd ed. London: Methuen, 1927.

Powe, B.W. *A Climate Changed: Essays on Canadian Writers.* Oakville, ON:
Mosaic, 1984.

Prentice, Alison. 'The Feminization of Teaching.' *The Neglected Majority:
Essays in Canadian Women's History.* Ed. Susan Mann Trofimenkoff and
Alison Prentice. Toronto: McClelland and Stewart, 1977.

Prentice, Alison, et al. *Canadian Women: A History.* Toronto: Harcourt Brace
Jovanovich, 1988.

Radway, Janice. *Reading the Romance: Women, Patriarchy, and Popular
Literature.* Chapel Hill: U of North Carolina P, 1984.

Ray, Sheila. 'School Stories.' *International Encyclopedia of Children's Literature.*
Ed. Peter Hunt. London: Routledge, 1996.

Reimer, Mavis, ed. *Such a Simple Little Tale: Critical Responses to L.M. Montgomery's 'Anne of Green Gables.'* Metuchen, NJ: Children's Literature Association and Scarecrow P, 1992.

Reischauer, Edwin O. *The Japanese Today.* Cambridge: Belknap P of Harvard
UP, 1988.

Rendall, Jane. *The Origins of the Scottish Enlightenment (1707–1776).* London:
Macmillan, 1972.

Rich, Adrienne. *Adrienne Rich's Poetry and Prose.* Ed. Barbara C. Gelpi and
Albert Gelpi. 2nd ed. New York: Norton, 1993.

Richardson, Theresa R. *The Century of the Child: The Mental Hygiene Movement
and Social Policy in the United States and Canada.* Albany: SUNY P, 1989.

Riesman, David. *The Lonely Crowd.* New Haven: Yale UP, 1968.

*The Road to L.M. Montgomery: The Newsletter of the Kindred Spirits Society of
Hamilton* 2 June 1996.

Roberts, Charles G.D. *The Collected Poems of Charles G.D. Roberts.* Ed.
Desmond Pacey. Wolfville, NS: The Wombat, 1985.

Roberts, Wayne. '"Rocking the Cradle for the World": The New Woman and Maternal Feminism, Toronto, 1877–1914.' *A Not Unreasonable Claim: Women and Reform in Canada, 1880s-1920s*. Ed. Linda Kealey. Toronto: Women's P, 1979. 15–45.

Robertson, Heather. *Driving Force: The McLaughlin Family and the Age of the Car*. Toronto: McClelland and Stewart, 1995.

Robertson, Ian Ross. 'Reform, Literacy, and the Lease: The Prince Edward Island Free Education Act of 1852.' *Acadiensis* (Autumn 1990): 52–71.

Robinson, Laura M. '"Pruned Down and Branched Out": Embracing Contradiction in *Anne of Green Gables.' Children's Voices in Atlantic Literature and Culture: Essays on Childhood*. Ed. Hilary Thompson. Guelph, ON: Canadian Children's P, 1995. 35–43.

Rooke, Patricia T., and R.L. Schnell. *Discarding the Asylum: From Child Rescue to Welfare State in English Canada (1800–1950)*. New York: UP of America, 1983.

Ross, Catherine Sheldrick. 'Readers Reading L.M. Montgomery.' *Harvesting Thistles: The Textual Garden of L.M. Montgomery*. Ed. Mary Henley Rubio. 23–35.

Rubio, Jennie. '"Strewn with Dead Bodies": Women and Gossip in *Anne of Ingleside.' Harvesting Thistles: The Textual Garden of L.M. Montgomery*. Ed. Mary Henley Rubio. 167–77.

Rubio, Mary Henley. *Anne of Green Gables:* 'The Architect of Adolescence.' *Such a Simple Little Tale: Critical Response to L.M. Montgomery's 'Anne of Green Gables.'* Ed. Mavis Reimer. 65–82.

– ed. *Harvesting Thistles: The Textual Garden of L.M. Montgomery*. Guelph, ON: Canadian Children's P, 1994.

– 'Lucy Maud Montgomery.' *Profiles in Canadian Literature*. Ed. Jeffrey M. Heath. Toronto: Dundurn, 1991.

– 'Subverting the Trite: L.M. Montgomery's "Room of Her Own."' *Canadian Children's Literature* 65 (1992): 6–39.

Rubio, Mary Henley, and Elizabeth Waterston. Introduction. *The Selected Journals of L.M. Montgomery*. Vol. I. By L.M. Montgomery. Toronto: Oxford UP, 1985. xiii–xxiv.

– *The Selected Journals of L.M. Montgomery*. Vol. III. By L.M. Montgomery. Toronto: Oxford UP, 1992. x–xxv.

– *Writing a Life: L.M. Montgomery*. Toronto: ECW, 1995.

Russell, R.W., D.W. Russell, and Rea Wilmshurst. *Lucy Maud Montgomery: A Preliminary Bibliography*. Waterloo, ON: U of Waterloo Library, 1986.

Said, Edward W. *Orientalism*. New York: Random House, 1978.

Savage, Candace. *Our Nell: A Scrapbook Biography of Nellie L. McClung*. Saskatoon: Western Producer Prairie Books, 1979.

Saxton, Martha. *Louisa May: A Modern Biography of Louisa May Alcott.*
Boston: Houghton Mifflin, 1977.

Scharff, Virginia. *Taking the Wheel: Women and the Coming of the Motor Age.*
New York: Free P, 1991.

Schatz, Thomas. *Hollywood Genres: Formulas, Filmmaking, and the Studio
System.* New York: Random House, 1981.

Scott, Paul H., ed. *Scotland: A Concise Cultural History.* Edinburgh: Mainstream, 1993.

Sheckels, Theodore F. 'In Search of Structures for the Stories of Girls and
Women: L.M. Montgomery's Life-Long Struggle.' *American Review of
Canadian Studies* 23 (1993): 523–38.

Sher, Richard B. *Church and University in the Scottish Enlightenment: The
Moderate Literati of Edinburgh.* Princeton: Princeton UP, 1985.

Showalter, Elaine. 'Feminist Criticism in the Wilderness.' *Critical Inquiry* 8
(1981): 179–205.

– 'Women's Time, Women's Space: Writing the History of Feminist Criticism.'
Feminist Issues in Literary Scholarship. Ed. Shari Benstock. Bloomington:
Indiana UP, 1987.

Silver, Harold. *The Concept of Popular Education: A Study of Ideas and Social
Movements in the Early Nineteenth Century.* London: Methuen, 1977.

Smart, Patricia. *Writing in the Father's House: The Emergence of the Feminine
in the Quebec Literary Tradition.* Toronto: U of Toronto P, 1991.

Smith, Donald. 'Culture and Religion.' *Scotland: A Concise Cultural History.* Ed.
Paul H. Scott. Edinburgh: Mainstream, 1993. 47–60.

Smith, W.O. Lester. *Education in Great Britain.* London: Oxford UP, 1964.

Smout, T.C. *A History of the Scottish People, 1560–1830.* London: Fontana,
1972.

Solomon, Stanley J. *Beyond Formula: American Film Genres.* New York:
Harcourt Brace Jovanovich, 1976.

Spivak, Gayatri Chakravorty. 'Three Women's Texts and a Critique of Imperialism.' *Critical Inquiry* 12.1 (1985): 43–61.

Spyri, Johanna. *Heidi.* 1880. Harmondsworth: Puffin Books, 1994.

Stevenson, Lionel. *Appraisals of Canadian Literature.* Toronto: Macmillan,
1926.

Stewart, Deborah. 'The Island Meets the Auto.' *The Island Magazine* (Fall/
Winter 1978): 9–13.

Stobie, Margaret. *Frederick Philip Grove.* New York: Twayne, 1973.

Strong-Boag, Veronica. 'Ever a Crusader: Nellie McClung, First-Wave Feminist.'
Rethinking Canada: The Promise of Women's History. Ed. Veronica Strong-
Boag and Anita Clair Fellman. Toronto: Copp Clark Pitman, 1986. 178–90.

Thomas, Gillian. 'The Decline of Anne: Matron vs. Child.' *Such a Simple Little*

Tale: Critical Responses to L.M. Montgomery's 'Anne of Green Gables.' Ed.
  Mavis Reimer. 23–8.
Tiffin, Helen. 'Post-Colonial Literatures and Counter-Discourse.' *Kunapipi* 9.3
  (1987): 17–34.
Turner, Graeme. 'The Idea of Cultural Studies.' *British Cultural Studies.*
  London: Routledge, 1996.
Tye, Diane. 'Multiple Meanings Called Cavendish: The Interaction of Tourism
  with Traditional Culture.' *Journal of Canadian Studies* 29.1 (1994): 122–34.
– 'Women's Oral Narrative Traditions as Depicted in Lucy Maud Mont-
  gomery's Fiction, 1918–1939.' *Myth and Milieu: Atlantic Literature and
  Culture, 1918–1939.* Ed. Gwendolyn Davies. Fredericton: Acadiensis, 1993.
  123–35.
Urquhart, Jane. Afterword. *Emily Climbs.* By L.M. Montgomery. Toronto:
  McClelland and Stewart, 1989. 330–4.
Valverde, Mariana. *The Age of Light, Soap, and Water: Moral Reform in English
  Canada, 1885–1925.* Toronto: McClelland and Stewart, 1991.
Wachowicz, Barbara. 'L.M. Montgomery at Home in Poland.' *Canadian
  Children's Literature* 46 (1987): 7–36.
Wardle, David. *English Popular Education, 1780–1970.* London: Cambridge UP,
  1970.
Waterston, Elizabeth. *Kindling Spirit: L.M. Montgomery's 'Anne of Green
  Gables.'* Toronto: ECW, 1993.
– 'Lucy Maud Montgomery.' *The Clear Spirit: Twenty Canadian Women and
  Their Times.* Ed. Mary Quayle Innis. Toronto: U of Toronto P, 1966. 198–220.
– 'Marigold and the Magic of Memory.' *Harvesting Thistles: The Textual
  Garden of L.M. Montgomery.* Ed. Mary Henley Rubio. 155–66.
– *Survey: A Short History of Canadian Literature.* Toronto: Methuen, 1973.
Watson, Albert Durrant, and Lorne Albert Pierce. *Our Canadian Literature:
  Representative Prose and Verse.* Toronto: Ryerson, 1922.
Walker, R.E. *Checklist of Canadian Literature and Background Materials, 1628–
  1960.* Toronto: U of Toronto P, 1972.
Weale, David. *Them Times.* Charlottetown: Institute of Island Studies, 1992.
Weber, Max. 'The Protestant Sects and the Spirit of Capitalism.' *From Max
  Weber: Essays in Sociology.* Ed. H.H. Gerth and C. Wright Mills. New York:
  Oxford UP, 1958.
White, Gavin. 'L.M. Montgomery and the French.' *Canadian Children's
  Literature* 78 (1995): 65–68.
Wiggins, Genevieve. *L.M. Montgomery.* Boston: Twayne, 1992.
Wilder, Laura Ingalls. *Little House on the Prairie.* New York: HarperCollins,
  1971.

Wilmshurst, Rea. Introduction. *Among the Shadows: Tales from the Darker Side*. Toronto: McClelland and Stewart, 1990. 7–15.

Yeast, Denyse. 'Negotiating Friendships: The Reading and Writing of L.M. Montgomery.' *Harvesting Thistles: The Textual Garden of L.M. Montgomery*. Ed. Mary Henley Rubio. Guelph, ON: Canadian Children's P, 1994. 113–25.

Young, Alan R. 'L.M. Montgomery's *Rilla of Ingleside* (1920): Romance and the Experience of War.' *Myth and Milieu: Atlantic Literature and Culture, 1918–1939*. Ed. Gwendolyn Davies. Fredericton: Acadiensis, 1993. 95–122.

Contributors

Yoshiko Akamatsu is an associate professor of English at Notre Dame Seishin University, in Okayama, Japan. She completed her doctorate in English literature at Hiroshima University with a focus on Montgomery's fiction and writing. Her Japanese translation of *Akin to Anne: Tales of Other Orphans* was published as *An no Nakamatachi* (1989) and *Zoku An no Nakamatachi* (1990) by the Shinozaki Shorin Press. She is also the author of a chapter entitled 'L.M. Montgomery' in *Kanada Bungaku Nyumon* (An Introduction to Canadian literature, 1998).

Margaret Atwood is one of Canada's most recognized and respected writers. She is the winner of many national and international awards. Her most recent works of fiction and poetry include *Alias Grace* (1996), *Morning in a Burnt House* (1995), *The Robber Bride* (1993), *Cat's Eye* (1989), and *The Handmaid's Tale* (1985). As a writer of non-fiction, Atwood has investigated Canadian culture in works including *Survival: A Thematic Guide to Canadian Literature* (1972) and *Strange Things: The Malevolent North in Canadian Literature* (1995). She lives in Toronto.

Roberta Buchanan is a professor of English and women's studies at Memorial University of Newfoundland. Born in South Africa and educated in England, with a PhD from the Shakespeare Institute at Birmingham University, she emigrated to Canada in 1964. She has been actively involved in the local feminist and writing communities. Buchanan is the editor of a sixteenth-century satire, Ulpian Fulwell's *Ars Adulandi or the Art of Flattery* (1986), and author of a collection of poems, *I Moved All My Women Upstairs* (1998). Her current research interests focus on women's autobiography.

Diana Arlene Chlebek is associate professor of bibliography in languages and literature in the library at the University of Akron, where she also teaches literature and film in the Canadian studies program. Her research interests include nineteenth- and twentieth-century narrative fiction, with a particular focus on children's and young adult literature. She has published articles on these topics in several volumes of the *Dictionary of Literary Biography*, in *Multicultural Authors of Books for Young People*, and in the *Children's Literature Association Quarterly*.

Adrienne Clarkson is a well-known television producer and writer in Canada. Her current program, *Adrienne Clarkson Presents*, now in its eighth season on CBC, is the only prime-time series devoted to Canadian culture. The show has won numerous awards nationally and internationally. Formerly Ontario's agent-general in France, Clarkson is an Officer of the Order of Canada and chairwoman of the Canadian Museum of Civilization.

Frank Davey is Carl F. Klinck Professor of Canadian Literature at the University of Western Ontario. He is the author of cultural studies books in a number of genres, including *Post-National Arguments: The Politics of the Anglophone Canadian Novel since 1967* (1993), *Canadian Literary Power* (1994), *Karla's Web: A Cultural Examination of the Mahaffy–French Murders* (1994), and *Cultural Mischief: A Practical Guide to Multiculturalism* (1996). His book *Reading 'KIM' Right* (1993), his examination of the electoral campaigns of ex-prime minister Kim Campbell, led to the essay in this volume.

Ann Dutton first read L.M. Montgomery's novels as a child and became reacquainted with the author's work when introducing the novels to her daughters. As an educator for many years in England, Ontario, and Prince Edward Island, she is especially interested in Montgomery's fictional portraits of students and teachers. Ann Dutton's poems have been published in several Irish journals and anthologies, including the *Waterford Review* (1984), *Women's Work* (1996), and *Tangerine Skies* (1996).

Owen Dudley Edwards is a reader in history at the University of Edinburgh, where he teaches Montgomery as part of his research seminar. He contributed a study of *Rilla of Ingleside* as a war novel to Mary Rubio's *Harvesting Thistles: The Textual Garden of L.M. Montgomery* and has also written for the journal *Canadian Children's Literature*. Owen Dudley Edwards's books include *Burke and Hare, P.G. Wodehouse: A Critical and Historical Essay, The Sins of Our Fathers: Roots of Conflict in Northern Ireland*, and *Macaulay*. He edited the

Oxford Sherlock Holmes and is currently writing a study of Ireland in the British imagination.

Elizabeth Epperly was most recently the president of the University of Prince Edward Island and was also the founding chair of the L.M. Montgomery Institute. A professor of English who specializes in nineteenth-century literature, she is the author of numerous articles on Lucy Maud Montgomery. Her most recent books include *The Fragrance of Sweet-Grass: L.M. Montgomery's Heroines and the Pursuit of Romance* (1992) and a co-edited volume, with F.W.P. Bolger, *My Dear Mr. M: Selected Letters of L.M. Montgomery* (1992). Her current research focuses on Montgomery's visual imagination.

Irene Gammel is associate professor of English at the University of Prince Edward Island, where she also serves as the co-chair of the L.M. Montgomery Institute. She has published widely on women's issues in twentieth-century literature and life writing. She is the author of *Sexualizing Power in Naturalism: Theodore Dreiser and Frederick Philip Grove* (1994) and the editor of *Confessional Politics: Women's Sexual Self-Representations in Life Writing and Popular Media* (1999). Her current research focuses on women's autobiographies during the twenties, and she is writing a cultural biography of Else von Freytag-Loringhoven, a Dada poet and performance artist in Greenwich Village.

Carole Gerson, professor in the Department of English at Simon Fraser University, has published extensively in the area of Canadian literary history. Her essay '"Fitted to Earn Her own Living": Figures on the New Woman in the Writing of L.M. Montgomery' appeared in *Children's Voices in Atlantic Literature and Culture: Essays on Childhood*, edited by Hilary Thompson (1995). She has edited Agnes Maule Machar's *Roland Graeme: Knight: A Novel of Our Time* (1996), and with Gwendolyn Davies she co-edited *Canadian Poetry: From the Beginnings through the First World War* (1994). Other titles include *Canada's Early Women Writers: Texts in English to 1859* (1994) and *A Purer Taste: The Writing and Reading of Fiction in English in Nineteenth-Century Canada* (1989).

Sharon J. Hamilton, professor of English, is currently associate dean for external affairs at the Indiana University School of Liberal Arts in Indianapolis, where she also serves as director of campus writing. She has published widely in journals such as *College English*, the *Journal of Teaching Writing*, and the *Writing Instructor*, and has edited three books on collaborative learning, most recently *Collaborative Learning in the Arts, Sciences, and Professional Schools.* In her own literacy narrative, *My Name's Not Susie: A Life Transformed by Literacy* (1995), she traces the influences of *Anne of Green Gables* on her own sense of identity and growing awareness of ethics and values.

Deirdre Kessler is a writer and broadcaster, and is co-chair of the L.M. Montgomery Institute. She is author of a dozen children's books and young adult novels, including a series about an Island cat named Brupp, which has been translated into other languages. Kessler's script on the life of L.M. Montgomery has been made into a video for the Parks Canada Green Gables site, and she has made a number of radio documentaries for CBC, including 'Becoming Wise' for *Ideas*, and 'Imagine a Castle of Blue: L.M. Montgomery, Romance, and Feminism.' She teaches children's literature at the University of Prince Edward Island, and has recently completed a full-length biography of Island centenarian and benefactor of the arts and culture, Wanda Lefurgey Wyatt.

Jennifer H. Litster is a doctoral candidate in history and Canadian studies at Edinburgh University. Her doctoral dissertation, prepared under the supervision of Owen Dudley Edwards and folklorist Margaret Bennett, is entitled 'The Scottish Context of L.M. Montgomery' and investigates archival sources in Prince Edward Island and at the University of Guelph. She has published her research in *Canadian Children's Literature.*

Dianne Hicks Morrow is executive director of the PEI Literacy Alliance. Her poetry has been published in various literary journals, such as the *Abegweit Review*, *Contemporary Verse 2*, and *Pottersfield Portfolio*. Her non-fiction articles and profiles of Islanders have been published in *Common Ground* and the *Island Magazine*. She is currently writing a non-fiction book about kindred spirits. She has lived on the north shore of PEI for over twenty years.

Sasha Mullally is a doctoral candidate in history at the University of Toronto. Her thesis focuses on the history of country doctors in the Maritimes and northern New England. She first explored the writings of L.M. Montgomery when she began analysing the portrayal of country doctors in popular literature. Also interested in the history of technology in rural North America, she is researching the early history of automobility on Prince Edward Island, which led to her chapter on Montgomery.

E. Holly Pike is an associate professor in the English literature program at Sir Wilfred Grenfell College in Corner Brook, Newfoundland. A specialist in nineteenth-century fiction and women writers, she is the author of *Family and Society in the Works of Elizabeth Gaskell* (1995) and has previously published on Montgomery in *Harvesting Thistles: The Textual Garden of L.M. Montgomery* (1994).

Laura Robinson teaches English literature at Queen's University and the Royal Military College. Her doctoral dissertation focuses on the work of L.M. Montgomery, Louisa May Alcott, and Charlotte M. Yonge. As part of this research, she has investigated Montgomery's manuscripts, scrapbooks, and memorabilia in Prince Edward Island. She has published on Montgomery in *Children's Voices in Atlantic Literature and Culture* (1995).

Erika Rothwell teaches composition and children's literature at the University of Alberta. Her doctoral dissertation focused on Georgian and Victorian women's fiction for children. She has recently published on E. Nesbit and is co-editor of *Intersections* (1998), a reader designed to introduce science and engineering students to rhetoric and composition. As a life-long reader of L.M. Montgomery, she hopes to make further contributions to the field of Montgomery scholarship.

Mary Rubio is the co-editor, with Elizabeth Waterston, of *The Selected Journals of L.M. Montgomery*, Volumes I–IV (1985–98). Rubio and Waterston are also authors of *Writing a Life: L.M. Montgomery* (1995). Rubio is the editor of *Harvesting Thistles: The Textual Garden of L.M. Montgomery, Essays on her Novels and Journals* (1994), and the author of 'L.M. Montgomery' in *Profiles of Canadian Literature*, Series #7 (1991). She is also a founding editor of *CCL: Canadian Children's Literature/Littérature canadienne pour la jeunesse*, a critical journal devoted to Canadian literature for young people.

Theodore F. Sheckels is professor of English and communications at Randolph-Macon College, Ashland, Virginia. He is the author of *Debating: Applied Rhetorical Theory* (1984) and *The Lion on the Freeway: A Thematic Introduction to Contemporary South African Literature in English* (1996). He is the author of essays on political communication in *Communication Quarterly, Argumentation and Advocacy, Southern Communication Journal*, and other journals. He is also the author of essays on L.M. Montgomery in the *American Review of Canadian Studies*, on Margaret Atwood in *Approaches to Teaching Margaret Atwood's 'The Handmaid's Tale' and Other Works*, and on Australian film in *Antipodes*.

Calvin Trillin is a prolific literary critic and editor. He has contributed numerous articles on issues of Canadian and American culture in the *New Yorker* and *Harper's*. His most recent books include *Messages from My Father* (1997), *Travels with Alice* (1990), and *Uncivil Liberties* (1987).

Elizabeth Waterston, Professor Emeritus at the University of Guelph, has published widely on Canadian, Scottish, and Victorian literature. With Mary Rubio, she is the co-founder of *Canadian Children's Literature* (in 1975) and co-editor of *The Selected Journals of Lucy Maud Montgomery* (1985–98). She is the author of *Children's Literature in Canada* (1993) and *Kindling Spirits: L.M. Montgomery's 'Anne of Green Gables'* (1993), and co-author of *Writing a Life: L.M. Montgomery* (1995).

Illustration Credits

Index